Published in the United States of America in 2004 by
Lynne Rienner Publishers, Inc.
1800 30th Street, Boulder, Colorado 80301
www.rienner.com

and in the United Kingdom by
Lynne Rienner Publishers, Inc.
3 Henrietta Street, Covent Garden, London WC2E 8LU

© 2004 by Wilson P. Dizard Jr. All rights reserved by the publisher

Library of Congress Cataloging-in-Publication Data
Dizard, Wilson P.
  Inventing public diplomacy : the story of the U.S. Information Agency /
  Wilson P. Dizard Jr.
  "An ADST-DACOR diplomats and diplomacy book"
  Includes bibliographical references and index.
  ISBN 1-58826-288-X (hardcover : alk. paper)
    1. United States Information Agency—History. 2. United States—Relations—
Foreign countries. 3. United States—Foreign relations—1945–1989. 4. United
States—Foreign relations—1989– .
  I. Title.
  E840.2.D59 2004
  327.1'1—dc22   2004001829

British Cataloguing in Publication Data
A Cataloguing in Publication record for this book
is available from the British Library.

Printed and bound in the United States of America

∞ The paper used in this publication meets the requirements
of the American National Standard for Permanence of
Paper for Printed Library Materials Z39.48-1992.

5 4 3 2 1

*For my former colleagues at
the United States Information Agency
and for those who continue its work of
telling America's story to the world*

Contents

List of Photographs	ix
Foreword, Kenneth L. Brown and Robert L. Funseth	xi
Preface	xiii

1	The United States and Ideological Warfare	1
2	USIA's Wartime Origins	17
3	From Hot War to Cold War	37
4	USIA: Getting Started	63
5	The Murrow Years	83
6	High Summer	103
7	Playing Bureaucratic Games	133
8	A Stone's Throw from the University	153
9	The Delicate Art of Exporting Culture	175
10	Sunset Years	199
11	The Future of Public Diplomacy	219

Selected Bibliography	233
Index	239
About the Book	255

Photographs

Edward R. Murrow, USIA's best-known director	123
Turkish visitors at a USIA trade-fair exhibit	123
USIA's Russian-language *Ameryka* magazine	124
Live television demonstration in Laos	124
English-teaching seminar in Togo	125
News Review, biweekly magazine printed in Arabic and English	125
Surrender leaflet produced by USIA during the war in Vietnam	126
USIA pamphlet featuring Jacqueline Kennedy	127
Actress Helen Hayes on the Voice of America	127
VOA master control board in Washington	128
San Francisco Ballet dancers on tour in Greece	128
"Working the cocktail circuit" as part of a USIA officer's routine	129
USIS-Portugal's *Let's Learn English* television program	129
USIA-translated books on display in Buenos Aires	130
Filming U.S. economic aid project in Bolivia	130
Specially designed USIS Jeeps for remote rural operations	131

Foreword

FOR MORE THAN 225 years, extraordinary men and women have represented the United States abroad under all sorts of circumstances. What they did and how and why they did it remain little known to their compatriots. In 1996, the Association for Diplomatic Studies and Training (ADST) and Diplomatic and Consular Officers, Retired (DACOR) created a book series to increase public knowledge and appreciation of the involvement of U.S. diplomats in world history. Toward this end, Wilson Dizard's *Inventing Public Diplomacy* recounts the instrumental role played by the U.S. Information Agency (USIA) in making public diplomacy integral to U.S. foreign policy. It should prove invaluable to students of international communications, media globalization, diplomacy, and the history of U.S. foreign relations.

Dizard has written the first comprehensive history of USIA, from its World War II antecedents to its legacy as a vital policy instrument in the face of today's rising anti-Americanism. Throughout, he balances the overall historical narrative with engaging personal anecdotes. He is also the first to document USIA's frequently overlooked role in the postwar expansion of U.S. media and cultural exports.

Drawing on his own distinguished careers as both diplomat and author, Dizard narrates, in delightful and informative ways, the day-to-day activities of USIA's overseas posts, the U.S. Information Service (USIS), and the Foreign Service officers who ran them. He tells, for example, how USIS in South Africa subtly undermined apartheid by opening its libraries to black patrons and helping train a generation of black leaders through scholarships and grants that brought them to the United States. Dizard describes not only the many successful public diplomacy operations but also the failures, as in Vietnam. He also examines the parallel Defense Department and CIA efforts to influence foreign audiences.

From 1951 to 1980, Dizard served in Washington and overseas in the State Department and USIS, emerging as a recognized expert on international communications. In *Inventing Public Diplomacy,* he has given us a fascinating, useful, and thoroughly accessible account of a remarkable, eclectic corps of dedicated men and women who spoke for the United States in the latter half of the twentieth century.

—Kenneth L. Brown, President
Association for Diplomatic Studies and Training

—Robert L. Funseth, President
Diplomatic and Consular Officers, Retired

Preface

IN MAY 1951, I arrived in Istanbul to begin my first Foreign Service assignment in the State Department's overseas information program. The program's aim was, in the then-current phrase, to win the hearts and minds of foreign audiences about the United States in general and its international policies in particular.

One of my first opportunities to change hearts and minds came improbably from an invitation to tea, extended by a Turkish admiral and his wife. It was a formal but pleasant affair in a sunny apartment overlooking the Bosporus. After tea was served, the admiral's wife went to fetch their son, a wide-eyed lad of about six. I was, she told me, the first American he had ever met. After a bashful introduction, he leaned over and whispered into his mother's ear. "Cevad wants to ask you a question about America," she said. "Fine," I replied, welcoming a chance to practice my new trade.

More whispering in Turkish between mother and son. "Well," she informed me, "he wants to know if cowboys live in skyscrapers." I explained the cowboy housing situation, hopefully without dispelling completely his friendly images of a far-off country.

I spent the next thirty years in the information program, moving on from Istanbul to Athens, Tehran, Dhaka, Warsaw, Saigon, and Geneva, dealing with men and women whose perceptions of the United States were often as confused, if not as innocent, as those of my young Turkish friend. This odyssey involved me in a unique part of the U.S. breakout into full world leadership after World War II. My employer for most of those years was the U.S. Information Agency (USIA), a government bureau with a mission to present a full and fair picture of the United States to the world. Created in 1953 in the early years of the Cold War,

USIA existed until 1999, when its operations were transferred to the Department of State.

This book is an overview of the information agency's record—its origin, purposes, and day-to-day activities, including its successes and failures. My aim is to identify USIA's contribution to the United States' worldwide ideological impact in the postwar decades. Its role was to portray the United States through the prism of national strategic interests. In a phrase, the agency was a propaganda operation, replicating similar programs of other governments, both friendly and hostile.

In the process, USIA added new dimensions to the old craft of propaganda, under the new rubric of public diplomacy. One of these was in the scope of its activities. In addition to its Voice of America radio service, the agency had posts in almost three hundred cities and towns abroad, making its activities more geographically dispersed than those of any other Washington agency, then or since. USIA was the first official U.S. presence in many of these population centers.

Its programs were an overlay on the U.S. commercial media's postwar expansion into global markets. This symbiotic relationship between Washington agencies and private organizations was an important part of U.S. influence on other cultures since World War II.

Cooperation between government and industry to promote information and cultural products is very much a part of this study of USIA's operations. These joint efforts were complex, and sometimes controversial. U.S. commercial media firms and cultural groups have been traditionally wary of association with government propaganda efforts. In part, this reflects First Amendment concerns about interference in their activities by federal agencies, including USIA. On the other hand, these private groups share a common interest with Washington policymakers in promoting information and cultural exports.

USIA played a unique role in this effort. It distributed massive amounts of commercial media and cultural goods and services through its own programs. It also sponsored programs that subsidized these products in ways that expanded international trade for U.S. exporters. This was particularly true of markets in Asia, Africa, and the Middle East, where U.S. media and cultural organizations had little or no presence before 1945. (A partial exception was the Hollywood film industry.) USIA helped make a wide range of commercial information products and services familiar for the first time to local audiences in these regions.

Beyond these efforts to promote commercial media and cultural exports, USIA made a record of its own, from the sophisticated salons of Paris to backwater towns across the developing world. Its programs touched literally billions of people, both directly through its local operations and indirectly through the radio Voice of America.

Public diplomacy's role in U.S. foreign policy has taken on new significance since September 11, 2001. The terrorist attacks in New York and Washington changed U.S. relations with the rest of the world, putting in doubt the prospects of a continued transition toward greater political and economic stability in the face of hostile forces. As in the Cold War era, there is no box score to tell who is winning or losing in this global ideological game.

What is needed now is not a return to the programs of the USIA era. The new communications environment created by the Internet and other transnational resources is too multidimensional for such an approach. Over and above the direct threat of terrorist movements, a different set of global relationships is forming. As in every major transition in human history, the ideas and perceptions of ordinary human beings count. The challenge of international terrorism calls for policies and actions that continue to respect the integrity of the world's many cultures along with a practical recognition of the crosscutting influences created by the information age.

Public diplomacy has a limited but necessary contribution to make in this effort, building on the experience gained in over forty years of USIA operations. As in the Cold War years, this will present a challenge to the task of defining the U.S. role in a disorderly world.

Scholarly study of the role of public diplomacy in U.S. foreign policy is still in its early stages, although important work has been done recently by David Krugler of the University of Wisconsin–Platteville, Kenneth Osgood at Florida Atlantic University, Richard Pells at the University of Texas, and Laura Belmonte at Oklahoma State, among others. I also had important help from many former USIA colleagues, in person and in their taped comments for the invaluable Foreign Affairs Oral History Project sponsored by the Washington-based Association for Diplomatic Studies and Training. The association agreed to sponsor this study as part of its book series on modern U.S. diplomacy. I am particularly indebted to the association's president, Kenneth L. Brown, and to Margery Boichel Thompson, its publishing director, for their support.

Finally, special thanks to Lynn Wood Dizard, my in-house editor and thoughtful critic on works in progress.

—*Wilson P. Dizard Jr.*

1

The United States and Ideological Warfare

INTERNATIONAL POLITICS IN the modern era has embraced the sophisticated use of information and cultural resources to support national interests. It is hardly a new idea: Niccolo Machiavelli codified its basic rules five centuries ago in his advice to Renaissance princes. The practice took on new importance during World War II and the Cold War that followed, spurred by the greater availability of electronic technologies (notably shortwave radio) capable of reaching mass audiences worldwide. The result was to give a new dimension to the old saw about ideas as weapons.

With the collapse of the Soviet empire, ideological confrontation has shifted from a bipolar focus to more complex patterns of doctrinal engagement. Nevertheless, such engagement remains a critical element in interstate relations. In particular, it has changed the ground rules of national sovereignty, challenged by new information-age forces and powered by advanced technologies, from computers to the Internet.

In considering the future of the nation-state system, does this promise a hopeful new era of peace and prosperity? Or will it result, as Harvard pundit Samuel Huntington suggests, in a clash of civilizations, a widening of the cultural fault lines separating a half-dozen distinct ideologies from Islam to Confucianism?[1] These questions took on urgent meaning following the terrorist events of September 2001. Given its current role as the dominant information power, the United States has a special stake in the answers.

This book describes the evolution of ideological policies and operations in U.S. foreign policy since 1940. The United States was a latecomer to this subject. In the years before World War II, it was the only major power that did not have a strategy, with a supporting bureaucracy, for carrying out ideological operations beyond its border.[2] The reasons for the United States' early disinterest in ideological operations centered around the national ambivalence over continental isolationism and evangelical engagement with the rest of the world. Political scientist Seymour Martin Lipset sees the roots of this dilemma in what he describes as "American exceptionalism."[3] It is reflected in, among many examples, Ralph Waldo Emerson's landmark 1837 Harvard lecture in which he called for U.S. emancipation from European cultural models.

Midwestern artist Thomas Hart Benton later pithily captured Emerson's proposal. Upon returning from his studies in Europe, Benton said that "a windmill, a junk heap and a Rotarian have more meaning for me than Notre Dame or the Parthenon." William James, the apostle of American pragmatism, declared early in the twentieth century, "Damn great empires. Give me individuals." Despite the siren calls of manifest destiny, these feelings had a strong pull on U.S. attitudes toward the outside world.

These attitudes resonate with a key element in this book—U.S. communications links with the rest of the world. In the nineteenth century, Americans saw the Morse telegraph and the Bell telephone primarily as domestic resources, useful for uniting a continental nation. There was little interest in expanding the new electrical networks to other countries. When Cyrus Field proposed the first transatlantic cable in the 1850s, he had to rely on European investors to finance most of the project.

At the same time, the United States refused to join the new International Telegraph Union (ITU), created to set technical standards for cross-border telegraph traffic, lest ITU membership open the way for other governments to regulate U.S. domestic networks. In the Radio Act of 1911, the first congressional legislation on electrical communications, the only international provision was a restriction on foreign control of domestic cable and telephone companies.[4] As one result of these inward protectionist policies, Britain, France, Germany, and other European powers dominated global network development before World War II.

Indifference toward developing strategies for projecting the country's information and cultural image abroad paralleled this general U.S. disinterest in promoting cross-border communications. The U.S. government lacked the political will to engage in the sharpening doctrinal conflict between communist, fascist, and democratic forces in the prewar years.[5]

The attack on Pearl Harbor shattered this ideological aloofness. Propaganda operations became part of a massive mobilization of resources to win the war. From a standing start, the U.S. government mounted an information and cultural offensive on a global scale. By the end of the conflict four years later, the United States dominated the contest to influence world opinion in support of national strategic aims and actions.

In this pursuit, Washington used most of the same conventional propaganda techniques as its allies and enemies, including a hastily created shortwave radio network, the Voice of America. However, it also had unique resources that have distinguished its ideological offensive ever since. These were the massive domestic networks of private information and cultural enterprises—from Hollywood to Harvard—that no other society could match. The government's overseas ideological operations during the past sixty years have constituted, in effect, an overlay on these private activities. This interplay of public and private interests was (and is) complex and, at times, confrontational. But decisions made under wartime pressures in the 1940s set the framework for public policies and private interests that have collectively defined the United States' current dominant position in an information-intensive postindustrial world.

The cumulative impact of this change has been summarized by political scientists Joseph Nye and William Owens: "Knowledge, more than ever, is power. The one country that can best lead the information revolution will be more powerful than any other. For the foreseeable future, that country is the United States. America has apparent strength in military power and economic production. Yet its more subtle comparative advantage is its ability to collect, process, act upon and disseminate information, an edge that will almost certainly grow in the next decade."[6]

It is a long distance, chronologically and otherwise, from mounting a wartime propaganda offensive in 1942 to defining the United States' role in the new information-intensive global order. Yet the connection is real, though often erratic and muddled. The wartime decision to become involved in ideological warfare led to the creation of a federal agency, the Office of War Information (OWI). When the Japanese surrendered in August 1945, the OWI's operations were cut back drastically, along with most other wartime programs. The onset of the Cold War reversed this decision with a dramatic expansion of overseas ideological programs in the 1950s. The Soviet regime's collapse in 1991 resulted in another cycle of cutbacks, until the September 2001 terrorist attacks in New York and Washington led to calls for another expansion of information and cultural programs.[7]

The recent threat of ideologically driven terrorism has sharpened the debate over the role of government-sponsored information operations in advancing U.S. strategic interests. The discussion is driven by doubts as to whether such operations can be effective in an age of complex information channels, from the Internet to mass-media products delivered by satellites and high-speed cable networks across the globe. In the early years of the new century, the debate is far from being resolved.

To get a better perspective on the subject, the following chapters examine U.S. government efforts to influence world public opinion from the early 1940s through World War II and the Cold War to the present. They focus on the organization that gave form and direction to these efforts for over forty-five years—the U.S. Information Agency (USIA).

Created in 1953, USIA became Washington's chosen instrument for ideological operations during the Cold War and in the decade that followed. It played a bellwether role in developing and carrying out a national strategy for overseas information and cultural operations. By the time the agency was closed down in 1999, the policy and operational framework was in place for public diplomacy.

USIA had an outsized role in projecting American ideas to the four corners of the earth. At the height of its Cold War operations, it had the most extensive overseas presence of any Washington agency. Its information and cultural posts—the U.S. Information Service (USIS)—operated in almost three hundred cities and towns. Overall, it was the biggest information and cultural effort ever mounted by one society to influence the attitudes and actions of men and women beyond its borders. USIA activities included:

- The Voice of America radio network, its best-known activity, broadcasting worldwide in over forty languages, heard by 100 million people weekly during the Cold War years
- Magazines, books, pamphlets, leaflets, and news bulletins in over one hundred languages printed and distributed in tens of billions of copies
- A global library network, the first to introduce open-shelf books in 150 countries abroad
- The largest English-teaching program ever mounted and, more significantly, training to improve the skills of tens of thousands of local English teachers abroad
- Exhibits on American life and ideas, drawing billions of visitors
- Thousands of agency-produced documentary films, newsreels, and television programs, including soap operas
- Exchange programs that brought millions of students, educators, artists, and other professionals to the United States and sent their

U.S. counterparts abroad. Over 200,000 academics and others participated in the best-known of these programs—the Fulbright awards. Fulbright grantees ranged from politician Daniel Patrick Moynihan and astronaut Harrison Schmitt to opera diva Anna Moffo.

What will be forever unmeasurable is the influence of these activities on foreign perceptions of the United States. The agency's objectives rested on the most elusive of human acts—changing someone else's mind. Television reporter Edward R. Murrow, the best-known of the USIA's directors, liked to say that no cash register rings when this happens. Over and above the cash-register test, considerable evidence suggests that the agency's activities made a difference in influencing foreign opinion, particularly in political situations where public attitudes played a definable role in affecting U.S. national interests.

USIA programs were only one strand in the web of official efforts to influence the rest of the world in the Cold War years. Other federal bureaucracies, in particular the Department of Defense and the Central Intelligence Agency (CIA), matched, and often outmatched, USIA's operations. The Defense Department's efforts centered around the military's new interest in psychological operations against hostile forces and civilian populations. The CIA, created in 1947, was assigned the role of carrying out covert ideological operations abroad, aimed at both Cold War adversaries and allies. These Defense Department and CIA operations alternately clashed with and complemented USIA activities, as we shall see.

These government operations were eclipsed by the massive global activities of private groups, which emerged as the largest force influencing America's ideological impact abroad in the past half-century. This private U.S. information sector, broadly defined, encompassed the mass media, the advertising industry, and cultural and educational institutions, along with multinational corporations and other organizations whose agendas included concerns about overseas public opinion.

The impact of these disparate groups gathered force as worldwide communications networks expanded, notably the Internet and the global information utility it helped form. Beginning in the 1990s, the Internet has played a special role as a multiplier of U.S. ideological influence abroad. At the turn of the century, about half of the world's Internet users were Americans.[8] All but 6 percent of the most visited World Wide Web sites were in the United States. Don Heath, former head of the Washington-based Internet Society, notes: "If the United States government had tried to come up with a scheme to spread its brand of capitalism and its emphasis on political liberalism around the world, it couldn't have invented a better model than the Internet."[9]

In summary, U.S. global ideological influences have evolved from a tangled relationship between two elements—the public Voice of America and the commercial voices of U.S. industry. This distinguishes U.S. practices from those of other countries, most of whom have some form of official controls over private information resources. The U.S. pattern, grounded in First Amendment law and tradition, involves a separate but symbiotic relationship between the government and private information sectors. This connection is particularly close at the international level, where the federal government has actively promoted the overseas expansion of domestic information firms, primarily through trade negotiations designed to assure them access to foreign markets.

Government promotion of information exports is relevant to this account of the U.S. Information Agency's role in national policy. At one level, the agency competed with private U.S. information providers. Commercial media companies generally acquiesced in this arrangement, while maintaining an arm's-length relationship with USIA activities to avoid public identification with government propaganda.

At another level, USIA was directly involved in promoting commercial information products in its overseas programs. In part, this resulted from its distribution of U.S. commercial-information products as part of its own activities. As the agency expanded its overseas operations, its annual budgets climbed toward the billion-dollar mark, making it a welcome client for U.S. media vendors. A significant part of this money involved contracts with U.S. companies to supply books, films, television programs, exhibits, and other information products. As a result, large quantities of commercial media materials were exported, paid for, and distributed by the agency. This factor had particular resonance in parts of the world, particularly Asia and Africa, that had little previous contact with U.S. media products.[10]

USIA subsidies significantly helped U.S. media firms gain a foothold in foreign countries where they previously had little or no market share. One example was the agency's role in creating Franklin Publications, a cartel of U.S. publishers, to challenge long-standing British and French domination of global book exports. Although formally separate from USIA, the cartel relied on the agency's overseas posts to support Franklin operations abroad, where Franklin's local publishers produced and distributed tens of millions of books in both English and local translations. This program gave U.S. publishers a significant overseas presence for the first time, particularly in Asia, Africa, and Latin America. As a result, they are now the dominant factor in the global book industry.

In another project designed to promote media exports, USIA managed a congressionally funded program known as Information Media Guaranty, which helped open overseas markets for U.S. newspaper, magazine, and film companies in the 1950s and 1960s by exchanging their often-worthless local currency receipts for dollars at favorable rates. Before the program was closed down in 1967, it had made possible the commercial sale overseas of periodicals, films, and other information materials worth over $80 million. As with the Franklin Publications project, the result was to give many U.S. media companies their first significant export markets.

The largest beneficiaries, both direct and indirect, from federal government assistance were academic and cultural organizations. The best-known example, the Fulbright grant program, begun in 1947 and managed overseas by USIA, was the forerunner of a wide variety of two-way exchanges of scholars and researchers with over 175 countries. Fulbright and other government-supported academic programs have accounted for over a quarter-million such exchanges.[11]

USIA also recruited foreign students for U.S. colleges and universities. In 1940 there were fewer that ten thousand overseas students in U.S. higher-education institutions; by the turn of the century, there were more than a half-million. Although many students arrived here through their own efforts, others came through arrangements that began in their home countries with financial and certification arrangements administered by USIS posts abroad.

Other government grants and subsidies in the postwar decades gave international exposure to a wide range of U.S. artistic groups, from symphony orchestras to Appalachian square dancers. Before World War II, such groups were virtually unknown abroad. Today, U.S. cultural attractions are familiar in live performances across the globe. In large part this happened because of direct government financial support of their overseas tours, particularly in the early postwar decades. Most of these programs, administered by USIS posts abroad, were subsequently phased out as such tours became financially self-supporting.

In summary, a major strength of America's cultural influences on the rest of the world came from reliance on a complex pattern of public policies and private initiatives over the past half-century. This effort did not spring from a master plan concocted by Washington bureaucrats to impose U.S. culture on the rest of the world, but rather from the overseas outreach of powerful domestic forces, encouraged by government programs but relying primarily on independent private resources.

This symbiotic mix of public and private interests often led to tensions between the two, centered around differences over what kinds of American culture should be exported. An early example was a 1946 State Department decision to sponsor an overseas exhibit of modern paintings that had originally been shown at New York's Museum of Modern Art. One congressman described the paintings as "Communist caricatures . . . sent out to mislead the rest of the world on what America was like." A senator suggested that taxpayer-supported art exhibits sent abroad should be limited to images of George Washington and Abraham Lincoln.[12] Attempts by beleaguered State Department officials to defend the collection were not helped by the offhand remark of President Harry Truman, upon viewing the paintings, that "if that's art, I'm a Hottentot." Despite the criticism, the paintings were shown abroad to great acclaim.

State Department and USIA plans in 1954 to underwrite the first major overseas tour of an American theatrical production, *Porgy and Bess,* brought a hailstorm of congressional criticism. Why, the critics asked, should U.S. taxpayers support a production that featured racism, drugs, rape, and poverty in a South Carolina slum? The answer came from a Yugoslav official following the first overseas performance of the Gershwin folk opera in Belgrade: "Only a psychologically mature people would have sponsored this work." *Porgy and Bess* went on to triumphal receptions in Moscow, Warsaw, and elsewhere.

Similar pressures to impose artistic conformity marked other USIA cultural efforts throughout its forty-five-year history. At times, the agency's leadership crumbled, particularly before congressional criticism. At other times, it resisted in ways that did credit to its legislative mandate of presenting a full and fair picture of the United States.

In the years before Pearl Harbor, the U.S. government had been ambivalent about overseas ideological operations. Among the many reasons for this, Americans' attitudes toward the European war were the most pressing. Overwhelmingly, public opinion favored neutrality. The Roosevelt administration's sympathies and actions tilted strongly toward aiding the British as they awaited an invasion that would have completed German hegemony over Europe and, by extension, other parts of the world.[13]

The White House carried out a largely covert strategy of economic and military assistance to the British. This help did not, however, include support for ideological warfare. In their secret negotiations with U.S.

authorities for aid in defending their homeland against a German invasion, the British had specifically requested help in mounting psychological-warfare operations against the Germans. It was not forthcoming, in part because of White House fears that it would raise public concerns about U.S. involvement in the war.

Meanwhile, Britain's sympathizers among the United States' eastern establishment pressed the Roosevelt administration to mount a domestic information campaign in favor of intervention. Dorothy Thompson, a popular newspaper columnist, called on the government to finance a "gargantuan propaganda campaign . . . at the cost of one battleship round the clock in all languages."[14] The president continued to turn down proposals to involve the administration in active ideological support for the British. At one point, he rejected as "an impossible suggestion" a State Department proposal for "an American version of a Ministry of Information," headed by a cabinet-rank official.[15]

These bureaucratic evasions were strongly challenged by two prominent New Yorkers, Nelson A. Rockefeller and William Donovan, both of whom wanted a more muscular response to the threat of a German victory in Europe. In different ways they laid the groundwork for the doctrine and organization of a modern U.S. strategy of global ideological operations in war and peace.[16]

Donovan was a colorful figure who will forever be attached to the nickname "Wild Bill." A lawyer and much-decorated World War I hero, he stood out from many Irish-Americans in 1940 for his belief that U.S. interests required strong support for the British war effort. Donovan took his case to Washington, where he set in motion two projects that played vital roles in the U.S. ideological response to Nazi aggression. The first was to create a foreign espionage service, which later evolved into the Central Intelligence Agency. The second project, directly relevant to this book, was a government-funded international propaganda campaign supporting the British.[17]

Nelson Rockefeller played a complementary role to Donovan's in criticizing what they both regarded as U.S. ignorance about the Nazi threat. Young, rich, and well-connected in the eastern establishment, Rockefeller had made a name for himself in the late 1930s as president of Rockefeller Center. He also harbored political ambitions focused on Latin America, where he had invested in business ventures.

Rockefeller combined these interests in a campaign to change U.S. policy about what he regarded as the Roosevelt administration's inadequate response to German attempts to undermine U.S. influence in Latin America. He lobbied the president successfully for an organization to deal with the problem. The result was the awkwardly named Office for Coordination of Commercial and Cultural Relations between the American Republics, a semiautonomous group within the State Department. The unit's name was mercifully shortened a few months later to the Office of the Coordinator of Interamerican Affairs (CIAA).[18]

Not surprisingly, the coordinator was Nelson Rockefeller. He proceeded to organize projects to strengthen U.S. strategic interests south of the border. His program included economic assistance for housing, roads, and similar projects—the forerunner of postwar U.S. foreign-aid programs. He had no hesitations, moreover, about using such aid directly to oppose Nazi activities in the region. At one point, he pressured a Washington agency, the Reconstruction Finance Corporation, to fund an $8 million takeover of a German-controlled airline in South America because it operated airfields within bombing range of the Panama Canal.[19]

Foreshadowing USIA's activities, the Rockefeller office set up Washington's first significant official cultural and information operations abroad. These early efforts relied heavily on shortwave radio news and entertainment broadcasts to Latin America, which later became part of the wartime Voice of America network. The most enduring of the Rockefeller ideological-warfare projects was a network of so-called binational centers in major Latin American cities that served as showcases for U.S. cultural wares through exhibits, lectures, and other activities. Six decades later, many of the centers are still active.

Rockefeller, who was a knowledgeable collector of modern art, also used his connections with the New York art world to build an alliance between private museums and collectors and the State Department to organize traveling art exhibitions in Latin America. The first such show in 1941 involved over three hundred paintings and watercolors. The exhibit drew audiences of over two hundred thousand. It was the beginning of a government-funded effort to showcase American art abroad that continues to this day.[20]

In sponsoring these activities, Nelson Rockefeller created the organizational template for what later became the U.S. Information Agency, the public arm of U.S. overseas ideological operations for four decades during the Cold War.

Meanwhile, "Wild Bill" Donovan was actively involved in pressing his case for U.S. intervention in the European war. President Roosevelt sent him on a secret mission to London in 1940 to assess the British government's resolve and staying power in the face of a direct threat to their homeland. Prime Minister Winston Churchill recognized the importance of Donovan's visit in winning U.S. support for a beleaguered Britain by giving him unprecedented access to military and intelligence information. Among other activities, Donovan was impressed with British successes in conducting "black operations," including radio stations that broadcast unattributed but seemingly credible news designed to undermine German civilian and military morale.[21]

Upon his return to Washington, Donovan submitted a plan to the president for strengthening U.S. intelligence operations, along with an activist program of covert and overt information programs. Roosevelt responded by appointing him head of the ambiguously named Office of the Coordinator of Information (COI). Its public role was to "collect and analyze all information which might bear on national security." It was also authorized to conduct "supplementary activities" to support its national security role. This loophole allowed the new agency to carry out psychological warfare activities along the lines that Donovan had witnessed in Britain.

The COI was the first bureaucratic step toward what became the Central Intelligence Agency. Beyond its role as a collector of intelligence information, the new office began planning covert propaganda operations. By September 1941 Donovan had been given White House authority to use unvouchered funds for such activities. These funds, the lifeblood of secret operations, required only Donovan's authorization, bypassing normal government accounting and auditing controls. It was the beginning of a vast network of covert operations, including ideological warfare, which later became the CIA's Directorate of Operations.[22]

Although Donovan was primarily interested in building up intelligence resources abroad, his new organization's charter included a small unit, the Foreign Information Service (FIS), to carry out open propaganda projects overseas. The FIS was the first acknowledgment by the Roosevelt administration that public ideological operations required a worldwide approach, well beyond the regional focus of Nelson Rockefeller's Latin American operations. The initial focus of FIS operations was on shortwave broadcasting. The project was hobbled by a shortage of U.S. transmitters capable of reaching international audiences, particularly in Europe and Asia. Despite this handicap, the Foreign Information Service began a schedule of overseas broadcasts in February 1942 under the newly minted name "the Voice of America."

Meanwhile, Nelson Rockefeller's CIAA steadily expanded its propaganda operations in Latin America. The agency's shortwave radio programs soon attracted a large audience throughout the region. The CIAA also set up a press service to supply news and feature materials to thousands of publications in the region. A film production unit enlisted the Disney organization to produce a cartoon series featuring José Carioca, a samba-dancing parrot whose adventures usually included a message of hemispheric unity. Rockefeller also negotiated with the Hollywood studios to withhold their products from Latin American theaters showing German propaganda films. Since American films, including the epochal *Gone with the Wind*, were enormously popular, Nazi products disappeared from local cinemas.

Nevertheless, CIAA made mistakes, reflecting the inexperience of its propaganda staff. Unwilling to copy the German practice of outright subsidies to Latin American publications, a plan was concocted to buy advertising in local papers touting the themes of democracy and hemispheric solidarity. Over $600,000—an enormous sum at the time—was allocated for the project.[23]

The ads featured the jaunty adventures of a young Latin American couple traveling in the United States. The project was a failure, not least because tourist visits to the United States were all but impossible at the time. Moreover, the advertising money went to newspapers on the basis of their circulation figures rather than their editorial policies. As a result, the largest pro-German paper in Brazil and a number of smaller ones were beneficiaries of CIAA money.

This and similar failed projects bolstered claims by State Department officials that the Rockefeller operation was, in the then-current phrase, a wasteful boondoggle. Tensions rose between Rockefeller's eager propagandists and old-line diplomats over what the latter regarded as fanciful public-relations attempts to influence the Latin American masses.

These criticisms were largely muted after the attack on Pearl Harbor. In Roosevelt's phrase, Dr. Win-the-War replaced Dr. New Deal as the national focus. Mobilization on a massive scale became the new priority. The emphasis was on military and economic plans, but it also included for the first time a major commitment to global ideological operations.

Despite his previous reluctance to become involved in overseas propaganda operations, Roosevelt had a bare-bones structure for expanding them in the hectic days after Pearl Harbor. It included Nelson Rockefeller's CIAA and Bill Donovan's COI. The Donovan operation was still in the early stages of getting organized. Rockefeller had the advantage of a two-year head start.

Fitting the two operations within the confines of the wartime Washington bureaucracy proved difficult. The COI problem was less pressing—

it was a small operation with no entrenched bureaucratic precedents to hinder its plans for covert espionage and psychological warfare operations. Moreover, Donovan proved himself adept at dealing with bureaucratic rivals, including the military, the FBI, and other civilian agencies. The COI was reconstituted as the Office of Strategic Services (OSS) in June 1942 with a broad mandate to conduct covert intelligence and information operations worldwide.

By and large, Donovan had a free hand to shape his operation outside the range of public, particularly congressional, scrutiny. He recruited a staff drawn heavily from the best and brightest of East Coast establishment lawyers, academics, and business executives. (This elitist tilt led Washington wits to dub the OSS the "Oh So Social" agency.) Despite the jibes, most OSS employees served credibly in their newly acquired duties as spies and propaganda warriors.

Creating an agency that would deal with public-information activities at home and abroad proved more difficult. A precedent had been set by the Rockefeller operation in Latin America. Despite occasional gaffes, the CIAA's propaganda activities provided useful policy and operational guidelines for mounting a wider global effort. Organizing the expanded operation quickly involved a bureaucratic battle, centered on Nelson Rockefeller's refusal to give up control over his Latin American information and cultural programs. Because of his considerable political clout in Washington, he won the battle.[24]

Latin America thus remained largely off-limits for the agency that was given responsibility for mounting a massive propaganda program in other regions of the world. That operation, the Office of War Information, created the form and substance of U.S. overseas ideological programs for the next six decades. Given OWI's influence on the activities of its successor, the U.S. Information Agency, the next chapter takes a closer look at its operations.

Notes

1. Huntington famously outlined his thesis in "The Clash of Civilizations," *Foreign Affairs* 72, no. 3, summer 1993, pp. 22–49.

2. Such strategies were central to the rise of aggressive dictatorships in the last century. The European democracies, notably Britain, adopted more subtle approaches to the problem after World War I. See Philip M. Taylor, *The Projection of Britain: British Overseas Publicity and Propaganda 1919–1939* (New York: Cambridge University Press, 1981). For an overview of the other major powers in the interwar years, see Philip M. Taylor, "Propaganda in International

Politics, 1919–1939," in K.R.M. Short (ed.), *Film and Radio Propaganda in World War II* (Knoxville: University of Tennessee Press, 1983), pp. 7–25.

3. Seymour Martin Lipset, *American Exceptionalism* (New York: W. W. Norton, 1996).

4. Daniel R. Hedrick, *The Invisible Weapon: Telecommunications and International Politics 1851–1945* (New York: Oxford University Press, 1991), pp. 119–121.

5. A short-lived experiment in U.S. propaganda operations was initiated during World War I. Known as the Committee on Public Information (CPI), it was active in both domestic and international win-the-war propaganda between April 1917 and March 1919.

6. Joseph S. Nye Jr. and William Owens, "America's Information Edge," *Foreign Affairs*, March-April 1996, p. 20.

7. "U.S. Message Lost Overseas," *Washington Post*, October 14, 2001, p. A-1.

8. "Worldwide Online Growth in the Digital Economy: Convergence and Regulatory Boundaries," Office of Policy and Plans, Federal Communications Commission, March 1995, p. 199.

9. "Welcome to the Internet: The First Global Colony," *New York Times*, January 9, 2000, p. WK-1.

10. For a useful history of the early evolution of this trend, see William H. Read, *America's Mass Media Merchants* (Baltimore, Md.: Johns Hopkins University Press, 1977).

11. A summary of this extraordinary exchange of people is given in "A Salute to Citizen Diplomacy," a study issued by the National Council of International Visitors, Washington, D.C., in 2000.

12. Frank Ninkovich, "The Currents of Cultural Diplomacy: Art and the State Department," *Diplomatic History* 1, no. 3, summer 1976, p. 228.

13. Steven Casey, *Franklin D. Roosevelt, American Public Opinion and the War Against Nazi Germany* (New York: Oxford University Press, 2001).

14. Quoted in Hu Shih, "The Conflict of Ideologies," *Annals of the American Academy of Political and Social Sciences*, No. 1218, November 1941, p. 26.

15. Memorandum for the Secretary of State, Box 4619, Executive papers, Franklin D. Roosevelt Library, Hyde Park, N.Y.

16. Richard W. Steele, "Preparing the Public for War: Efforts to Establish a National War Agency," *American Historical Review*, October 1970, pp. 1640–1653. See also Lowell Mellett, "Government Propaganda," *Atlantic Monthly*, September 1941, pp. 311–313. Mellett was a prominent official in the Roosevelt administration.

17. Allan M. Winkler, *The Politics of Propaganda: The Office of War Information 1942–1945* (New Haven, Conn.: Yale University Press, 1978), p. 13.

18. Nelson Rockefeller's role in establishing the Latin American program is described in James Desmond, *Nelson Rockefeller: A Political Biography* (New York: Macmillan, 1964), pp. 71–91.

19. Ibid., p. 100.

20. Ninkovich, "Currents of Cultural Diplomacy," p. 219.

21. The origins of these black operations are described in Selfton Delmer, *Black Boomerang* (London: Secker & Warburg, 1962), pp. 43–76. See also

Charles Cruickshank, *The Fourth Arm: Psychological Warfare* (London: Davis-Poynter Publishers, 1976).

22. An incomplete but interesting description of the origins of Donovan's involvement in what became the Office of Strategic Services is given in a Central Intelligence Agency publication, *The Office of Strategic Services: America's First Intelligence Agency,* issued by the agency's historical division in May 2000.

23. Desmond, *Nelson Rockefeller,* pp. 88–89.

24. In the process, the Coordinator's Office was renamed the Office of Interamerican Affairs.

2

USIA's Wartime Origins

IN JUNE 1942, seven months after Pearl Harbor, a White House executive order created the Office of War Information (OWI). The order gave OWI a double mandate to carry out information programs both within the United States and overseas. There was little public opposition to propagandizing foreigners about U.S. war aims, but the idea of similar operations aimed at U.S. citizens created tensions from the start.

Republicans in Congress saw the OWI as a New Deal agency designed to publicize the accomplishments of the Roosevelt administration among domestic constituencies. Though overwrought, the charge resulted in drastic congressional cutbacks in the agency's budget, effectively phasing out most of its domestic programs by 1944.

As a result, the OWI focused largely on reaching overseas audiences. Its overall success resulted, in large part, from President Roosevelt's choice of Elmer Davis as the organization's director. Davis, a lean, lank Hoosier, had been the chief news analyst for the CBS radio network at the time. An enigmatic man, he combined a flair for writing slick magazine fiction with a shrewd astuteness in political analysis.

Davis brought both professional expertise and a crusty integrity to the new agency. "A good many people," he announced, "seem to think that we are specifically charged with the maintenance of national morale. We are not, and in my opinion there is no need for such an agency . . . we intend to see that the American people get just as much information as genuine considerations of military security will permit."[1]

Davis began his OWI assignment without clear instructions on how to carry out the organization's mandate. As a result, he found himself on a collision course with Washington agencies whose interests lay primarily in saying as little as possible about what they were doing. One of these, the State Department, had been given general policy oversight over what the OWI said and did abroad. It was an impossible assignment, in part because the department did not have the personnel to monitor the flood of print, radio, and other materials that the OWI churned out daily from its New York headquarters. Policy guidance consisted primarily of telephone conferences between New York and Washington, a situation that inevitably led to mixed signals and policies.

One instance of poor coordination occurred in 1943 when an OWI Italian-language radio program broadcast a commentary that referred to Italy's King Umberto as a "moronic little king." No one in Washington had bothered to inform the OWI that the allied powers were conducting secret negotiations aimed at Italy's surrender that hinged in part on the future of the royal family. The moronic-little-king episode typified a perennial cycle of policy differences between cautious diplomats and eager propagandists that persisted into the era of the OWI's successor, the U.S. Information Agency.

Meanwhile, pressure mounted on Elmer Davis to staff the global information service. Bill Donovan's Office of Strategic Services had recruited its work force from the eastern establishment—academia, banking, and the upper reaches of corporate America. The OWI tapped another personnel resource—the brash worlds of mass media and advertising—a choice that set the tone and direction not only of the OWI's operations but also those of USIA throughout the Cold War decades. As one OWI veteran later recalled, "Never had there been assembled in one organization a higher concentration of talent, a greater diversity of personalities, and a more paradoxical blend of craftsmanship and incompetence, creativeness and crackpottery, selfless dedication and cutthroat power hunger, brilliant improvisation and organizational chaos."[2]

The antics of a few incompetents gave the organization a tarnished name it did not deserve. One radio operator, hired to send Morse-code news to North Africa, garbled the transmissions so badly that the OWI office in Algiers responded: "If must send with foot, please use right foot."[3]

Much of the criticism of the OWI and its staff was politically inspired. Westbrook Pegler, a prominent conservative newspaper columnist, saw the agency as "a hideout for privileged intellectual New Deal cowards and Communists." The ratio of New Deal Democrats (as well as Communist sympathizers) on the staff was undoubtedly higher than the national average, thanks in part to political patronage as well as to what Arthur Krock, the conservative *New York Times* chief political columnist, ruefully called "the superior articulation of the left."

The OWI's hastily recruited employees brought a great deal of professional media expertise to their jobs. In general, however, the intricacies of international political propaganda exceeded their experience. Their skills had been honed in domestic industries, particularly media and advertising, that were the largest and most successful examples of their kind in the world. They knew how to package and market soft drinks, automobiles, and breakfast cereal for large corporations. Now their client was the United States government, and their job was to sell Washington's policies on war and peace.[4]

The OWI staff suffered in particular from general ignorance of the cultural barriers involved in reaching out to foreign audiences. Coming from a consumer-marketing background, they brought with them an insouciant belief that U.S. advertising techniques would work in the wider world: if you could sell it in Kalamazoo, you could sell it in Karachi, Kuala Lumpur, and Kyoto.

Their attitudes were strongly influenced by the ideas of a small group of U.S. academics working in the new field of public-opinion studies. From modest beginnings in the 1920s, research in this field had expanded in volume and influence in the prewar years. Writing in arcane journals and speaking at obscure conferences, opinion researchers advanced the theory that public attitudes could be scientifically identified through polling and other survey techniques. The corollary to this proposition was that the results could be used to develop appeals that would influence public opinion.[5] These theoretical findings became guidelines for U.S. overseas cultural and information operations over the next half-century.

The researchers who advanced these theories were a diverse group, working mostly in universities where communications studies seemed an often unwelcome intruder on older disciplines. They brought a new interdisciplinary attitude to their work. "Communications is the crossroads where all the disciplines meet," declared Wilbur Schramm, one of the pioneers in the field. He and his colleagues drew upon anthropology, economics, history, mathematics, sociology, and psychology, among other scholarly areas, in their research. Harold Lasswell, the acknowledged leader of the group, summed up their basic approach when he defined mass communications as answering the questions, "Who says what, in what channel, to whom, with what effect?"

Lasswell has a special place in this survey of the U.S. role in the global war of ideas, primarily because of his groundbreaking research in international communications. His 1927 doctoral thesis at the University of Chicago, later published as *Propaganda Techniques in the World*

War, took a detached view of propaganda.[6] He saw it as "the control of opinions by significant symbols . . . and other forms of social communications." It was, he added, "an inescapable fact of life; democracies must adjust to it, not rail against it." The argument did not impress a young New York lawyer, John Foster Dulles. In a review, Dulles described *Propaganda Techniques* as a "Machiavellian textbook which should promptly be destroyed!"[7]

Lasswell's views on the relevance of propaganda did not match popular feelings on the subject at the time. A series of congressional hearings after World War I documented the extent to which the British and German governments had used propaganda to influence U.S. attitudes on participation in the war. A 1934 congressional investigation had uncovered evidence that large U.S. public relations firms were in the pay of the Nazi regime in Germany. These accounts about foreign attempts to manipulate U.S. public opinion reinforced the idea that propaganda was a bad thing.[8]

Lasswell continued his interest in international communications throughout his long career. He wrote about the need to establish "world weather maps in public opinion" as a form of "preventive politics" in dealing with crises. After Pearl Harbor, Lasswell set up a research unit at the Library of Congress to advise the OWI and other war agencies on overseas opinion trends. In later years, he served as an adviser to the U.S. Information Agency.

Most of Harold Lasswell's fellow researchers concentrated on studies of domestic public opinion in the 1930s, with results that later influenced OWI operations. One early practitioner, George Gallup, a trained psychologist, was hired in 1933 by the Young and Rubicam advertising agency to carry out surveys for its clients. Two years later, he founded the American Institute of Public Opinion to conduct his own studies.

Gallup made his mark in the new field of political polling, beginning with the 1936 presidential election in which Franklin Roosevelt sought a second term. Gallup pollsters used scientific sampling to select interviewees who represented a demographic cross section of U.S. voters. When their polling results closely matched the final vote, opinion research came into its own as a permanent feature of U.S. politics. Similar polling techniques were later used in the country's global ideological operations. USIA hired foreign affiliates of the Gallup organization to track overseas opinion trends during the Cold War.

The prospect of identifying consumer preferences was particularly appealing to U.S. radio broadcasters. By the mid-1930s, radio sets had become a standard fixture in over 85 percent of U.S. homes. The

Columbia Broadcasting System (CBS) took the lead in underwriting public-opinion polling, led by Frank Stanton, its young research director. Stanton's early measurements of listener attitudes demonstrated radio's power to deliver compelling advertising messages to mass audiences.[9]

CBS engineers developed a small handheld device called a program analyzer to record and tabulate the responses of a roomful of people listening to a radio program. The device, known affectionately at CBS headquarters as "Little Annie," had two buttons, one red and one green. At regular intervals, audience members indicated, by pressing one of the buttons, whether or not they liked what they heard. For CBS executives, the results were akin to discovering the magic formula that would unlock the secrets of how to sell toothpaste and breakfast cereal on the radio.

The men and women that OWI recruited came mostly from jobs in the media and advertising sectors, in which Little Annie and other new survey techniques were changing U.S. mass-media practices. Unlike their counterparts in ideological-warfare units abroad, they were not oriented to propaganda but to marketing. As a result, the new public-opinion research techniques adopted by the OWI staff often reflected the slick, hyped-up messages of commercial media and advertising.

A sardonic (and unofficial) poster created by the OWI's graphics section belittled this approach. It depicted the Statue of Liberty, whose upraised arm held four bottles of Coca-Cola. The caption read: "The War That Refreshes: The Four Delicious Freedoms." A group of OWI staff members, including a young historian, Arthur M. Schlesinger Jr., later resigned in protest against the agency's feel-good messages. In their resignation letter, they declared that OWI operations were dominated by "high pressure promoters who prefer slick salesmanship to honest information. . . . They are turning the Office of War Information into an Office of War Ballyhoo."[10]

Most OWI employees had little or no experience in media operations abroad. U.S. media involvement in overseas markets was a shadow of their present-day global outreach: the war had cut off or reduced most of their foreign sales after 1939. The Hollywood studios in particular suffered because overseas revenues accounted for over a third of their earnings by 1940. The other U.S. media—books, newspapers, and radio broadcasting—had not yet developed strong markets abroad. Lacking any large media presence in most parts of the world, the OWI had to create its own media channels and products to reach foreign audiences.

What the agency's international division had going for it was the strong curiosity among ordinary people abroad about the distant land that now had become involved in the war. Their understanding of the United States ranged from the sketchy to the nonexistent. Even now, despite the Internet and global television, it is probably still true that most of the world's population knows the United States primarily as the name of a large foreign country. To use the familiar opinion-polling phrase, the "don't knows" outnumber those who have a reasonably accurate idea of American life. Their concerns are bound geographically by their village and perhaps a nearby market town, socially by their family and clan, and by heavens and hells that make our own traditions seem pale by contrast.

What is often real to them has been a mythic perception of a far-off country whose citizens are acquiring what the rest of the world thinks it wants. Malcolm Muggeridge, the acerbic British journalist, once summarized this phenomenon:

> Driving at night into the town of Athens, Ohio (pop. 450), bright colored lights stood out in the darkness: "Gas." "Drugs." "Beauty." "Food." Here, I thought, is the ultimate, the logos of our time, presented in sublime simplicity. It was like a vision in which suddenly all the complexity of life is reduced to one single inescapable proposition. These signs could have shone forth as clearly in Athens, Greece, as in Athens, Ohio. They belonged as aptly to Turkestan or Sind or Kamchatka. All the world loves Lucy.[11]

This is the psychic environment in which most foreigners placed the United States—and (with reservations) continue to do so. Despite active and often violent opposition to specific U.S. policies, their fascination with American culture and lifestyles set the context within which the OWI, and later the USIA, operated. It was the unique edge that U.S. ideological operations had overseas during the long decades of hot and cold wars.

In 1942, OWI director Elmer Davis faced the immediate problem of creating, largely from scratch, a broad array of media channels for reaching foreign audiences. At the time, the U.S. government had few capabilities in this area. This deficit was particularly acute in radio broadcasting, which had emerged as the most powerful tool for national propaganda efforts around the world. In the years before World War II, radio had become, in the words of British communications scholar Anthony Smith, "the supreme cultural instrument of the nation-state . . . a vast socializing instrument by which all the members of a society could be contacted simultaneously. With the wireless radio would arrive the possibility of defining cultural policy as deliberately as economic policy; it created national markets for cultural production, national arbitrage for artistic reputation and a new constituency for politics."[12]

Mindful of these factors, most governments took direct control of the structure and content of radio broadcasting as it expanded throughout the 1920s. The United States was the exception. In the very early days of radio, anyone could get permission to operate a transmitter simply by sending a postcard to the Department of Commerce in Washington, notifying it which frequency they planned to use.

At the same time, there was little U.S. interest in international broadcasting. The domestic radio market was big, booming, and increasingly profitable; commercial broadcasters had no motivation to reach out to foreign audiences who could not buy the wares advertised on their stations.

Overseas governments did not share these attitudes. They saw the value of broadcasting as a political instrument, capable of influencing foreign as well as domestic audiences. One of the earliest advocates of this use of radio was V. I. Lenin, the leader of the Bolshevik revolution. Before his death in 1924 he ordered a massive expansion of Soviet domestic radio broadcasting to allow Communist authorities in Moscow to consolidate their authority across the new Soviet Union. They soon expanded these broadcasts to include foreign-language versions reaching neighboring countries. Radio Moscow grew into an international network accessible to listeners in all parts of the world. The Nazi regime in Germany followed suit, installing shortwave transmitters capable of reaching beyond Europe into Asia and the Western Hemisphere.[13]

In Western Europe, the British and French governments developed similar facilities, designed primarily to reach their colonies in Africa and Asia. In 1932, the British Broadcasting Corporation (BBC) inaugurated overseas shortwave transmissions, known as the Empire Service. The corporation later expanded its overseas operations into Europe and North America. Because few Americans had shortwave-capable radio sets, the BBC negotiated with local medium-wave stations to rebroadcast its programs. Within a year, about 130 stations had agreed to do so. Although these programs had relatively few listeners, they helped bolster the BBC's reputation as a reliable information source. This well-earned reputation obscured the fact that British government officials subtly managed the content of the BBC's overseas broadcasts.[14]

The United States meanwhile lagged badly in establishing a global radio presence. Early efforts to do so were dominated by the New York commercial networks' attempts to develop advertising-supported programs beamed overseas. The Columbia Broadcasting System was the first network to broadcast internationally, beginning with experimental programming to Latin America in 1930.[15] However, the networks' plans for full-scale overseas broadcasting in the 1930s were slow to materialize.

The federal government played no role in these developments until 1939 when the Federal Communications Commission (FCC) ruled that foreign transmissions by U.S. broadcasters should be limited to programs that "reflect the culture of this country and which will promote international goodwill, understanding and cooperation." The FCC withdrew its ruling when CBS, NBC, the National Association of Broadcasters, and the American Civil Liberties Union opposed it on First Amendment grounds.

Meanwhile both CBS and NBC had achieved some success in attracting commercial sponsors for their Latin American transmissions, including the United Fruit Co. and Standard Oil, both of which had large economic interests in the region. Another shortwave station operator, the Crossley Company in Cincinnati, had a more eclectic list of advertisers that included Kleenex, Alka-Seltzer, Planter's Peanuts, and Carter's Little Liver Pills.[16]

This commercial pattern changed abruptly in 1940 when Nelson Rockefeller's Office of the Coordinator of Interamerican Affairs (CIAA) began operations as a semi-independent unit within the State Department. Shortwave radio was central to Rockefeller's plans for countering Nazi propaganda within Latin America. After contentious negotiations, he contracted for air time on several commercial transmitters, broadcasting a mix of news and entertainment programming. It was a small beginning for the United States' entry into the global radio wars, a contest in which it eventually became the biggest player.

At the time of Pearl Harbor, the United States had fewer than a dozen shortwave transmitters capable of overseas broadcasting. (The German government had sixty-eight.) All of these transmitters, including those already broadcasting into Latin America as part of Nelson Rockefeller's operations, were pressed into service by the Office of War Information when it established the Voice of America (VOA) service.

The OWI's immediate problem after Pearl Harbor was to reach out to new radio audiences across two wide oceans. This goal was met with a crash program of transmitter construction that, by war's end, gave the Voice of America a global presence. The most pressing need was to reach European audiences in occupied countries and in Germany and Italy. The OWI arranged with the BBC to share the corporation's medium-wave facilities in Britain. OWI radio teams followed Allied troops into North Africa and Europe, taking over transmitters in Tunis,

Palermo, Bari, and other cities. The agency also developed its own medium-wave facilities, the American Broadcasting Station in Europe, which operated out of BBC studios in London.[17]

Starting up operations in Asia was more difficult. Only one transmitter, in California, was capable of reaching Asian audiences at the time of Pearl Harbor. New transmitters in Hawaii and, later, in the Philippines, eventually gave the Voice of America a presence in Japan and on the Asian mainland.

By 1945, the OWI had thirty-nine transmitters worldwide, broadcasting in forty languages. For the first time, hundreds of millions of overseas listeners had a direct information connection with the United States. They were also were being introduced to a new, faster-paced way of presenting news and entertainment programming that contrasted sharply with the stilted government-controlled broadcasts to which they were accustomed.

This change was reinforced by another innovation: U.S. military radio stations that followed the troops as they moved out overseas. The first such station was set up in London in 1942 when the advance contingent of U.S. units arrived. Their numbers swelled to over a million by the time of the invasion of France two years later. General Dwight Eisenhower, the supreme Allied commander for the invasion, saw home-style radio broadcasting as one solution to easing morale problems as his troops trained for the invasion. He ordered planning to begin for an Armed Forces Network (AFN), a series of low-powered, medium-wave stations throughout Britain that would feature news and entertainment programming, the latter mostly repeats of popular stateside shows.

BBC officials took exception to the AFN proposal, seeing it as a threat to their broadcasting monopoly and, specifically, to the prospect that the stations would lead to the introduction of commercial broadcasting.[18] Upset by this opposition, Eisenhower took his case to Prime Minister Winston Churchill. A longtime maverick in British politics who had had his own battles with BBC authorities, Churchill issued an order authorizing the AFN project.[19]

In addition to being an important morale booster for the troops, the AFN stations attracted millions of British listeners, particularly young people intrigued by the breezy style of the American programs. The AFN stations in Britain were the first in a string of similar installations that operated across the globe by the end of the war. AFN stations became an important resource in the overall U.S. ideological war effort, particularly in introducing foreign audiences to cultural information as well as to a new media style.[20]

The OWI also benefited from cooperative arrangements with U.S. commercial media organizations. It is useful to summarize these since they set important precedents for later relationships between USIA and private media companies during the Cold War decades. These relationships varied widely, ranging from close cooperation to tense hostility. The net result, however, was that USIA played a useful role in helping domestic media firms establish a commercial base for their overseas expansion in the postwar decades.

In the weeks after Pearl Harbor, U.S. media pledged strong support for the war effort. This included agreeing to voluntary guidelines for dealing with news about military movements, war production activities, and other sensitive subjects. This cooperation eventually expanded into active collaboration with the OWI in wartime propaganda operations.

The most reluctant among the media firms offering such cooperation were the three U.S. press agencies—the Associated Press, United Press, and the International News Service. They tended to regard the OWI as a competitor, particularly in overseas news distribution. By the end of the war, the OWI was operating a global press service that transmitted 100,000 words a day to sixty overseas posts, as well as a global radio-photo network and its own transatlantic cable facilities. Although the three commercial agencies agreed to self-censorship of their news copy, they resisted more direct government involvement in their operations. The extent of their cooperation was to let the OWI use their news output on a cost-for-transmission basis.[21] Overall, the three press agencies maintained most of their editorial independence during the war, despite occasional government attempts to influence their products through overzealous censorship.

Other print media organizations developed closer relations with the OWI. The agency was particularly interested in expanding distribution of U.S. newspapers and magazines abroad. Both the OWI and Nelson Rockefeller's CIAA provided direct assistance to the editors of the *Reader's Digest* in launching the first of their international language editions in Sweden and in Latin America.[22]

U.S. book publishers also became the direct beneficiaries of an OWI program to introduce their products abroad. Overseas markets had been largely closed to them before the war, in part because British and French publishers dominated the field through longtime alliances with foreign book distributors. The OWI publications unit took the first steps toward breaking up this arrangement by sponsoring an extensive paperback book series, Overseas Editions, which was distributed in neutral countries and, clandestinely, in occupied territories. The unit also negotiated contracts with publishers-in-exile for U.S. books that appeared soon after their countries were liberated.

The OWI also recognized the influential role played by Hollywood films in reaching foreign audiences. Commenting on the global impact of American films, London's staid *Times Literary Supplement* later observed:

> What the Tower of London is to England in foreign imaginations, so is Hollywood to the United States in those parts of the world which do not fly the Stars and Stripes. The Tower, however, is static and in that sense it runs true to symbolic form, but the products of Hollywood go all over the world, flown in jet aircraft and climbing the goat trail. They are dynamic, ubiquitous, brash, shameless, persuasive, compelling the cultures of ancient, alien countries to copy their formula and imitate their style. . . . Here is the Voice of America made visible.[23]

Although the OWI produced its own documentary films, it also enlisted the help of the California film studios in its overseas operations. A "war activities committee" was created by the industry to coordinate its mobilization efforts, with the OWI as the group's primary point of contact with the government. The industry's support consisted largely in shifting its production emphasis to war-related products, from lightweight comedies (*Blondie for Victory*) and musicals (*Star-Spangled Rhythm*) to combat epics in which familiar stars such as John Wayne and Clark Gable triumphed over snarling Germans and Japanese, the latter usually portrayed as subhuman creatures.[24]

In New York, OWI officials fretted about the deficiencies of Hollywood's wartime products in delivering a clear ideological message. The industry's output was "escapist and delusionary," one agency official complained. "Hollywood is letting its imagination carry it away," OWI director Elmer Davis declared.[25] In an effort to improve the film studios' performance, the agency set up a "bureau of intelligence" to assess the industry's output in terms of its contribution to the government's propaganda effort at home and abroad. To its credit, the OWI never directly attempted to censor Hollywood films. It limited its efforts to suggesting ways in which a film could deliver stronger win-the-war messages.

In a few instances, the OWI's suggestions were sound, and script changes were made. At other times, the advice was naïve, as in the case of *Casablanca*, probably the most effective film in terms of propaganda impact produced by wartime Hollywood. The OWI reviewers saw all kinds of opportunities to improve the film to fit their purposes. In the last memorable scene, Humphrey Bogart, the cynical American, and Claude Rains, the collaborating French police chief, walk into the foggy night as Bogart utters the classic line: "Louie, this could be the beginning of a beautiful friendship." As one commentator noted later, the OWI reviewers would have preferred an uplifting sermonette explaining Nazi aggression and the justice of the Allied cause.[26]

The OWI closed down its movie-review unit in 1943. The agency's attempt to improve the industry's products began what in later years became a long and occasionally testy relationship between Hollywood and Washington on the role of commercial films in the nation's overseas ideological efforts.

Wartime Hollywood did cooperate fully with the government in one important area of its production activities. This involved newsreels, a now-forgotten film product that in pretelevision days gave domestic and foreign filmgoers their most dramatic view of current events. At the government's request, the Hollywood studios set up the United Newsreel Co., which made all of their newsreel footage available to the OWI. The agency selected appropriate segments, which United Newsreel turned into a weekly newsreel, incorporating OWI-written commentary. The company then produced and distributed the final product through theater outlets overseas.[27]

The OWI also collaborated with Hollywood in distributing the industry's commercial products abroad during the war. This was a tit-for-tat operation. The agency was allowed to choose forty feature films for distribution as part of its own activities in neutral countries and in liberated territories. In exchange, it facilitated Hollywood's initial entry into the postwar overseas film market by shipping and distributing over 250 features abroad.

As the war progressed, the OWI devoted more time to setting up operational posts abroad, under the newly minted name of the U.S. Information Service (USIS). The first and largest of these posts, in London, had 1,600 employees at the height of its wartime operations. London was a major OWI production center for materials intended for audiences in Europe. It also served as a redistribution center for pamphlets and other products developed at the agency's New York headquarters. These included a mix of the useful and the irrelevant, the latter often reflecting the consumer-marketing background of the OWI staff.

One successful product was *Victory*, a lavish, *Life*-style magazine sold or given away in friendly or neutral countries around the world. Another successful product was a four-page tabloid newspaper, *L'Amérique en Guerre,* 7 million copies of which were air-dropped weekly over cities in occupied France before D-Day. Other newspapers were produced for occupied Norway and for neutral Spain and Ireland.[28]

The New York office also promoted so-called specialty items. These included matchbooks, shoelaces, and sewing kits, each including a liberation message for audiences in enemy-occupied areas.[29] Inevitably some of these air-dropped messages wound up in the wrong place. Five years after the war ended, a USIS officer assigned to Oslo found that the post was overstocked with cartons of red-white-and-blue soap bars, each imprinted with a liberation message printed in Spanish.[30]

Following the Allied invasion of Europe in June 1944, USIS posts were set up in Paris, Toulouse, and Lyon, just behind advancing troops. Bob Hickok, an OWI officer assigned to the Lyon office, later recalled that one of his first projects was to mount a hastily prepared photo exhibit in a local town hall, responding to criticisms by local Communist resistance leaders that the United States was not doing as much as the Soviet Union to defeat the Germans. The exhibit was a popular success, and the Communists muted their criticisms.

Meanwhile, an effort to establish a USIS post in Moscow was thwarted by Soviet officials. They also turned down a proposal to station a VOA radio reporter in Moscow in exchange for free time for a Soviet correspondent on a U.S. station. OWI efforts to reach Soviet citizens through Russian-language VOA transmissions were limited by the general lack of shortwave receivers in the country. Eventually, a daily news bulletin was issued by the U.S. embassy, using material from a State Department radio bulletin, a U.S. Army news file from Tehran, and OWI materials relayed through London. Although the bulletin was distributed to Soviet news agencies, little of its contents was used by them.

The most successful OWI operation in the wartime Soviet Union was the publication of a slick-paper magazine, *America Illustrated*. After protracted negotiations, the Soviet government agreed to its distribution, with the proviso that its editorial content be approved by Foreign Ministry censors. Although its circulation was only 32,000 copies, the magazine was a popular success, with copies passed from hand to hand until they became shredded from use.

Setting up OWI posts in other parts of the world proved equally difficult. In the Middle East and South Asia, the agency operated in regions where the British and French had colonies and other longstanding political interests. The American ideological emphasis on the Atlantic Charter's Four Freedoms, including political self-determination, clashed with the intent of these two allies to maintain their colonial influence in the region after the war.[31]

The gap between U.S. and British policy was particularly acute in India, where the OWI had established posts in several large cities. Britain's prime minister, Winston Churchill, had earlier made it clear that, in his words, he did not intend to preside over the liquidation of the British Empire. Meanwhile, Americans, including President Roosevelt, were generally sympathetic to the Indians' attempts to gain independence.

The OWI was caught in an ideological bind. The agency, one of its officials declared, "is not in India to fortify the cause of British imperialism." Eventually, the OWI had to moderate its stance, agreeing at one point not to distribute one of its pamphlets, "The United Nations Fight for the Four Freedoms," which the State Department deemed "unsuitable for India as it might incite the Indians against the British."[32] Further difficulties were avoided after an Anglo-American coordination group agreed in August 1942 to a common propaganda policy in dealing with India, one that recognized the priority of winning the war first and dealing with colonialism later. The controversy foreshadowed later controversies between the United States and its wartime allies as dozens of former colonies moved toward independence in the postwar years.

China also presented a difficult problem for U.S. policymakers. Japanese military units had occupied large parts of the country since 1936. For the U.S. government, this had the immediate advantage of tying down enemy troops who might otherwise be facing U.S. forces. But it also had the disadvantage of complicating the prospects of ending an ongoing Chinese civil war involving Nationalist forces under Chiang Kai-shek and Communist guerrillas headed by Mao Zedong. Both Chiang and Mao had one eye on the Japanese and the other on each other.

The OWI, along with twenty other U.S. government agencies, set up shop in Chungking, the bomb-battered capital of the Nationalist government. Each of the agencies had ambiguous and often conflicting missions to enlist both Nationalist and Communist support for the Allied war effort. This included ideological operations, a project that was initially undertaken before Pearl Harbor by Bill Donovan's Office of the Coordinator of Information (COI). In December 1941, McCracken Fisher, a longtime United Press correspondent in China, was named as the COI's representative at the U.S. embassy at Chungking.

Fisher proceeded to set up the first official overseas U.S. information outpost outside those in the Western Hemisphere that formed part of Nelson's Rockefeller's information and cultural operations. Fisher rented a thatch-roofed mud bungalow in the Nationalist Ministry of Information's compound and put up a sign identifying it as the American Information Service.[33]

The OWI took over the Chungking outpost several months later. The renamed U.S. Information Service operated an extensive press and publications program while trying to avoid the convoluted politics involving other U.S. agencies, including the Office of Strategic Services (OSS), in their negotiations between the Nationalist and Communist forces.[34]

U.S. ideological operations in wartime China also included the first cultural relations program outside the Western Hemisphere. The project resulted from a strong plea by the Chungking embassy to the State Department to set up an exchange program involving Chinese and U.S. academic and technical experts. After some delays, several dozen Chinese educators and other professionals came to the United States between 1943 and 1947. A similar number of U.S. specialists went to China in the same period. The exchange program was unique in another way, namely that the embassy officer in charge of the program, Wilma Fairbank, was the first woman to manage an overseas U.S. cultural operation.[35]

Meanwhile, Elmer Davis and his staff in New York were under pressure to adapt their operations to the changing nature of the war. The OWI had an amorphous charter that, in its international operations, emphasized the need to give foreign audiences a credible account of the United States at war as well as its postwar aims. The agency's leitmotif was the Atlantic Charter, the statement of war aims drafted by President Roosevelt and Prime Minister Churchill in their August 1941 meeting on a British battleship off the coast of Newfoundland. OWI overseas media output emphasized the importance of destroying fascist forces in Europe and Asia and of promoting self-determination for all people after the war.

It was a high-minded message, heavily promoted by the OWI around the world. However, Allied military planners regarded it as increasingly irrelevant to their immediate problem of mounting two unprecedented operations—the invasions of Europe and Japan. By 1943, pressures intensified to redirect the OWI's operations toward tactical psychological warfare operations supporting the invasions.

This tougher approach was closer to the already proven British model of information warfare. In London, a top-secret Political Warfare Executive became increasingly effective in undermining enemy morale through covert operations. Among the most successful of these British projects were "black radio" transmissions that falsely identified themselves as coming from German stations. These transmissions used military-intelligence information to spread doubt and confusion among enemy audiences, both military and civilian.[36]

The United States had lagged in planning such operations until 1941, when William Donovan successfully urged President Roosevelt to authorize similar capabilities for the U.S. defense effort. Black radio transmissions became an important part of the covert information operations carried out after Pearl Harbor by Donovan's OSS.

These "psywar" operations got their first test when U.S. troops landed in North Africa in November 1942. Small teams took over radio stations and newspaper facilities, turning them into effective instruments for encouraging enemy troops to surrender as well as seeking civilian cooperation. Millions of surrender leaflets were air-dropped, with effective results.

In London, these efforts impressed the new supreme commander for European operations, Dwight Eisenhower. "I don't know much about psychological warfare, but I want to give it every chance," he declared.[37] A Psychological Warfare Branch organized under his command included the military, the OSS, the OWI, and two British groups—the Ministry of Information and the Political Warfare Executive.

In Washington, President Roosevelt issued an executive order placing the OWI under military command in war theaters and requiring Joint Chiefs of Staff approval of OWI materials.[38] The agency's original focus on strategic political operations would henceforth be subordinated to tactical military needs. In effect, the high-minded ideological crusade gave way to targeted objectives. These circumstances would be repeated, with variations, in USIA's operations in Vietnam twenty years later.

In the months before the invasion of Europe in June 1944, the OWI helped plan and carry out a massive campaign to shake German army morale, involving over 800 million air-dropped surrender leaflets. Most frontline military commanders accepted the operation's usefulness. The flamboyant General George S. Patton was among the early skeptics. Reacting to a suggestion that he use more leaflet operations against enemy soldiers, he declared: "I'm not here to write 'em letters. I'm here to kill the sons of bitches."[39] He later recognized the value of surrender appeals when enemy soldiers began crossing the lines, leaflets in hand.

Meanwhile, the new U.S. Information Service posts on the European continent were being integrated into the military-tactical effort. A particularly effective operation was carried out in neutral Switzerland. The USIS post was a one-man operation in Berne run by a young OWI officer, Gerald Mayer, working with the local OSS station chief, Allan Dulles, who later became one of the first directors of the CIA.

Ostensibly there to provide general information about the United States to the local Swiss burghers, Mayer and Dulles extended their activities to neighboring occupied countries. OWI publications were smuggled onto railway trains and, on occasion, floated down rivers on little rafts, wrapped in waterproof containers.

Mayer also planted news stories, written by OWI editors in New York, by telephone to Express Telegraph, a private press agency permitted by the Nazis to serve local newspapers throughout occupied Europe. The arrangement worked until one day a guttural voice broke into the phone call. In thickly accented English, it announced: "The American news now stops." Click, and the line was cut off.[40]

As Allied troops closed in on the German heartland, the OWI used radio broadcasts effectively to convince both German civilians and the military that they were losing the war. Although the German army tried to destroy radio transmitters as it retreated, it failed to do so with Radio Luxembourg, the second most powerful station on the continent. A daring tank raid by U.S. troops captured the station intact. This success gave the Allied forces a medium-wave broadcasting signal that could reach most of Germany. OWI and army radio experts reconfigured the station's frequencies so that it could operate both as a regular station transmitting music and news, and as a clandestine station, Radio 1212.

The latter was ostensibly run from within Germany by anti-Nazi dissidents. It featured, among other news items, accurate accounts of the damage being done by Allied bombers to German cities, information suppressed by the Berlin government. Although German authorities tried to jam Radio 1212 transmissions, the station attracted a large audience of civilians and soldiers, despite the fact that listening to it was punishable by death.[41]

When European hostilities ended in May 1945, OWI officials turned their full attention to the Pacific war. Unlike Europe, there was no central Allied command in the region, making it difficult to coordinate OWI operations. Moreover, U.S. military commanders, particularly those in the navy, were suspicious of a civilian agency with a rogue reputation. These suspicions were reduced somewhat when President Roosevelt brought Elmer Davis to a conference of military commanders in Honolulu in July 1944. The president extracted a pledge from them that they would work more closely with the OWI. Psychological warfare operations in the region improved considerably, as U.S. troops moved from island to island, closing in on Japan. As in Europe, radio broadcasting played a central role in the OWI's Pacific operations.[42]

High-powered shortwave transmitters were constructed in Hawaii and in the Philippines to augment the single installation that existed in California before Pearl Harbor. The capture of the island of Saipan in the western Pacific allowed the OWI to build a medium-wave station that could be heard on ordinary home receivers in Japan. The station gave the civilian population information about the grim realities that their country faced, including the inevitability of a massive U.S. invasion of their homeland. It was the beginning of an ideological campaign by the United States to bring Japan back into the family of nations, a process in which USIA later played an important role.

The war ended with the Japanese surrender in August 1945. The Office of War Information and other temporary wartime agencies suddenly had no visible mission. For the OWI, officially there was nothing more to explain. When the agency was closed down, less than a month after the Japanese surrender, it left a mixed legacy of successes and failures. On balance, the successes outweighed the failures, particularly as the agency itself gained confidence and experience during its three years of operations.

The OWI created the pattern for a continuing U.S. presence overseas in the field of ideological operations. By the end of the war, it had established (together with Nelson Rockefeller's Latin American operation) a physical presence in over forty countries, along with a global Voice of America radio network.

In August 1945, these were important national assets. Questions remained, however, as to whether the U.S. government would sustain its overseas ideological operations in the postwar era. As we shall see in the next chapter, doubts about the issue persisted for years after the last shots were fired in World War II.

Notes

1. "A Giant Named Elmer," *Washington Journalism Review,* December 1991, p. 37.
2. Theodore Olson, "We Told the World," *Foreign Service Journal,* August 1968, p. 16.
3. Wilson Dizard, *The Strategy of Truth: The Story of the United States Information Service* (Washington, D.C.: Public Affairs Press, 1961), p. 36.
4. The OWI did make an attempt to train its employees for propaganda work at a posh Long Island estate: "Psychological Warfare: The OWI Runs a School for Propaganda," *Life,* December 13, 1943, pp. 81–84.
5. The early history of public opinion research in the United States is detailed in: Wilbur Schramm (Stephen Chaffee and Everett M. Rogers, eds.), *The Beginnings of Communications Study in America: A Personal Memoir* (Thousand Oaks, Calif.: Sage Publications, 1997). The book, written by one of the pioneers in the field, was edited following Schramm's death in 1987.

6. Harold Lasswell, *Propaganda Techniques in the World War* (London: Kegan Paul, 1927). A paperback edition was issued by MIT Press in 1971.

7. Schramm, *Beginnings of Communications Study,* p. 35.

8. U.S. public opinion attitudes on propaganda in the interwar years are described in: O. W. Riegel, *Mobilizing for Chaos: The Story of the New Propaganda* (New Haven. Conn.: Yale University Press, 1934).

9. Schramm, *Beginnings of Communications,* p. 55. Frank Stanton later became president of CBS. In that role, he served as an adviser to USIA, including leading a study on the agency's organization in the 1970s.

10. Allan M. Winkler, *The Politics of Propaganda: The Office of War Information 1942–1945* (New Haven, Conn.: Yale University Press, 1978), pp. 64–65.

11. Malcolm Muggeridge, *Things Past* (London: Collins Publishers, 1978), p. 125.

12. Anthony Smith, "The Wire and the Wavelength—An Historical Study," in *Cable: An Investigation of the Social and Political Implications of Cable Television,* Report of the Standing Conference on Broadcasting, London, 1974, p. 29.

13. Philip E. Jacob, "The National Socialist Theory of Radio Propaganda," in Harwood L. Childs and John B. Whitton (eds.), *Propaganda by Shortwave* (Princeton, N.J.: Princeton University Press, 1943), pp. 51–108.

14. Daniel Katz, "Britain Speaks," in Harwood L. Childs and John B. Whitton (eds.), *Propaganda by Shortwave* (Princeton, N.J.: Princeton University Press, 1943), p. 111.

15. Douglas A Boyd, "The Prehistory of the Voice of America," *Public Telecommunications Review,* December 1976, p. 41.

16. Ibid., p. 42.

17. Robert Bauer, "D-Day, June 6, 1944," in *United States Information Agency: A Commemoration,* U.S. Information Agency Office of Public Information, 1999, p. 8.

18. The BBC's fears were realized after the war when British commercial radio and television stations were approved by Parliament. Wilson Dizard, *Television: A World View* (Syracuse, N.Y.: Syracuse University Press, 1966), pp. 30–33.

19. "Allied on the Airwaves," *History Today* (London), January 1999, pp. 29–34.

20. For a summary of AFN's early impact, see: Donald R. Browne, "The World in the Pentagon's Shadow," *Educational Broadcasting Review* 5, no. 2, April 1971, pp. 31–48.

21. Charles A. W. Thomson, *Overseas Information Service of the U.S. Government* (Washington, D.C.: Brookings Institution, 1948), p. 59.

22. Ibid., p. 128.

23. Quoted in Dizard, *Strategy of Truth,* p. 88.

24. For an overall survey of the film studios' activities during the war, see: George R. Koppes and Gregory D. Black, *Hollywood Goes to War: How Politics, Profits and Propaganda Shaped World War II Movies* (New York: Free Press/Macmillan, 1987).

25. Winkler, *The Politics of Propaganda,* p. 58.

26. George R. Koppes and Gregory D. Black, "OWI Goes to the Movies," *Foreign Service Journal,* August 1974, p. 18.

27. Thomson, *Overseas Information Service*, pp. 65–67.
28. Thomas C. Sorensen, *The Word War: The Story of American Propaganda* (New York: Harper & Row, 1968), p. 17.
29. Winkler, *The Politics of Propaganda*, p. 80.
30. Olson, "We Told the World," p. 17.
31. Seth Arsenian, "Wartime Propaganda in the Middle East," *Middle East Journal*, October 1948, pp. 417–429.
32. Winkler, *The Politics of Propaganda*, p. 84.
33. F. McCracken Fisher, "Which USIS Came First?: Reminiscences of an Old China Hand," *USIA Alumni Association Newsletter*, September 1983, p. 3.
34. Yu Maochun, *OSS in China: Prelude to the Cold War* (New Haven, Conn.: Yale University Press, 1997).
35. Wilma Fairbank, "Experiment in China," *Exchange*, Bureau of Educational and Cultural Affairs, Department of State, spring 1976, pp. 9–16.
36. The Political Warfare Executive's activities, including its relationship with U.S. organizations, are described in: Charles Cruickshank, *The Fourth Arm: Psychological Warfare 1938–1945* (London: Davis-Poynter, 1977).
37. Winkler, *The Politics of Propaganda*, p. 129.
38. "Defining the Foreign Information Activities of the Office of War Information," Executive Order 9312, March 9, 1943, *Federal Register* 8, no. 50, p. 3021.
39. Winkler, *The Politics of Propaganda*, p. 129.
40. Olson, "We Told the World," p. 18.
41. Lawrence W. Soley, *Radio Warfare: OSS and CIA Subversive Propaganda* (New York: Praeger Publishers, 1989), pp. 138–150.
42. Winkler, *The Politics of Propaganda*, p. 66.

3

From Hot War to Cold War

THE OFFICE OF WAR INFORMATION (OWI) ranked high on the list of wartime agencies slated to be closed down in the weeks after the Japanese surrender in August 1945. The agency was particularly vulnerable because its overseas activities were little known to the public.

Moreover, powerful political forces, including the commercial media establishment, regarded the OWI with suspicion. Media companies tended to see the OWI as the thin wedge of government control over their activities, eroding First Amendment protections. The federal establishment's ability to organize media operations worldwide loomed as a potential threat to their plans for postwar expansion into overseas markets—a recurring theme in the history of the OWI's successor, the U.S. Information Agency.

The most immediate threat to the continuity of the overseas information program came from Congress. The OWI's budget had been under steady attack during the war by a coalition of conservative Republicans and Southern Democrats, who constituted a majority in a legislature nominally controlled by the Democratic leadership. Even before the Japanese surrender, one Republican, Representative Leon Gavin of Pennsylvania, suggested that the OWI be abolished "to save $50 million for the taxpayers and a lot of headaches for the American people." For good measure, the conservative coalition in Congress also questioned the need for the State Department's Division of Cultural Relations.[1] Few legislators were prepared to defend a controversial government program whose activities had little relevance to their home districts.

Given these political factors, the White House moved quickly to close down the OWI less than two weeks after the Japanese surrender.

President Truman signed an executive order transferring the agency's functions to the Department of State and redesignating the program as the Interim International Information Service.[2] His decision was in line with earlier State Department studies on postwar foreign policy organization. Each proposed, with variations, that overseas information and cultural programs be consolidated in a single bureau within the department.[3]

The new organization's mandate was ambivalent, befitting its interim status. The White House executive order said that the United States "would endeavor" to conduct an international information program giving foreign audiences a "full and fair picture" of the United States and its policies.

However, some provisions in the presidential order, if carried out, would have severely restricted the program. These included a stipulation that future overseas information activities should supplement rather than compete with U.S. commercial media companies. The order required the State Department to limit its information programs to overseas areas where these companies did not operate. Interpreted literally, this would have confined the program to a few remote areas of Asia and Africa. It was a formula for future trouble.

In a less-noticed White House move, most of the functions of the Office of Strategic Services (OSS), including its covert psychological warfare activities, were transferred to the War Department as the ambiguously named Strategic Services Unit until a permanent plan for conducting covert activities could be decided upon.[4] The resulting bureaucratic cycle set the postwar pattern for both overt and covert propaganda operations.

These initial decisions about overseas information operations were codified into more permanent arrangements eighteen months later in the National Security Act of 1947. The act authorized the creation of a National Security Council (NSC) in the White House to advise the president on major foreign policy issues. In addition to the State Department, the council included two new agencies—the Defense Department, incorporating the former War and Navy Departments, and the Central Intelligence Agency, successor to Bill Donovan's Office of Strategic Services.

Propaganda and psychological warfare operations were not mentioned in the National Security Council legislation. However, the act contained catchall language authorizing the NSC to conduct "functions and duties . . . affecting the national security."[5] This gave the new council sufficient leeway to plan and carry out a national strategy for conducting overseas ideological operations in the early postwar years and during the Cold War that followed.

This strategy eventually included a role for an international information and cultural infrastructure, building on precedents set in the wartime operations of both the OWI and the OSS. In the months after the Japanese surrender, however, there was reason to doubt whether these operations would continue, even in a limited way. As noted above, the OWI's remaining assets had been assigned to a third level of the State Department as an *interim* international information service. It was an orphan operation, underfunded, understaffed, and unwanted by State Department officers who remembered the rocky relationship between OWI and the department during the war years.

The department's immediate problem was to find a credible director for its newly acquired information unit. The job was offered to Walter Lippman, the most distinguished newspaper commentator on U.S. foreign policy at the time. Lippman turned down the offer with the observation that he was opposed to the government's propaganda programs. Secretary of State James Byrnes then recruited William Benton, a partner in Benton and Bowles, a leading New York advertising agency. Benton had strong media credentials, but he was a tyro in Washington politics. He took over his job in October 1945 as head of the department's Bureau of Public Affairs, with responsibilities for both domestic and overseas information programs.

The latter included the bureaucratic shards of the OWI's wartime operations. Within a few months of the Japanese surrender, 90 percent of the agency's 13,000 employees were let go. Program time on transmitters used by the Voice of America (VOA) was cut back drastically, in part because they had been leased to the government from private broadcasters only for the duration of the war. The transmitters were returned to their commercial owners, with VOA programming limited to a few hours a day.

A more stubborn problem was the fact that Benton's office did not control most of the content being broadcast by the Voice of America. This was the result of a congressional stipulation, outlined in appropriations legislation, that private broadcasting companies be given contracts to provide the majority of VOA scripts. By the autumn of 1947, the NBC and CBS radio networks were producing 75 percent of the Voice's broadcasts. Among other consequences, this meant that most of the VOA's scriptwriters did not receive any substantive policy guidance from the State Department.

William Benton, the information program's new director, moved vigorously to give the program higher visibility in the department. Though not a foreign policy specialist, he had a better understanding than most Washington officials of the Soviet expansionist threat and of the role that information resources could play in dealing with it. In February 1946, Benton warned department officials about the impact of Moscow's ideological operations, pointing out that, in the Soviet view, "propaganda is in fact 'psychological warfare' all the time, not merely during war."[6] At the time, neither Secretary Byrnes or his successor, General George C. Marshall, paid much attention to his warnings. It was a clear sign that Benton was outside State's high-policy loop.

Despite this and other setbacks to the overseas information program, Benton could point to one postwar program that proved the value of information operations in foreign policy strategy—the U.S. success in introducing democratic concepts and practices to the leadership and populations of two former enemies, Germany and Japan. The approaches to this problem differed in the two countries, given their individual political and cultural situations. Nevertheless, a major ideological effort in each produced results that were critical in turning two former enemies into major U.S. allies throughout the Cold War and in the years since. The German and Japanese democratization campaigns were the most successful single events in postwar U.S. overseas ideological operations. They prepared much of the groundwork for the later policy and operational style of the U.S. Information Agency.

It was by no means a foregone conclusion in 1945 that democratization programs would succeed in Germany and Japan. The United States and its allies were prepared to impose a harsh occupation regime in both countries, in line with their war aim of unconditional surrender. The problem became most immediate with the end of hostilities in Germany in April 1945. The country's economic and political structure was in ruins. The population was dispirited, particularly as a result of credible reports of massacres, looting, and rape by Soviet troops that had swept in from the east in a successful effort to reach Berlin before Western forces.

The German populace also harbored nagging fears about U.S. intentions. Such fears were fueled by reports about a plan advanced by Secretary of the Treasury Henry M. Morgenthau to reduce postwar Germany to a country "primarily agricultural and pastoral in character."[7] The proposal was turned down by President Roosevelt, but not before Nazi domestic propaganda exploited it as an "international Jewry plot" to turn the country into (as one German official declared) a potato patch.

In fact, the occupation proved to be less harsh than feared in the zones controlled by U.S., British, and French military authorities. Government officials were rounded up, and preparations began for convicting the top leaders of war crimes. For ordinary Germans, the occupation meant taking the first steps toward restoring their day-to-day lives in a new situation. U.S. and other Allied occupation troops in the western zones turned out to be less menacing than Nazi propaganda had predicted. Despite strict rules laid down by military commanders about fraternization, contacts between Allied troops and the local population were soon rampant, from handing out chewing gum to children to informal couplings between Allied soldiers and German women.[8]

These individual contacts played a special role in advancing a major goal of western-zone authorities, namely the ideological reeducation of an entire population following years of exposure to Nazi propaganda. Variously known as "democratization" and "denazification," the program had gotten under way before the war ended. It included orientation lectures for the 360,000 German soldiers in U.S. prisoner-of-war camps, supervised by a War Department "POW special projects division."

Although the prisoners reacted initially to the lectures with attitudes ranging from skepticism to hostility, they were curious about a country they knew little about. Their images of the United States were often dominated by the writings of a popular German novelist, Karl May, whose stories featured an improbable cowboy, Old Shatterhand, who outlassoed, outshot, and generally outwitted Yankees and Indians alike on the Great Plains. Although May had traveled no further west than Buffalo, New York, on his one visit to the United States, his eighty Shatterhand books created an enduring myth about American culture for generations of Germans, selling over 100 million copies.[9] The POW orientation experiment, focused on explaining the workings of U.S. democracy, was intended, in part, to redirect the prisoners' Karl May images as they were repatriated to Germany.

Within the U.S. occupation zone, the Office of Military Government (OMGUS) set up an "information control division" to manage the denazification program. It closed down all information and cultural organizations in the zone, including newspapers, publishing houses, film studios, libraries, theaters, and opera companies. Occupation authorities then began the laborious task of investigating and licensing new proprietors for these enterprises. Within a year, they had cleared nearly 58,000 Germans for return to work in the music and theater trades alone.[10]

Strict censorship was ordered for newspaper and radio stations. To demonstrate a model of open journalism, the U.S. Army created a newspaper, *Die Neue Zeitung*, published in Munich, with a front-page banner that read: "An American newspaper for the German population." The paper was staffed by a combination of "clean" Germans and naturalized Americans who had fled Nazi rule in the 1930s. It quickly reached a circulation of 14.5 million, with an estimated 18 million readers, before it was closed down in 1955.[11]

A significant role in the denazification program was played by hundreds of U.S. army personnel and civilians. Known as "resident officers," they were assigned to towns and villages to supervise the democratization program at the local level. (One of them was Sergeant Henry Kissinger.) It was a grass-roots project from the start. The tone was set by Charles Thayer, the State Department's chief officer in Munich, in a briefing session for the resident officers: "Get out to towns and villages, buy the burgermeisters a beer, and talk with them about the United States and what we are trying to do here."[12] Many of the resident officers later joined USIA after it was set up in 1953.

Resident officers set up the first of what became an extensive network of America Houses ("Amerika Haüser"), small cultural institutes that included libraries, lecture rooms, and English-teaching facilities.[13] These installations served as a model for a global network of similar cultural centers created later by the U.S. Information Agency.

OMGUS authorities also managed a massive exchange operation that brought thousands of German journalists, teachers, businessmen, and anti-Nazi political leaders to the United States for a firsthand look at how a democratic society operated. Among the political leaders included in the exchanges was a young socialist activist, Willy Brandt, who later became the mayor of West Berlin and then chancellor of the reconstituted Federal Republic of Germany. The German exchange program, like the America Houses, was a model for similar programs managed by USIA posts throughout the world in later years.

In its early months of the occupation, the OMGUS reeducation program focused on positive themes such as civil liberties, media freedoms, and the like. There was little discussion of worsening postwar political relations between the three Western occupying powers and the Soviet Union. In part, this was the result of a four-power agreement on dealing with German media, whose rules were managed by an information control commission. Among other provisions, the occupying powers pledged not to issue "malicious information" about each other.

It soon became evident that Soviet occupation authorities were ignoring the agreement. Radio stations under their control were broadcasting a steady diet of anti-American material.[14] The U.S. Army's Munich newspaper, *Neue Zeitung,* was banned in the Soviet zone. Occupied Germany was becoming a major propaganda battlefield in Soviet-Western relations.

In October 1947, General Lucius Clay, military governor of the U.S. zone, ordered an information counteroffensive ("Operation Backtalk"), which took a decidedly tougher line toward the Soviet Union in general and its occupation policies in Germany in particular. Among other actions, a special pocket-sized edition of *Neue Zeitung* was printed for clandestine distribution in the Soviet zone.[15]

The most potent weapon in the new hard-line approach was a radio station in West Berlin—RIAS (Radio in the American Sector). RIAS had originally been set up as a small transmitter on the flatbed of a Signal Corps truck when U.S. soldiers moved into the devastated city during the final days of the war. As in other German towns, RIAS was intended to be a temporary substitute for the Berlin radio stations closed down by Allied authorities until a denazified national network could be set up. Sixty years later, a civilianized RIAS continued to broadcast in Berlin.

Within months after it went on the air in 1945, RIAS began its long career as the most striking example of radio's effectiveness in modern psychological warfare. The station soon emerged as a potent influence on public attitudes and actions in the Soviet zone. Moscow authorities had tightened their control over the zone as part of their plans for setting up a puppet communist government. RIAS, located in the center of the zone, had a clear signal throughout eastern Germany despite attempts by Soviet authorities to jam its signals. The station was regarded by its listeners as a German station, although they were well aware of its American connection.

The major concession to RIAS's U.S. sponsorship was a daily Voice of America German-language relay that accounted for less than 5 percent of the station's programming. The rest of its schedule was taken up with news and information programs prepared by the station's German staff. These transmissions included reports on Soviet-zone events, much of it supplied clandestinely by volunteers in the zone. Descriptions of closed communist meetings and other Soviet-sponsored activities were often aired within a few hours.

This RIAS capability was described at the time by a U.S. observer, foreign correspondent Edmund Taylor, as "the Gandhian strategy of constructive subversion, a technique against which the Communists seem to have no effective psychological defense."[16] RIAS and other American information and cultural activities in occupied Germany and Austria constituted the largest overseas ideological operation mounted by the United States then or since. At its height in the early 1950s, the program included a staff of over three thousand civilian and military men and women. Eventually, the program was cut back and its activities transferred to the new U.S. Information Agency in 1953.

Meanwhile, the democratization program in Japan faced different problems. In addition to the cultural distance between the Japanese and their U.S. occupiers, the country had been traumatized by the atom-bomb attacks on Hiroshima and Nagasaki. The occupation's tone was set by its leading personality, General Douglas A. MacArthur, who had assumed the imposing title of Supreme Commander, Allied Powers (SCAP). His mark was on every detail of the democratization effort, which was managed by a SCAP "civil education and information division" that reported directly to him.

Unlike the situation in Germany, the Japanese government, including the emperor's court, continued to function throughout the occupation. Most media organizations were allowed to continue their normal operations; only radio stations were subject to direct censorship. Newspaper content was monitored in conferences between Japanese editors and occupation authorities based largely on consensus agreements that were dutifully obeyed by the Japanese.[17]

Meanwhile, an extensive program of American-style libraries, exchange programs, and publishing ventures was set up throughout the country as part of the democratization effort. With the signing of the Japanese peace treaty in September 1951, these programs were taken over by the civilian U.S. Information Service (USIS) as part of the State Department's overseas information operations. Japan remained one of the largest single USIS programs abroad throughout the Cold War years.

Despite the success of the postwar democratization efforts in Germany and Japan, Republicans in Congress continued to attack the State Department's information program. William Benton's International Information Administration (IIA) endured a tenuous existence, unloved and largely ignored by the State Department's top command. Meanwhile, congressional critics of the program had strengthened their ranks as a result of the Republican Party's victories in the 1946 midterm elections. Both houses of Congress were returned to GOP control after the party's two decades in the political wilderness. This led to a new legislative assault on allegedly socialistic Roosevelt-era projects, including the overseas information program.

Despite threats by conservative Republicans to close it down, the information program's prospects began to improve. Congressional criticism of the Voice of America and other IIA operations continued, but it was muted by louder concerns over hostile Soviet moves in Eastern

Europe and in the Balkans. In March 1947, President Truman made an extraordinary request to Congress for direct military and economic aid to Greece and Turkey, aimed at resisting Soviet military pressures on both countries. The "Truman Doctrine" was the first significant drawing of lines against Moscow's aggressive moves.[18]

The role of propaganda in countering these Soviet actions soon emerged as a congressional issue. The leader in this effort was a South Dakota Republican, Representative Karl Mundt, previously best known for supporting legislation favoring his farmer constituency. An improbable candidate for the role of defender of the State Department's information program, Mundt was a vocal supporter of his party's attacks on the program, particularly its efforts to root out alleged Communist infiltration of the Voice of America staff. However, he also saw the VOA and other information programs as critical resources in countering Soviet ideological warfare.[19]

Mundt teamed up with a fellow Republican, Senator Alexander Smith of New Jersey, to sponsor legislation that would give permanent status to the State Department's information and cultural programs. Their proposal was treated skeptically at first by Republican leaders, longtime critics of the programs. Mundt assured them that his legislation included safeguards that "no Communists or parlor pinks or crypto-Communists or fellow travelers would have any part of this program in any way, shape or form."[20]

Mundt's pledge did not end his colleagues' suspicions. Senator Robert Taft of Ohio, the nominal leader of the congressional Republicans, called for postponing the legislation, arguing that it didn't make sense to give the information program permanent status while Congress was investigating mismanagement of its operations. Mundt and Smith stood their ground, however, firm in their belief that the United States needed a strong ideological response to Soviet aggression.

The event that tipped the balance in their favor was a congressional study tour of overseas information operations they organized in September 1947. Made up of a bipartisan group of a dozen senators and representatives, the group visited twenty-two countries in Europe and the Near East in five weeks. State Department officials recognized the importance of the tour in determining the future of the information program, particularly in relating its activities to Soviet aggressive moves. The congressional tour members were given a carefully scripted presentation of this theme at embassies and consulates along the study tour's route. The visit to Vienna was typical, as described later by a USIS officer who accompanied the group:

We took them first to the downtown Soviet Information Center, an eight-story blocklong building complete with a movie theater, lecture halls, exhibition floors, libraries with deep leather armchairs, and even a plush retreat for chess players—a showplace that lacked only one thing—customers, of whom barely a dozen could be seen in the whole establishment. Then we took our guests across the square to our own Amerika Haus—a bomb-shaken building at the city's busiest intersection, in which we occupied a string of rooms, some of them in a basement, and all of them so crowded that many readers had to stand. And yet checkers clocked an average of four thousand visitors a day.[21]

Most of the touring members of Congress were impressed. Their trip report strongly favored strengthening the State Department's overseas information and cultural programs, but rearguard opposition to the idea persisted. In the floor debate on the Smith-Mundt legislation, one congressman argued that the academic exchange program would enable foreign radicals "to poison the minds of students of this nation."[22] Despite this and similar objections, the Smith-Mundt bill was approved by both houses as Public Law 402, signed by President Truman on January 30, 1948.[23] The new law established ideological operations as a permanent part of U.S. foreign policy, a concept that continued to be attacked and compromised over the years but which remains the basic law governing overseas information operations to this day.

The Smith-Mundt legislation had another important effect on foreign policy. The debate leading up to its passage underscored the urgency of strengthening Western Europe against political and economic collapse. Three months before the Smith-Mundt study tour, Secretary of State George Marshall had proposed, in a commencement speech at Harvard, a program against "hunger, poverty, desperation and chaos" in the region.

State Department officials had seen the Smith-Mundt study tour as a special opportunity to demonstrate the need for what later became known as the Marshall Plan. Embassies along the tour were instructed to link support of a strong information effort with Europe's immediate requirements for economic assistance. The strategy worked. The study group's report highlighted the threat of Soviet "aggressive psychological warfare against us in order to discredit us and drive us out of Europe." Expanding the State Department's overseas information program, the report concluded, was a "necessary corollary to the European recovery plan."

The Smith-Mundt legislation gave the State Department's international information program a new lease on life. Congressional pressure led to the resignation of William Benton, the program's director, long suspected by the Republicans of New Deal tendencies. He was replaced by career diplomat George V. Allen, who brought to the job longtime experience with State Department attitudes and practices. Under Allen's direction, the program gained sizable budgetary increases.

The Voice of America doubled its language services, and added 900 employees. An elaborate plan to build fourteen high-powered transmitters was approved, allowing the VOA to reach hitherto poorly served regions and also to begin to override increased Soviet jamming of its programs. George Allen's influence also helped the VOA break free of the congressional mandate requiring the contracting out of most of its script-writing to private radio networks such as NBC and CBS.

The impetus for this change came from the political ineptitude of the networks themselves. A series of NBC scripts written for the VOA described the fictional travels of two foreign visitors to the United States. The program, *Know North America,* was a bumbling project from the start in its portrayal of life in the United States. Brigham Young was described as "a primitive priest," Pennsylvania Quakers were "a social problem," and members of Congress were portrayed as using their status to become millionaires. These and similar gaffes raised legislative hackles. Congress quickly ordered the network contracts canceled and script-writing authority restored to the VOA.[24]

Meanwhile, the State Department information program benefited indirectly from the Marshall Plan, which Congress approved in 1948. Over the next four years, Congress budgeted $13 billion for the plan. A small but significant portion of these funds was allocated to publicizing Marshall Plan operations at home and abroad. This publicity campaign was organized separately from the State Department's information program, primarily because the two leading Marshall Plan officials, auto executive Paul Hoffman and banker W. Averell Harriman, wanted to bypass the department's bureaucracy and its budgetary restraints. Within two years, the Marshall Plan publicity budget in Europe, with $65 million allocated to West Germany alone, far exceeded that of the department's worldwide information operations.[25]

The Marshall Plan's publicity headquarters in Paris created some of the most freewheeling and imaginative information projects carried out then or since. These included a striking series of documentary films about the plan's accomplishments, directed by up-and-coming young European filmmakers such as Vittorio DeSica and Roberto Rossellini. In Greece, the local Marshall Plan office outfitted a traditional fishing caique, named it the "Samuel Gridley Howe" after an American who had fought in the Greek wars of independence, and sailed it around the Greek islands distributing fishing hooks and propaganda leaflets. The hooks, in short supply in postwar Greece, were a small but critical part of the U.S. effort to restore the country's fishing industry.

Meanwhile, the State Department's overseas information program was adjusting its operations to new concerns in the Truman White House and in Congress about alleged Soviet superiority in propaganda operations. The Democratic Party saw the need to focus on the subject not only as a national security issue but also to counter Republican claims that it was, in the then-current phrase, soft on communism. The issue was to resonate strongly in the political maneuvering leading up to the 1952 presidential election.

As part of their effort to emphasize their anticommunist credentials, the Democrats discussed a plan in early 1950 for a dramatic expansion of the State Department's overseas information programs. The idea was surfaced in a speech by the program's first postwar director, William Benton, by then a Democratic senator from Connecticut. Benton proposed a worldwide "Marshall Plan of ideas" to counter Soviet propaganda.

His somewhat overwrought title was dropped, but the proposal became the centerpiece for a major speech by President Truman, delivered before the annual convention of the American Society of Newspaper Editors in April 1950. The president declared that the challenge of "imperialistic communism" was, above all, a struggle for the minds of men. He proposed a "Campaign of Truth" in which the United States would coordinate its information activities with those of other free nations "in a sustained, intensified program to promote the cause of freedom against the propaganda of slavery."[26]

The speech was well-received by the assembled editors, as reflected in their editorial columns. It also resulted in a welcome increase in congressional funding for the overseas information program. The White House submitted an $89 million supplemental budget request for the program, which exceeded by $5 million the State Department's request for the entire year. Although Congress finally authorized a somewhat smaller amount, the information program was in better fiscal and operational shape than it had ever been. As part of the Campaign of Truth initiative, the Voice of America was given funds to expand its services from twenty-three to forty-six languages.[27]

The State Department's overseas information division, now renamed the International Information Administration, was able to activate long-shelved plans to open new USIS posts in the Middle East, Asia, and Africa, focusing particularly on former colonies that had become independent states since the end of the war. By 1952, the IIA had expanded its overseas operations to eighty-eight countries.

Despite these changes, the IIA faced a continuing problem in identifying its place in overseas propaganda operations. The problem was complex, but it came down to defining the role of covert and overt ideological operations in U.S. strategy. The issue had its origins in the hastily arranged division of responsibilities for overt and covert operations during World War II. The Office of War Information carried out public operations and the Office of Strategic Services took on the covert role, the so-called "dirty tricks" assignments. Under wartime pressures, there was relatively little operational confusion between the two roles.

This pragmatic arrangement broke down in the early months after the Japanese surrender. As we have seen, the OSS's assets were sequestered away in the lower depths of the War Department. The OWI's remaining operations were relegated to third-level status in the State Department.

Defining the relationship between overt and covert propaganda operations in peacetime proved more difficult. The first attempt to do so took place at the second meeting of the National Security Council in November 1947. One of the agenda items was the organization of psychological warfare operations to counter Soviet challenges in this area. The Council recommended coordination of all information and psychological activities within the State Department's bureau of public affairs. It assigned responsibility for overt information operations to the State Department. Covert operations would be the responsibility of the new Central Intelligence Agency, acting under guidelines established by State.[28]

These coordination arrangements never worked smoothly. However logical the idea of an integrated national policy on ideological operations, it was bypassed in the general confusion of purposes among powerful interests to "do something" about Soviet aggression. Congress supplied a loud voice in the debate, imposing its will primarily through budget decisions.

In the private sector, the advertising industry weighed in with numerous suggestions on using its marketing skills to counter Soviet propaganda moves. The industry set up a task force to recommend a solution. After studying the problem for several months, the group invited a Foreign Service officer, Walter Schwinn, to come to New York to hear their recommendations. Schwinn had years of experience in dealing with Soviet propaganda methods, having been stationed in Eastern Europe.

Gathered in a conference room, the admen told Schwinn that the key to U.S. propaganda success was to create a distinctive symbol, one that would be instantly recognizable like Winston Churchill's V-for-victory sign in World War II or (one of the participants suggested) the sign of the cross. Moreover, they informed Schwinn, the committee had come up with just such a symbol. The committee chairman walked over to a blackboard and drew a Valentine-style heart. The idea, he said, is that our side had heart and the other side was heartless. Hearts could be scribbled on walls and sidewalks throughout the communist world as a sign of opposition. Music incorporating heart themes could be broadcast by the Voice of America. And so on, and so on. Schwinn was appalled. He held his tongue, and took the proposal back to Washington where it was quietly forgotten.

The academic community also offered advice on how to organize the U.S. ideological offensive. Research units at MIT, Harvard, Columbia, and the Rand Corporation each prepared specific recommendations for exploiting Soviet propaganda vulnerabilities.[29] All this was grist for the bureaucratic tug-of-war in Washington over basic decisions on psychological warfare operations.

The doctrinal underpinnings for the debate were largely defined by a high-level State Department Foreign Service officer, George F. Kennan. Following a tour as ambassador in Moscow, Kennan became director of the State Department's newly formed Policy Planning Staff (PPS) in 1947. He outlined his views on Moscow's postwar policies in a seminal article, "The Sources of Soviet Conduct," in the July 1947 issue of *Foreign Affairs*. Kennan's article has usually been summarized as advocating containment of Kremlin expansionism, an essentially defensive strategy. Actually, he saw drawing the line on Moscow's aggressive moves as only the initial stage in a longer-range project. Kennan envisioned a strategy in which the pull of Western cultural and economic forces would undermine Soviet domination of Eastern Europe. Dissension and unrest would follow, forcing Kremlin leaders to modify their international behavior or face internal collapse.

Kennan expanded on this second-stage theme in a December 1947 lecture to military officers at the National War College in Washington. He cited the Marshall Plan, then being debated in Congress, as part of an overall strategy that could lead to the liberation of Soviet-dominated nations in Eastern Europe. He then outlined a scenario for the "psychological dissolution of Soviet power" through the establishment of what he called a "salient of free political institutions in the region."[30]

Kennan did not mention psychological operations as such in his War College lecture, but he clearly appreciated their potential. Moreover, as head of the State Department's Policy Planning Staff, he had a bureaucratic base for carrying out his ideas. Two months after the lecture, the PPS made its initial recommendation that covert operations, including information programs, be extended to Eastern Europe. Among its proposals, the staff suggested recruiting Soviet-bloc refugees for "political-psychological operations," organized in part through "freedom committees" in the West. It was the first major plan for a covert campaign intended (in the then-current phrase) to roll back Soviet aggression in Europe.[31]

The proposed campaign put a heavy emphasis on radio broadcasting. Plans were drawn up for a network of stations designed to reach Soviet-bloc audiences with a liberation message. By 1950, two Munich-based operations, Radio Free Europe and Radio Liberation, clandestinely funded and run by the CIA, were broadcasting respectively into Eastern Europe and the Soviet Union. Both stations attracted significant audiences from the start, making them the most effective of the propaganda operations plans advanced by Kennan and others in the late 1940s.

Another successful project was a tightly coordinated campaign to influence the first postwar Italian elections in April 1948, in which the well-organized local Communist Party, subsidized from Moscow, threatened to dominate the central government. U.S. agencies, including the CIA, played a critical role in drumming up popular support for opposition parties, particularly the Vatican-backed Christian Democrats.[32]

U.S. support for centrist forces in the 1948 Italian elections resulted in a setback for the Communists, but other psywar projects in early postwar Europe were less successful. Many of them were impractical or preposterous, including the sending of small helium-filled balloons into Eastern Europe, carrying liberation messages.[33] The general failure of these psywar efforts was due, in part, to dissension between the State Department and the CIA about control of such operations. After months of negotiations, the outcome was a compromise brokered at the National Security Council. In June 1948, a council directive, NSC-10/2, authorized an Office of Policy Coordination within the CIA, with a State officer, Frank Wisner, as director.[34]

For the time being, the State Department's policy planning staff appeared to be in control of covert psywar plans and operations, with a veto power over individual projects. His office, Kennan declared, would be a directorate of political warfare. The arrangement soon broke down. The CIA had superior assets, including access to large unvouchered funds, to mount its own operations.

Kennan's incursions into psychological operations also did not sit well with many of his State Department counterparts. Their opposition became more pointed after Dean Acheson became Secretary of State in January 1949. Kennan's emphasis on long-range political strategy, including psychological operations, did not fit with the new secretary's focus on a military buildup along the ideological fault line separating Western and Eastern Europe, centered around the newly created North Atlantic Treaty Organization (NATO). Kennan saw this as the militarization of U.S. policy.[35] He left the department a year later to take up residence at Princeton's Institute for Advanced Studies. His subsequent writings reflected his struggle to resolve his dual role as both an architect and a critic of Cold War strategy, including its ideological aspects.

Under Acheson's leadership, psychological operations were given a somewhat different role in U.S.-Soviet relations than that envisioned by George Kennan. This role was outlined in the most important statement of U.S. policy goals in the early Cold War era, the National Security Council's NSC-68 document, approved by President Truman in 1950.

NSC-68 called for a full-scale mobilization of U.S. military and economic power to match Soviet efforts. It also outlined a more focused psychological strategy, including information operations. The aim, the document stated, was "the intensification of affirmative and timely measures and operations by covert means in the fields of economic warfare and political and psychological warfare with a view to fomenting and supporting unrest and revolt in selected strategic satellite countries."[36]

NSC-68 recommended the creation of a Psychological Strategy Board to coordinate these operations at the White House level. The new board proceeded to analyze the prospects for effective psywar operations. After eight months of studying the options, its conclusions disappointed Washington's psywar enthusiasts. There were, the board declared, no quick-fix solutions in dealing with Soviet aggressive policies and actions. It suggested a more moderate long-range psychological operations plan to counter Moscow's actions.

The Psychological Strategy Board's recommendations set the stage for a bitter debate over the role of psychological warfare that spilled over into the 1952 presidential elections. As historian Arthur M. Schlesinger Jr. noted at the time:

> For the Truman administration, psychological warfare was essentially an auxiliary weapon—auxiliary both to diplomatic policy and to military power. But for an increasingly vocal minority during the last years of the Truman administration, psychological warfare came to be seen as an independent weapon, powerful in its own right, whose uninhibited use could take the place of diplomacy and rearmament and change the whole atmosphere of the Cold War.[37]

Support for a more muscular psywar strategy to force a Soviet retreat from Eastern Europe came from the Republican Party, anxious to recapture the White House after twenty years in the political wilderness. The subject became a centerpiece issue for the party in the 1952 election campaign, which resulted in a stunning victory for Dwight Eisenhower.

Once in office, the Eisenhower administration reviewed the options for implementing campaign promises of an aggressive liberation strategy. A week after his inauguration, the new president appointed a Committee on International Information Activities, headed by William H. Jackson, a former CIA deputy director. Time Inc. executive C. D. Jackson was named a presidential assistant to deal with psywar activities.[38]

The first challenge to the administration's psywar plans took place a month later. It was brought on by the death of Josef Stalin, an event which had been anticipated for over a year. The dictator's demise fueled expectations in Washington of a succession struggle within the Kremlin that could be exploited in ways that would weaken overall Soviet power. The succession struggle took place, but the new Eisenhower administration was unable to exploit it.

The White House reaction to Stalin's death was limited largely to an ambiguous presidential message to the Soviet people, suggesting that they put their faith in God and in an "abiding political system." It was not a message designed to send disaffected Russians into the streets demanding an end to Communist rule. In Washington, discretion, based on imperfect intelligence about the succession struggle, ruled out calls for militant liberation.[39]

Similar cautions limited most other psywar operations. The highwater mark in the liberation crusade took place during an uprising of East German workers against their Soviet rulers in June 1953. It began as a strike by construction workers protesting stringent new work rules. Although the offending rules were canceled, the demonstrations spread to hundreds of towns and villages.

In Washington, the Psychological Strategy Board informed the president that the event created "the greatest opportunity for initiating effective policies to help roll back Soviet power that has yet come to light."[40] Plans were drawn up for a wide range of covert operations to encourage the protesters. It soon became apparent, however, that any attempts to capitalize on East German unrest would set off a direct confrontation with the powerful Soviet military presence in Germany, particularly in Berlin where Russian and U.S. troops faced each other directly.

Most of the psywar plans were eventually shelved as higher political priorities, notably the pending integration of West German armed forces into NATO, dictated restraint. The one success in influencing the East German uprising involved RIAS, the U.S. government radio station in Berlin. RIAS broadcasts maintained strong credibility among Soviet-zone listeners during the tense weeks of confrontation following the initial demonstrations.

Eventually, the station's most important message was that the West, and particularly the United States, would not intervene in the uprising. This message deflated any hopes by East German citizens that their political lot would be improved. It also marked the beginning of the end of Washington's hopes for a quick rollback of Soviet power in Eastern Europe. The Jackson committee, appointed by Eisenhower in the first days of the new administration, recommended abolishing the Truman-era Psychological Strategy Board as part of a general policy of downgrading the role of psychological operations in any quick-fix attempts to turn back Moscow's aggressive international actions. The committee concluded its report on the following sobering note:

> "Cold War" and "psychological warfare" are unfortunate terms. In reality there is a psychological aspect or implication to every diplomatic, economic or military policy and action. This implication should receive more attention both in the planning and execution stage of policy. But not to the exclusion of other vital factors. Except for propaganda, there are no psychological warfare instruments distinct from traditional instruments of policy.[41]

The Jackson committee's recommendations were adopted, with results that defined the general tone and organization of U.S. overseas ideological operations abroad for the next forty years. The more strident aspects of psywar operations in countering Soviet power were quietly shelved. The CIA was given responsibility for covert operations, with loose supervision by the National Security Council.[42]

These changes in organizing covert projects were relatively easy to carry out because the projects were planned largely behind closed doors, with decisions hidden from public scrutiny. Restructuring overt ideological operations proved more difficult. It involved the future of the State Department's International Information Administration and its major operations—the Voice of America and the network of U.S. Information Service posts abroad.

The key player in influencing the information program's role in the new Eisenhower administration was the new secretary of state, John Foster Dulles. He took over his duties with the firm intention of moving the International Information Administration out of the department.

Among other factors, this reflected his general disdain for international public opinion as a factor in foreign policy.[43]

Dulles's plans to get rid of the IIA were complicated by the fact that its operations were the subject of four investigations—one at the White House, one in the House of Representatives and two in the Senate. Each played an important role in the Eisenhower administration's eventual decision to create an independent information agency to manage overseas cultural and media operations.

The House investigation concentrated largely on budgetary and other administrative problems within the IIA. The Senate investigation, headed by Bourke Hickenlooper, an Iowa Republican, was generally supportive of the idea of taking the program out of the State Department. An effective overseas program, it declared in its final report, "could hardly be met within the outlines of a cautious, tradition-bound, bureaucratic foreign office."[44]

The White House investigation of the IIA's future was managed by two men, Abbott Washburn and Henry Loomis, each of whom would later play prominent roles as U.S. Information Agency officials. They were a Mutt-and-Jeff contrast: Washburn was a rumpled soft-spoken public relations executive from Minneapolis; Loomis was a bona fide member of the eastern establishment who had taken a job at the CIA after an impressive career as a policy analyst at MIT. Assigned by the incoming Eisenhower administration to come up with recommendations on the future of the overseas information program, their original intention was to propose that it remain within the State Department.

In addition to Secretary Dulles's opposition to the idea, they had to deal with demands by powerful political forces for a more aggressive bureaucratic solution to the problem. The American Legion, the influential veterans' group, called for a new cabinet-rank agency to manage overt and covert psychological warfare operations.[45]

Senator Karl Mundt, the coauthor of the information program's congressional charter, advanced the idea of a "Department of International Public Relations," based on the premise that advertising professionals could do a better job than State Department employees in projecting a positive overseas image of the United States and its policies.[46] The head of the American Association of Advertising Agencies proposed that the government use paid advertising in overseas media to promote its foreign policies.[47]

Washburn and Loomis ignored these quick-fix solutions. Their major concern was to assure that the overseas information program be given a stronger role in strategic policy formation. This could best be done, they concluded, by giving the program independent bureaucratic status. Together the two men guided the process that led to the White House decision to create the U.S. Information Agency.

Before this happened, the information program was seriously threatened by a rogue investigation of its activities in the Senate Government Operations Committee, dominated by Wisconsin senator Joseph R. McCarthy. The senator's theme was that the program was controlled by leftist officials who were undermining U.S. policy. His investigation came as close to laying low the information program as any event in its short history.

During the black days of spring 1953, the State Department's overseas information operations sagged and groaned to a virtual halt. Except for routine operations such as Voice of America broadcasts, there was little direction in the program and no inclination on the part of the staff to start anything that would attract the attention of the congressional investigators.[48]

The Campaign of Truth was stopped short. Many of the shiny knights who initiated it had fled or were removed from their jobs in the wake of the Republican electoral landslide. The troops left behind wondered what they were doing in this army. Day in and day out, investigators poked around the camp, trying to prove that the communist enemy was not somewhere over the horizon but right here in the ranks.

One of the wry amusements of the staff, while waiting for the next barrage of accusations from the McCarthy committee, was to compose fictitious documentary film scripts. One such twisted masterpiece was called *Napalm—The Story of an Idea;* another was *A Day in the Life of a Small Town Call Girl.* These exercises in misdirected talent were little compensation for the dreary course of Senator McCarthy's attacks.[49]

Thrashing around for good headline-making topics to document the left-wing conspiracy in the information program, McCarthy focused on two areas—the overseas library program and the Voice of America. In backing up his allegations, he was aided by a self-appointed group of State Department employees that referred to itself as "the loyal American underground." (The implication was that the rest of the staff consisted of leftists, if not bomb-toting Bolsheviks.) One by one, members of the underground made appearances before the committee as "friendly witnesses," each with a tale of sinister influences in the information program.

A Voice of America secretary denounced her supervisor, the head of religious programming, as an atheist. Another VOA employee burst into the headlines with the revelation that she had been importuned by her boss to join a free-love colony in a New York suburb. It turned out that he had suggested that she might be interested in buying land in an FHA housing cooperative. But the facts never caught up with the original headline charge, nor did any of the actual faults in the information program get a serious hearing before the committee.[50]

The overseas library program came under attack for allegedly having communist propaganda among its holdings. McCarthy dispatched two aides, Roy Cohn and David Schine, overseas to ferret out the offending books. In Paris, the chief librarian, Ann Davis, a feisty New York Irisher, won an honored place in USIA annals by refusing to allow the two investigators access to the library's holdings.

In Washington, the State Department panicked. It issued a directive prohibiting books by "Communists, fellow travelers, etc." in its overseas libraries. It then faced the job of identifying communists (as well as fellow travelers and "etc.") among the authors of the library system's 2 million volumes, together with those who wrote the three thousand new books ordered every month.[51] The department's task was not made any easier by an offhand press conference remark by President Eisenhower that he would have left the works of one of the banned writers, left-wing author Dashiell Hammett, on the shelves.

As it turned out, the actual number of books by known or avowed communists in all USIS libraries at the time was thirty-nine copies involving twenty-five titles by eight authors. Many of them, leftovers from wartime OWI library operations, were out-of-date descriptions of U.S.-Soviet relations, reflecting the wartime political honeymoon with the Russians.[52] Nevertheless, hundreds of books were put in storage by cautious librarians, awaiting State Department approval of their authors.

In his attacks on the information program, Senator McCarthy had a special advantage in that his hearings were covered live on television across the country. National networking was relatively new at the time, and coverage of congressional committee meetings even newer. The McCarthy hearings were the first of their kind to gain a large television audience, intrigued by their circuslike atmosphere.[53]

The hearings also attracted attention overseas. Informed public opinion abroad expressed astonishment at the blatant unfairness of the committee's attacks. Raymond Aron, one of the few French intellectuals who supported U.S. policy, attended the hearings and announced that he could no longer defend the United States against those who argued that its politics were dominated by fear and hysteria.

In Berlin, a university professor informed the USIS post that he was boycotting its library until it restored the books that had been removed.

The USIS post in Tokyo received a query from a Japanese scholar asking for information about U.S. "thought police." The Oslo newspaper *Verdens Gang* declared editorially that "McCarthy and his associates have damaged the cause of the United States much more than any Commie they could conceivably uncover."[54]

The McCarthy hearings provided a useful target for communist propaganda outlets worldwide. Their theme was American hysteria, immaturity, and weakness. "For whom does the bell toll?" asked a Radio Prague commentator, with a rhetorical flourish. "The bell tolls today for the Voice of America." This gratuitous death knell was premature, however. Slowly then quickly U.S. public opinion began to turn against the McCarthy hearings.

In the early weeks of the hearings, the Eisenhower White House had attempted to be deferential to McCarthy. The administration was newly installed, and it did not want to go head-to-head with a popular Republican senator, one who was repeating some of the charges against the information program made by party spokesmen during the presidential election. The White House, Eisenhower announced, would not interfere with the right of Congress to investigate as it pleased. As the hearings progressed, he backed off, declaring in a March 1953 press conference that he might intervene if the hearings reached a point where they invited "international misunderstandings."[55] The White House cautiously stiffened its attitude toward the McCarthy hearings as Congress became more alarmed at the harm they were doing to the legislative system. Individual members of both the Senate and the House of Representatives began to speak up not only against McCarthy but also in support of the overseas information program.

They were aided by the final report of the Senate Foreign Relations Committee on its own quiet investigation of the program. Although the document (usually referred to as the Hickenlooper report, after the committee chairman) was critical of many aspects of the program, it backed the Eisenhower administration's effort to improve its operations and endorsed the suggestion that the program be moved out of the State Department.[56] The report gave valuable support to the White House's own legislative proposal for an independent information agency, which was submitted to Congress and approved by both houses three weeks later.[57]

In addition to promising more efficient information operations abroad, the reorganization plan stipulated that the new U.S. Information Agency's output would be subject to policy guidance from the State Department. The plan also called for USIA input to National Security

Council decisionmaking in order to strengthen the role of ideological and public-opinion factors in foreign policy.

For a number of reasons, this formula for defining the agency's role as an adviser on foreign policy never fully succeeded. But all this was in the future as the U.S. Information Agency embarked on a course that lasted, with bureaucratic twists and turns, for over forty-five years.

Notes

1. David F. Krugler, *The Voice of America and Domestic Propaganda Battles 1945–1953* (Columbia: University of Missouri Press, 2000), p. 33.
2. "Termination of O.W.I. and Disposition of Certain Functions of O.I.A.A.," *Department of State Bulletin,* September 23, 1945, p. 306.
3. "The Organization and Administration of the Department of State," U.S. Bureau of the Budget, Washington, D.C., August 15, 1945.
4. The decision to protect OSS resources is described in Michael W. Dravis, "The 'Cadre Strategy' of Covert Action: Preserving U.S. Secret Operations Capability, 1945–1947." Paper delivered at the annual conference of the Society of Historians of American Foreign Relations, Georgetown University, June 21, 1997.
5. Section 102 (d), National Security Act of 1947.
6. Krugler, *The Voice of America,* pp. 41–42.
7. Robert H Ferrell, *American Diplomacy* (New York: W. W. Norton, 1969), p. 651.
8. Allan M. Winkler, *The Politics of Propaganda: The Office of War Information 1942–1945* (New Haven, Conn.: Yale University Press, 1978), pp. 134–135. The overall social impact of U.S. troops during the occupation is described in: "The American Occupation of Germany in Cultural Perspective: A Round Table," *Diplomatic History* 23, no. 1, winter 1999, pp. 1–69.
9. "Ich bin ein Cowboy," *The Economist* (London), May 26, 2001, p. 84.
10. For a detailed account of OMGUS directives and their effect on postwar German media and cultural organizations, see: Charles A. H. Thomson, *Overseas Information Service of the United States Government* (Washington, D.C.: Brookings Institution, 1948), pp. 243–271.
11. Claus Jacobi, "A New German Press," *Foreign Affairs,* January 1954, pp. 323–330.
12. Yale Richmond, "Beer for Burgermeisters," in United States Information Agency, *Commemoration: Public Diplomacy, Looking Back, Looking Forward* (Washington, D.C.: USIA Office of Public Information, 1999), p. 10.
13. Terry R. Hamblin, "Selling America: The Amerika Haus and U.S. Cultural Diplomacy in Germany and Austria 1946–1956." Paper presented at the annual conference of the Society of Historians of American Foreign Relations, American University, Washington, D.C., June 2001.
14. Thomson, *Overseas Information Service,* pp. 250–265.
15. Jessica C. E. Gienow-Hecht, "Art Is Democracy and Democracy Is Art," *Diplomatic History* 23, no. 1, winter 1999, pp. 21–23.

16. Edmund Taylor, "RIAS—The Voice East Germans Believe," *The Reporter,* October 10, 1953, p. 53.

17. Thomson, *Overseas Information Service,* pp. 271–280.

18. For a useful survey of congressional actions affecting propaganda operations in the early Cold War period, see: Robert David Johnson, "Congress and the Cold War," *Journal of Cold War Studies* 3, no. 2, spring 2001, pp. 76–100.

19. Krugler, *The Voice of America,* p. 58.

20. Ibid., p. 22.

21. William Harlan Hale, "We've Muffled Our Own Dreams," *The Reporter,* April 13, 1954, p. 33.

22. Krugler, *The Voice of America,* p. 63.

23. United States Educational and Cultural Exchange Act of 1948, Public Law 402, 80th Congress, 2nd session, January 27, 1948.

24. Krugler, *The Voice of America,* p. 80.

25. The Marshall Plan information program is described in: Harry Bayard Price, *The Marshall Plan and Its Meaning* (Ithaca, N.Y.: Cornell University Press, 1952), pp. 242–250; Waldemar A. Neilson, "Information to Win Public Support and Sustain Morale," in Constantine Menges (ed.), *The Marshall Plan from Those Who Made It Succeed* (Lanham, Md.: University Press of America, 1999), pp. 199–212.

26. The text of the speech is given in "Going Forward with the Campaign of Truth," Department of State Bulletin, September 2, 1950, p. 669 et passim.

27. Krugler, *The Voice of America,* p. 139.

28. "Coordination of Foreign Information Measures," National Security Council NSC-4-A, December 12, 1947.

29. Gregory P. Mitrovich, *Undermining the Kremlin: America's Strategy for Subverting the Soviet Bloc 1947–1950* (Ithaca, N.Y.: Cornell University Press, 2000).

30. Kennan's role in fostering psywar operations is described in: Douglas E. Selvage, "Strategy of Liberation: Kennan, Containment and Covert Operations 1948–1950." Paper delivered at the annual conference of the Society of Historians of American Foreign Relations, Georgetown University, June 1997. Kennan's activities in this area are described in: Wilson D. Miscamble, *George Kennan and the Making of American Policy* (Princeton, N.J.: Princeton University Press, 1992), pp. 199–205.

31. The origins and operations of the liberation campaign are described in: Peter Grose, *Operation Rollback: America's Secret War Behind the Iron Curtain* (Boston: Houghton Mifflin, 2000). See also: Edward P. Lily, "The Development of American Psychological Operations," in *Declassified Documents Reference System,* vol. 1 (Washington, D.C.: Carrollton Press, 1981).

32. For a summary of the U.S. involvement in the 1948 Italian elections, see: Robert T. Holt and Robert W. van der Velde, *Strategic Psychological Operations and American Foreign Policy,* (Chicago: University of Chicago Press, 1960), pp. 159–205.

33. "Balloons for Captive Audiences," *The Reporter,* November 18, 1954, pp. 28–31.

34. The bureaucratic sequence defining responsibility for covert and overt psywar operations is outlined in "The CIA's Office of Policy Coordination from NSC-4 to NSC-68." Paper presented at the annual conference of the Society of

Historians of American Foreign Relations, American University, June 2001, by Michael Warner, deputy chief of the CIA history staff.

35. The origins of the differences between Acheson and Kennan are described in: James Chace, *Acheson* (New York: Simon & Schuster, 1998), pp. 149–151.

36. For an analysis of the links between NSC-68 and the Campaign of Truth, see: Walter L Hixson, *Parting of the Iron Curtain: Propaganda, Culture and the Cold War* (New York: St. Martin's Griffin, 1997), pp. 14–15.

37. Arthur M. Schlesinger Jr., "Psychological Warfare: Can It Sell Freedom?" *The Reporter,* March 31, 1953, pp. 7–11. See also: Monteagle Stearns, "Democratic Diplomacy and the Role of Propaganda," *Foreign Service Journal,* October 1953, pp. 24–25.

38. Kenneth A. Osgood, "Form Before Substance: Eisenhower's Commitment to Psychological Warfare and Negotiations with the Enemy," *Diplomatic History* 24, no. 3, summer 2000, pp. 405–433.

39. "Cold War Setup in U.S. Unprepared," *New York Times,* March 6, 1953, p. 8.

40. "Interim U.S. Psychological Strategy Plan for Exploiting of Unrest in Satellite Europe." PSBD-45. Psychological Strategy Board, July 1, 1953.

41. White House press statement on the report, June 8, 1953, p. 2. The report was not made public at the time.

42. The CIA's early postwar covert operations focused largely on Western Europe and the Soviet bloc. Trevor Barnes, "The Secret Cold War: The CIA and American Foreign Policy in Europe 1946–1956," *The Historical Review* (London) 24, no. 2, 1981, pp. 399–415. See also: Volker R. Berghahn, *Americans and the Intellectual Cold Wars in Europe* (Princeton, N.J.: Princeton University Press, 2001) for the special role that U.S. academics played in covert operations.

43. Dulles outlined his views on the subject in a discussion with Abbott Washburn and Henry Loomis, staff officers of the Jackson committee, shortly after he took office. Loomis interview, Foreign Service Oral History Project, February 25, 1989, p. 16.

44. "Overseas Information Programs of the United States." Report No. 406, Senate Committee on Foreign Relations, 83rd Congress, 1st session, June 15, 1953, p. 2.

45. "Cold War Agency in Cabinet Backed," *New York Times,* March 15, 1953, p. 7.

46. "Big Sell in the Cold War," *Saturday Review of Literature,* October 10, 1959, p. 14.

47. "Cunningham Bids U.S. Buy Space to Sell Self," *New York Herald-Tribune,* April 23, 1953, p. 16. In fact, paid newspaper ads extolling American democracy had been used by U.S. Information Service posts at the time in at least two countries, Greece and Egypt, with little apparent benefits.

48. "Cold War Staffs Riddled with Low Morale," *New York Times,* April 14, 1953, p. 3.

49. Wilson P. Dizard, *The Strategy of Truth* (Washington, D.C.: Public Affairs Press, 1961), p. 42.

50. "3 Witnesses Brand 'Voice' Aide as Atheist," *Washington Times-Herald,* March 3, 1953, p. 1.

51. "State Dep't. Bogs Down in Task of Seeking Out Red Authors," *Washington Post,* April 23, 1953, p. 1.

52. Dizard, *The Strategy of Truth,* p. 141.

53. "Voice Hearings Here Tomorrow on National TV," *New York Herald-Tribune,* February 27, 1953, p. 16.

54. For overall European reactions to the McCarthy investigations, see: "State Department Deference to McCarthy Alarms Europe," *New York Times,* February 27, 1953, p. 3.

55. "President May Take Hand If Inquiry Imperils Unity," *New York Times,* March 6, 1953, p. 1.

56. "Overseas Information Programs of the United States," p. 8.

57. "Ike Revamps Information, MSA Setups," *Washington Post,* June 2, 1953, p. 1.

4

USIA: Getting Started

TWO BLOCKS WEST of the White House, 1776 Pennsylvania Avenue is an unassuming gray brick building that architects might classify as Warren Harding Gothic. For over fifty years, it served as the headquarters for the overseas information program, the hub of a network that extended from the staid precincts of London's Grosvenor Square to the upcountry Laotian town of Luang Prabang.

August 1, 1953, was a special day in the building's history. The program's staff streamed into its offices for the first time as employees of the new U.S. Information Agency (USIA). Their mood was subdued, a mix of hopes and doubts, after months of bureaucratic turmoil centered on the McCarthy investigation.

But they had reason for hope. After probing fruitlessly for communists in the State Department, McCarthy turned his attention to another improbable source of subversion—the U.S. Army. His committee focused on an army dentist with leftist views stationed at Ft. Monmouth, New Jersey. By this time, however, public interest in the McCarthy investigation had largely collapsed as a result of the committee's own witless mistakes. The Senate finally took steps to curb its activities, including a vote to censure McCarthy himself several months later.

The prospect of deep budget cuts posed a more immediate threat to the new agency. Republican oratory during the 1952 presidential campaign had focused heavily on what was described as "the mess in Washington" resulting from two decades of Democratic control of the White House. Moreover, the Republicans now dominated both houses of Congress. Given their longtime suspicions about the information program's alleged role as a haven for liberal Democrats, conservative Republicans regarded USIA as a prime candidate for budget cutbacks. The new agency was in danger of losing a large part of its assets before it had a chance to establish its credentials.

These fears were soon realized. Within months Congress cut USIA's appropriation by 36 percent, including a 25 percent reduction in its staff, and closed down thirty-eight of the agency's overseas posts. It was a jolting reversal for a program that had built up considerable momentum in recent years, thanks to the expanded budgets sparked by the Truman administration's 1950 Campaign of Truth initiative. The information agency had used that infusion of new money to expand program activities in dozens of newly decolonized countries in Asia and Africa. The 1953 budget reductions put a sudden stop to this expansion.

The cutbacks were especially harmful to USIA operations in India, where the ruling Congress Party, led by Jawaharlal Nehru, faced serious challenges from Soviet-sponsored Communist groups. An important element in publicizing U.S. support for the newly independent republic was a biweekly U.S. Information Service (USIS) newspaper, *American Reporter,* published in seven local languages and subscribed to by almost a half-million influential Indians (a circulation four times greater than that of the country's leading newspaper). Following the 1953 congressional budget constraints, four of the paper's language editions were eliminated and circulation on the rest was cut back.[1] Similar reductions were made in local USIS programs in other parts of the world.

The budget cuts also had a traumatic effect on Washington operations. Current operations were reduced; new initiatives were put on hold. Layoff notices flowed out of the personnel office. One group was prepared for them: the Democratic patronage appointees who made up a large segment of the information program's top leadership. Many had been with the program since the Office of War Information (OWI) days. Although some were political hangers-on, most were competent managers who had set the bureaucratic style and direction of the program in its early years.

One of these political appointees, Herbert Edwards, headed the motion picture division. When the Republicans took over the White House, Edwards knew that he would be moving on, an insight reinforced by the fact that his wife, India, was cochair of the Democratic National Committee. At his going-away party, his retirement speech was short. "I have," he declared, "only one wife to give to my country."[2]

Following this political purge—a traditional Washington exercise—the USIA settled down to the task of restoring operational stability to its worldwide operations. That it succeeded was due largely to the White House's choice for the agency's first director, Theodore Streibert, a

New York broadcasting executive. A bluff, gruff man, Streibert took on the job with no interest in postmortems about the former glories or failings of the information program. He started fresh and showed a sure sense for giving the program what it needed—firm leadership and a solid managerial framework. As one agency employee noted at the time: "Ted Streibert gave us the feeling that we were in the information *business*."

The new director knew his staff's morale had been shattered by the McCarthy investigations. He had a chance to turn this situation around early in his new job, and he seized it. The occasion was a letter from Senator McCarthy demanding that two anticommunist books written under his name be added to all USIS libraries overseas. The books contained scattershot accusations about alleged communist infiltration into the U.S. government; one of them suggested that former secretary of state George C. Marshall was guilty of treason. Streibert summarily turned down the senator's request. News of his decision spread quickly throughout the agency, reinforcing the staff's hopes that a tough new leader was in charge.

Streibert could be decisive in other ways. One day he called in his director for European operations, Walter Roberts, and asked him to arrange an appointment with the pope. Roberts was stunned. "Before even thinking of how to arrange such a meeting," he recalled later, "I asked Streibert why he wanted to meet the pope. His answer: 'Don't you understand, Walter? He is in the anticommunist business. I am in the anticommunist business. Shouldn't we exchange ideas?'" After some delays, a meeting between Streibert and the pope was arranged.[3]

Streibert's new management team included the two men largely responsible for the Eisenhower administration's decision to restructure the information program—Abbott Washburn and Henry Loomis. They had worked as a team in negotiating the transfer of the program from the State Department to its new autonomy as an independent agency. Streibert appointed Washburn as his deputy, a position he held with distinction for almost eight years. Loomis became Streibert's special assistant. Thus, the new director had close-at-hand advice from men who knew the bureaucratic twists and turns involved in the creation of the agency. In particular, they understood USIA's sensitive relationship with the State Department, beginning with Secretary John Foster Dulles's disdain for public opinion in general and for the information program in particular.[4]

Some of Streibert's other appointments were less inspired. University of Maryland professor Franklin Burdette was put in charge of the agency's overseas library operations. A conservative Republican, Burdette proposed a "gray list" of four hundred U.S. authors whose works were to be banned from USIS libraries abroad. The list included, among other writers, Ernest Hemingway and Dorothy Parker. Burdette also questioned use of the works of Henry David Thoreau, not on the grounds of his allegedly radical views but because his writings had influenced foreigners who became communists. Aware of how such censorship would harm the new agency's credibility, Abbott Washburn squelched the project before it caused a public uproar.[5]

Another Streibert personnel mistake was to appoint a famous Hollywood director, Cecil B. DeMille, as an adviser on the agency's film operations. An ardent conservative, DeMille flew into Washington and gave an impassioned speech to agency officials in which he extolled the potential of films in general, and of Hollywood productions in particular, in defeating the communist menace. He then packed his bags and went back to California, never to return.

Despite these early gaffes, Streibert's pragmatic style caught on at Washington headquarters. He visited dozens of USIS posts abroad, something no previous manager had done. These visits convinced him that basic decisions about program activities in individual countries should be made primarily at the embassy level by ambassadors and USIS public affairs officers, not long distance by the Washington staff. The agency's management structure was reorganized to reflect this change.

Streibert's success in revitalizing the information program depended heavily on how President Eisenhower viewed its operations. From his earliest days in the White House, the new president showed a good instinct for the role of public opinion in foreign policy. "Eisenhower had a soft spot for the information program. He was a sentimentalist; he thought of it as people-to-people togetherness," according to George Allen, a State Department diplomat who served as USIA's director in the final years of the Eisenhower administration.[6] Moreover, the president had direct experience (as commander of Allied forces in wartime Europe) with the effective use of propaganda in achieving political and military objectives. Overall, he was more sympathetic to the idea of an overseas information program than any other chief executive in USIA's forty-five-year history.[7]

Eisenhower, meanwhile, faced the problem of squaring his moderate approach on propaganda with the Republican Party's insistence on a muscular liberation strategy to deal with the Soviet takeover of Eastern Europe. "Surely what they can accomplish, we can accomplish," the new secretary of state, John Foster Dulles, told a Senate committee. "Surely if they can use moral and psychological force, we can use it."[8]

Once in office, the president had appointed the Committee on International Information Activities, headed by William H. Jackson, that reviewed the role of psychological operations. After five months of deliberations, the Jackson committee had recommended that psyops projects be integrated into existing political, economic, and military planning procedures, not treated as an easy answer to the long-term problem of dealing with Soviet aggression.[9] The CIA, however, continued to be active in covert operations designed to undermine Soviet influence in Western Europe and in many of the newly independent nations in Asia and Africa.

The problem of identifying the role of the government's overt information operations was more complex. Secretary Dulles had been insistent that these programs be transferred from the department as part of his plan to focus its activities on what he regarded as traditional diplomatic duties. In his view, dealing with foreign opinion was not a part of these duties. On the other hand, the president's election campaign speeches called for closer coordination of national security policymaking, specifically including ideological operations. This theme also had strong support in the new Republican-controlled Congress, particularly in the influential Senate Committee on Foreign Relations.[10]

USIA's role in a reorganized foreign policy structure was tied to White House plans for restructuring the Truman-era National Security Council (NSC). Foreign policy experts, in and out of government, generally agreed that NSC operations were seriously flawed. It was understaffed, and its recommendations often did not carry weight, largely because of internal bureaucratic disputes between the State and Defense Departments.

A small part of the Eisenhower administration's plan to reorganize the NSC involved USIA. The White House directive creating the agency said that its director would be responsible "under the National Security Council" to the president.[11] This provision was vague enough to give White House officials considerable leeway in determining the details of USIA's responsibilities in a revamped NSC.

It soon became clear that key officials in the Eisenhower administration were not enthusiastic about giving the agency a significant role within the NSC structure. Henry Loomis, who served as liaison with White House officials during this period, later described their reluctance to make classified reports available to agency officials. When he complained to Robert Cutler, an NSC official, Cutler replied that he didn't trust USIA officials. "They're really a bunch of Commies over there," he informed Loomis. Cutler finally agreed to make the reports available to Loomis alone. Loomis then made them available to agency policy officers. "People came to my office and read the papers there. After a while, we relaxed a little and let the policy staff hold some. In about six months, we had the papers go straight to [the policy staff] as they should have gone."[12] The incident was a small indicator of USIA difficulties over the years in positioning itself as a policy adviser on national security issues.

Under the Eisenhower reorganization, the NSC continued to be dominated by the State and Defense Departments and the CIA. The council was given stronger staff support, including a new planning board to provide the backup research and analysis for its decisions. The Operations Coordinating Board, another innovation, supervised a roster of working groups, each assigned to deal with a specific foreign policy issue. The groups then monitored each agency's compliance with the NSC's decision on the issue involved.

The overall plan was a clear improvement over the NSC's previous loose organization. It reflected Eisenhower's military experience with a chain-of-command structure. He regularly presided over the weekly two-hour council meeting, missing only six of the first two hundred sessions.[13] However, a flaw in the new structure was the virtual exclusion of USIA from a significant role in council operations. The agency's participation was limited largely to the Operations Coordinating Board and its working groups. Ted Streibert was a member of this board, which met weekly to sort out interagency responsibilities for the current agenda of foreign policy problems. This had the advantage of giving USIA a policy voice in the NSC structure, albeit at the lowest level of the council's operations.

The agency's role was further limited by the unwillingness of many State Department officials, beginning with Secretary Dulles, to give credence to overseas public opinion factors in general or to USIA proposals to build these factors into the foreign policy process in particular. Attempts to give more attention to public opinion within the NSC structure foundered largely on these State Department attitudes.[14]

The Eisenhower administration's approach to psychological operations, both overt and covert, was flawed overall. A 1955 attempt to correct this situation ultimately failed. It involved the creation of a White House "Planning Coordination Group," specifically charged with integrating psyops planning with political and military operations. The group was headed by Nelson Rockefeller, who had both the experience and enthusiasm to deal with the issue, based on his wartime direction of propaganda programs in Latin America. Now his assignment was extended to dealing with communist propaganda across the globe, using all the resources of the Washington bureaucracy.

The bureaucracy, in particular the State and Defense Departments, did not take kindly to such outside interference. Their opposition was aided by the Rockefeller group's lack of funding. (The operation was eventually financed, largely by the CIA and Rockefeller's personal funds.) The group's small staff spent its time drawing up position papers, including one that identified 177 Soviet-bloc vulnerabilities that could be addressed by coordinated psyops programs. A great deal of time was also spent planning a "Position Room," a sort of command center decorated with graphics that would provide up-to-date information on various communist threats around the world. These efforts produced no results, and the Planning Coordinating Group was eventually abolished in December 1955, less than a year after it was set up.[15]

USIA played almost no role in the Rockefeller operation. It was not a member of the group, nor were its advice and resources called upon in the group's deliberations, despite the fact that the agency had been created by the Eisenhower administration to deal at an overt level with precisely the kind of psyops planning envisioned for the Rockefeller office.

USIA's limited role in national security planning during the Eisenhower years had continuing implications for the agency's role during the long decades of Cold War confrontation. The agency's influence at the highest level of policymaking—the White House—was at best sporadic. Exceptions to this pattern included, most notably, the 1962 Cuban missile crisis, when the agency's policy and program resources became an important element in reversing what could have been an apocalyptic confrontation in U.S.-Soviet relations.

Denied a major policy role at the Eisenhower White House, USIA officials turned in its first few months to restructuring the agency's internal operations. This exercise included first assessment of the information program's operating assumptions, a survey carried out with the help of a group of social scientists led by Leo Bogart of Columbia University. The resulting five-volume study came up with mixed recommendations. The most important of these was to strengthen the agency's ability to influence foreign policy decisionmaking in the early stages of its formation by working-level officials in Washington and at overseas embassies.[16]

Meanwhile, USIA focused on shaping its products and their messages to President Eisenhower's foreign policy initiatives.[17] The president had set the tone for his administration in a major speech before the American Society of Newspaper Editors (ASNE) three months after he took office, unveiling the first U.S. effort to propose a "thaw" in U.S.-Soviet relations, a strategy repeated with variations by all U.S. presidents throughout the Cold War. In his speech to the editors, Eisenhower challenged the Soviets by proposing disarmament talks, an end to the war in Korea, a united Germany, and a joint effort to provide economic assistance to third-world nations.

The Kremlin curtly dismissed the Eisenhower proposals. However, the White House initiatives gave USIA a platform to exploit a dual message of U.S. peaceful intentions and Soviet intransigence. The ASNE speech was followed by more detailed Eisenhower proposals, including an "atoms for peace" plan, announced by the president at the first postwar summit meeting between U.S. and Soviet leaders in Geneva in 1955. The plan suggested a gradual shift in nuclear resources by both sides from military to civilian uses, such as medical research, agriculture, and electricity production.

These and similar conciliatory themes set the tone and content of a major part of USIA program themes for the next forty years. In particular, the sharp confrontational tone that had marked much of Voice of America's programs in the early postwar years was dropped.[18] This shift was a critical step in establishing the VOA as a more credible source of news and information among its audiences. The Voice's listenership rose steadily, particularly in the Soviet Union and Eastern Europe, because of this new moderation.

The introduction of a new two-hour nightly jazz show, *Music USA*, played a special role in expanding listenership. Originally targeted to audiences in Soviet-controlled areas, the show was soon expanded to reach a worldwide audience. Washington disc jockey Willis Conover, the host of *Music USA*, was a knowledgeable jazz enthusiast with a personal record collection of over sixty thousand selections. His program regularly featured interviews with popular artists from Duke Ellington to Frank Sinatra. (He drew the line at Elvis Presley.)

Conover let the music speak for itself, although he often added his own program notes such as his explanation of the meaning of the title of one of Sinatra's hits, "I've Got the World on a String." His occasional trips abroad were triumphal processions, particularly in the Soviet Union and Eastern Europe. It is no exaggeration that, for over three decades, Willis Conover was the most influential single USIA employee in reaching out to overseas audiences, especially younger people, about American ideas and values. That a considerable number of his interviews involved talented black musicians carried its own message.[19]

Another innovation in USIA operations during the 1950s was U.S. participation in overseas trade fairs. Such fairs were an established tradition abroad, particularly in Europe. Originally intended as showpieces for local industrial wares, they were increasingly used in the postwar years to deliver political messages. The decision to provide an official U.S. presence at such fairs resulted from President Eisenhower's reading a report that the Soviet Union was expanding its role in trade fairs for propaganda purposes. A special $2.2 million congressional appropriation authorized a joint program managed by USIA and the Department of Commerce to support U.S. government participation in major fairs abroad.

The U.S. exhibits were a big hit. One of the first shows, "America at Home," drew as many as seventy thousand people a day in Paris. It included a five-room house through whose windows people could look while "Mother" prepared meals in a model kitchen filled with American gadgetry. Outside, "Father" puttered with the car in the garage, worked with power tools in the home shop, and broiled steaks on the terrace. This general pattern was repeated in hundreds of other exhibits that served as windows on American life for overseas audiences during the next forty years.[20]

A regular feature of every U.S. exhibit was a trade mission, usually a six-member panel drawn half from the Commerce Department and half from industry. The panel's role was to answer questions about importing from and exporting to the United States. The trade panels were an early example of USIA's direct involvement in promoting U.S. exports.[21]

Not all of the agency's plans for promoting trade worked out. One of its projects proposed refurbishing a mothballed navy aircraft carrier at a cost of $4 million and sailing it around the world as a floating trade exhibit, complete with a movie theater on the flight deck where an audience of two thousand could view films about the U.S. economy and its products. The ideological focus of the project was "people's capitalism," a maladroit twist on a Soviet propaganda theme.[22] The aircraft-carrier project was torpedoed before it ever reached a congressional appropriations committee.

Exhibits played a special role in the Eisenhower administration's efforts to open long-closed information channels to the Soviet Union. Beginning in 1956, the two countries concluded a series of agreements for information and cultural exchanges, which the Soviets insisted should be carried out under carefully balanced reciprocal arrangements. The first agreement permitted the United States to resume distribution of a new version of *Ameryka* magazine, the wartime Russian-language publication whose distribution in the Soviet Union had been abruptly closed down by the Kremlin in 1945. The editorial style of the new publication, now called *America Illustrated,* matched that of *Life* magazine. The agreement included arrangements for a similar Soviet publication, *USSR* (later changed to *Soviet Life*), to be sold in the United States and called for strict reciprocity regarding the number of copies to be sold in each country.[23]

The magazine project hit a snag that was never fully resolved throughout the decades of U.S.-Soviet information negotiations. It involved the fact that *America Illustrated* was highly popular among Soviet readers, with copies exchanged at black-market prices, while copies of *USSR* languished unsold on U.S. newsstands. Among other factors, the contrast was in the editorial content of the two publications.

USSR tended to emphasize articles with pictures of happy peasants and brawny steelworkers in heroic poses as they filled their production quotas. *America Illustrated*'s first issue featured five color pages of Detroit automobile models, with a price chart indicating that a Nash Rambler could be bought for the equivalent of 6,000 rubles, less than half the price of a Pobeda, a comparable Soviet car. The same issue also included stories about other aspects of American life, including the Philadelphia Orchestra, the Mt. Palomar telescope, and modern architecture in San Francisco.

A year after the magazine agreement was signed, a small U.S.-Soviet exchange-of-persons program was negotiated. As with the magazine exchange, it was a modest beginning—"poking peepholes in the Iron Curtain," as one USIA official put it. Both the U.S. and Soviet governments had severely limited citizen exchanges between the two countries since World War II. This pattern was broken in 1955, when an Iowa newspaper responded to a Kremlin domestic campaign for increased corn production by inviting a Soviet agricultural delegation to visit the Midwest "to see how we do it." To the newspaper's astonishment, the Soviet agricultural ministry accepted the invitation. After some bureaucratic foot-dragging at the State Department, the reciprocal visits took place in the summer of 1955, a few months before the first Eisenhower-Khrushchev summit meeting in Geneva.[24]

In Washington, USIA officials lobbied the White House for a proposal to expand cultural and information exchanges at the Geneva meeting. It was an idea that reflected the president's gradualist approach to dealing with Moscow in contrast to the aggressive psychological warfare stance of the conservative wing of the Republican Party. USIA's director, Ted Streibert, saw increased exchanges as, in his words, a beachhead to reach the Soviet people. He suggested the proposal include an information center in Moscow in return for a similar Soviet facility in Washington.

State Department officials, reflecting Secretary Dulles's hard-line attitudes, declared in an internal memo that Streibert's proposal "smacks too much of the shotgun, grandiose spending of money for spending's sake." The statement added, somewhat gratuitously, that the Streibert plan reflected "our own lack of leadership and policy direction over USIA."[25] Despite the department's attitude, the first U.S.-Soviet cultural exchange agreement was negotiated after the Geneva summit.

The exchanges were orchestrated with careful attention to reciprocity. The U.S. Marine Band would play in Moscow and the Red Army Chorus would perform in New York. In other exchange areas, it was difficult to get a precise balance, particularly in academic exchanges. From the beginning, the Soviet side emphasized scientific researchers, with the aim of catching up on U.S. developments in their individual fields.[26] American academic exchanges were weighted toward practitioners in the social sciences and the humanities—economists, historians, sociologists, and the like, all interested in Soviet developments in their respective fields.

The most visible and successful part of these early exchange agreements involved a decision to sponsor exhibits on a reciprocal basis. Again there was an imbalance, one that favored U.S. interests. As with their magazine, the Soviet exhibits within the United States drew relatively small audiences. Their shows were, by and large, stolid, uninspired depictions of the same workers and peasants who dominated the pages of *USSR* magazine. Overall, Moscow's exhibits were a sharp contrast, both in themes and in audience reaction, to the American shows that toured the Soviet Union.

The first U.S. exhibit (the "American National Exhibition") opened in Moscow's Sokolniki Park in July 1959. It provided an outsized view of American life for the 2.7 million Soviet citizens who trooped through its buildings, which included a Buckminster Fuller geodesic dome and a house decorated by Macy's department store. Free Pepsi Cola was served. Exhibit goers were interviewed in a studio featuring color television, a technology that had not yet been adopted by Soviet stations.

The surprise hit of the show were the seventy-five young American exhibit guides. They were Russian-speaking volunteers who were given free transportation to Moscow and a $16 per diem. The guides were hired to explain the individual exhibits, but they spent most of their time answering questions from skeptical Russians on all aspects of American life. Are American slums underground? Is it true you publish *Anna Karenina* as a twelve-page comic book? Are Marx and Engels banned or published only with critical annotations? What is your family's income? The direct good-natured replies given by the guides were effective enough to set off a propaganda barrage in the Soviet media in which the guides were variously accused of giving misleading answers, of offending the Soviet people, and, in one case, of pinching a hotel maid.

The exhibit earned a footnote in diplomatic history as the scene of a confrontation between Soviet premier Nikita Khrushchev and then–vice president Richard Nixon in the kitchen of the show's model American house. The "kitchen debate" covered a range of U.S.-Soviet issues in an exchange that was alternately good-natured and confrontational. Khrushchev (who visited the American pavilion twice) then moved on to an exhibit of American paintings, a project that had raised congressional hackles back in Washington because of its alleged bias in favor of modern works. President Eisenhower ended the Washington dispute in a Solomonic decision that some representational nineteenth-century paintings should be included.[27]

Khrushchev reacted as violently as the members of Congress to the modern art on display. Walking past a large nude female statue on loan from New York's Museum of Modern Art, he commented, "Only a pederast would have done this." Gazing at a John Marin watercolor, he declared that it looked as if someone had peed on the canvas. Nixon's interpreter, USIA officer Hans Tuch, gave a somewhat gentler version of his remarks. Khrushchev countered with a demand that Tuch make a precise translation of what he said.[28]

Modern art was not the only display that drew objections from Soviet officials. In the months before the exhibition opened, they complained about several other U.S. plans for the show. One of these was to construct large color-tiled restrooms for exhibit-goers that would include modern toilet facilities of a type nonexistent in the USSR. The U.S. plumbing industry offered to provide, free of charge, 150 toilets and a similar number of urinals and washbasins. The Soviet government vetoed the proposal and installed its own old-fashioned facilities a short distance from the U.S. exhibit.

A more serious dispute involved a display of American books. Soviet officials insisted on censoring the collection, including the current edition of the *World Almanac*. In a compromise, a few of the more explicit anti-Soviet volumes were removed, but this did not end the dispute. On the exhibition's first day, six hundred books were stolen by visitors. Soviet officials demanded that all the books be bolted down securely under plexiglass. Again an uneasy compromise was reached, with only a few books given the plexiglass treatment.[29]

The 1959 Moscow exhibit was the first in a series of large shows that USIA mounted under other U.S.-Soviet cultural agreements during the next thirty years. Each exhibit featured a specific theme, ranging from architecture to farming. The shows traveled across the Soviet Union from its western borders to Siberia, attracting long lines of visitors at each stop. Smaller versions of the exhibits also toured most of the Communist-dominated countries of Eastern Europe, under arrangements similar to those in the initial 1957 U.S.-Soviet exchange agreement.

Overall, these exhibits were visually stunning. They drew on the talents of leading American designers including two USIA employees, Robert Sivard and Jack Masey. The impact of the shows was in many ways ephemeral, but (as subsequent audience surveys showed) they played a special role in the range of forces that led to the final implosion of the Kremlin's authority and the collapse of the Soviet Union in 1991.

The 1959 Moscow exhibit and those that followed had little immediate effect on the continuing political confrontation between the United States and the Soviet Union. The Kremlin leadership was adept at using the limited Eisenhower-Khrushchev thaw to press its own claim to be the leading practitioner of what it termed peaceful coexistence. It financed front organizations throughout the world to organize, among other events, international youth rallies promoting the coexistence theme. Soviet authorities also helped launch the Stockholm Peace Appeal, a fuzzy but effective manifesto that cast the United States in the role of international aggressor. The peace appeal had a respected British philosopher, Bertrand Russell, as its most prominent sponsor. It was supported by other leading intellectuals around the world and gathered tens of millions of signatures from ordinary citizens.

Throughout the Eisenhower-Khrushchev thaw, U.S. responses often appeared to be overwhelmed by these Moscow initiatives. Despite the exchange agreements, access to audiences in the Soviet bloc was severely restricted. Shortwave radio–jamming techniques obstructed the day-to-day exposure of these audiences to outside information from the Voice of America, the BBC, and other Western broadcasters. Moscow authorities played a game of on-and-off relaxation of shortwave jamming, a tactic that became a barometer of their current assessment of the Soviet Union's relations with the West. When they did reduce jamming, it usually involved transmissions in English and other languages not widely understood by Soviet listeners.[30]

The tone and direction of Soviet propaganda during the peaceful-coexistence years was set by political events. The abortive 1956 French and British attempt to regain control of the Suez Canal (quickly ended by U.S. diplomatic intervention) was characterized by Moscow as a return to colonialism. In the same vein, Western moral support for the 1957 attempt by Hungarians to overthrow their Communist government was described as a threat to world peace. In their attacks on the United States, Soviet spokesmen played the racial-discrimination card very effectively. They exploited the civil rights demonstrations of the late 1950s, in particular, the 1957 confrontation in Little Rock following a federal court decision requiring the admission of black schoolchildren to a previously all-white school.

The biggest propaganda boon to Moscow during the Eisenhower-Khrushchev thaw was *Sputnik*. The 1957 launching of the first man-made object to orbit the earth was a spectacular Soviet achievement. *Sputnik*'s beeper signals, repeated endlessly by Radio Moscow and other propaganda outlets, affirmed in popular imagination around the world the Soviet Union's status as a superpower. Although the United States had a broader range of space projects at the time, none of them matched the *Sputnik* project or the later Soviet success in putting the first man into space. It would take a decade before the United States could challenge the initial impact of these two events on world opinion.

Meanwhile, USIA was going through a managerial shakedown. Ted Streibert resigned in 1957, to return to his broadcasting duties in New York. He was replaced by Arthur Larson, a Republican labor lawyer, whose political instincts were less than subtle. In a speech at a Republican gathering in Hawaii shortly after he was appointed. he castigated the Roosevelt and Truman administrations as having held the country "in the grip of a somewhat alien philosophy, imported from Europe."

Larson's gaffe was particularly ill-timed, given the fact that the Democrats had taken control of the Senate several months earlier. It was now their chance to harass a Republican administration on a range of subjects, including the overseas information program. The attack was led by the Senate majority leader, Lyndon Johnson, who lambasted Larson in committee hearings for the agency's alleged failings. "Nobody but nobody loves the USIA," the *New York Times* declared. Congress proceeded to cut the agency's budget. A plan to return the agency to the State Department, initiated by a respected Democratic senator, Mike Mansfield of Montana, was revived.[31]

Tensions between Congress and the agency were lowered somewhat when Larson resigned, to be replaced by George V. Allen, a veteran State Department diplomat, late in 1957. It was a repeat performance for Allen: he had headed the State Department's overseas information operations a decade earlier.[32] He brought nonpartisan credentials to the job as well as a sharp instinct for what USIA could and could not do to advance foreign policy objectives. Moreover, he was well respected in Congress, a factor that helped restore a large share of congressional confidence in USIA during the last years of the Eisenhower administration.

Larger budgets allowed the agency to expand its overseas operations, particularly in Asia and Africa, where dozens of new nations were being drawn into the orbit of U.S.-Soviet confrontation. Although most of these countries professed nonalignment in this wider political struggle, their general tilt favored policies that gave the edge to Soviet peaceful-coexistence claims. Moscow's intentions in developing regions were made clear when Premier Khrushchev's called for "wars of national liberation" against alleged U.S. imperialism in Asia, Africa, and Latin America. The Chinese Communist leadership had adopted a similar stance, but their approach was different enough from that of the Soviets to lead to a serious ideological rift with Moscow in the late 1950s.

Communist-led insurgencies supported by Moscow and Beijing in the Philippines, Thailand, and Malaysia underscored the urgency of the threat to U.S. interests. One of these insurgencies was taking place in French Indo-China, a colonial possession that included present-day Cambodia, Laos, and Vietnam. At first, this event did not attract much attention in Washington, primarily because the French were intent on ending the insurgency on their own terms, which were to restore their authority in a region that had been overrun by the Japanese during World War II.

This indifference changed in 1954 when French military units suffered a major defeat by a ragtag Vietminh guerrilla force at Dien Bien Phu. The French appealed for major U.S. assistance, a proposal supported by John Foster Dulles and rejected by President Eisenhower. Nevertheless, a small group of Defense Department advisers were dispatched to Vietnam. It was the beginning of direct U.S. military involvement in the region.

This involvement soon affected USIA. The U.S. legation in Saigon had included a small information unit since the early 1950s, directed by Lee Brady, a soft-spoken scholar who had previously taught French literature at a small Midwestern college. As the French came under greater pressure from Vietminh guerrilla forces, the unit was expanded. One of its younger officers, Howard Simpson, was assigned as the U.S. representative on a Franco-Vietnamese Psychological Warfare Committee run by the French military mission.[33] It was the start of USIA's involvement in a shadow colonial war, one which was to expand to a major commitment of the agency's personnel and other resources over the next fifteen years.

As the Eisenhower presidency wound down in the late 1950s, USIA was in healthy organizational shape. Despite Democratic sniping in Congress, its budgets were relatively steady. The agency's expansion into newly decolonized countries in Asia and Africa involved a steady shift of its overseas resources from European and Japanese posts. Although its role in national security policymaking in Washington was still shaky, USIA's influence on policy decisions at the embassy level increased, as more ambassadors recognized the value of U.S. Information Service resources in their day-to-day dealings with local political issues.

In large part, USIA's limited but growing acceptance as a foreign policy resource could be attributed to President Eisenhower's gradualist policies, in particular his willingness to broaden contacts with the Soviet Union at both the Kremlin and public-opinion levels. Although his approach was often rejected (for different reasons) in Moscow and in conservative circles at home, it set a tone that favored the kind of resources the USIA could bring to bear on foreign policy.

Eisenhower gave a special boost to what he called people-to-people diplomacy in the last months before the 1960 presidential campaign got under way. It was a trip that took him to eleven countries in Asia, the Middle East, and Europe in December 1959.

Such globe-trotting travels by world leaders have since become routine occurrences, but none have matched the scope and impact of Eisenhower's triumphal tour. Tens of millions of people saw the president in person and hundreds of millions watched him on television as the tour progressed. The trip was a major test of USIA's ability to organize a multimedia campaign, not only in the countries visited by the president but also for audiences in other countries. It became a model for dealing with later presidential trips abroad, an activity in which the agency developed considerable expertise over the years.

Inevitably, there were glitches during the Eisenhower trip. In Athens, where a million Greeks lined the streets on a late December afternoon to see the president, American flags flew on every building along the route from the airport. The exception was the U.S. embassy. A panicked embassy officer told the U.S. Marine guard on duty in the lobby to display the flag. No, the guard replied, his orders were to take the flag down at five o'clock every afternoon. After a series of increasingly frenzied phone calls, the order came down to make an exception in this one case.

Although the Eisenhower administration gave the overseas information program strong operational support overall, it never managed to fully exploit USIA as a policy resource. In 1959, the president appointed a blue-ribbon commission, headed by industrialist Mansfield Sprague, to examine the program. By and large, the Sprague commission validated the program's effectiveness, except for its weak role in policy formation. The report recommended strengthening USIA's role within the NSC structure, but no actions were taken in the final lame-duck months of the Eisenhower administration.[34] It was one of the many projects put aside as Washington prepared for the transfer of presidential power from a distinguished warrior-statesman to a young senator from Massachusetts, whose credentials were yet to be tested on the national scene.

Notes

1. "Budget Cuts Mute U.S. Voice in India," *New York Times,* September 20, 1953, p. 9.
2. "Farewell to an Old Friend: The Roger Smith Hotel," in United States Information Agency, *Commemoration: Public Diplomacy, Looking Back, Looking Forward* (Washington, D.C.: USIA Office of Public Information, 1999), p. 46.
3. "Recalling Directors Streibert and Allen," in United States Information Agency, *Commemoration: Public Diplomacy, Looking Back, Looking Forward* (Washington, D.C.: USIA Office of Public Information, 1999), p. 22.
4. Interview with Henry Loomis, Foreign Affairs Oral History Project, February 25, 1989, p. 24.
5. Thomas C. Sorensen, *The Word War: The Story of American Propaganda* (New York: Harper & Row, 1967), p. 51.
6. Ibid., p. 105.
7. Eisenhower's overall relations with USIA are described in: Hans Tuch and G. Lewis Schmitt (eds.), *Ike and USIA: A Commemorative Symposium* (Washington, D.C.: USIA Alumni Association and the Public Diplomacy Foundation, 1991).
8. Quoted in: Arthur Schlesinger Jr., "Psychological Warfare: Can It Sell Freedom?" *The Reporter,* March 31, 1953, p. 9.
9. Walter L. Hixson, *Parting the Curtain: Propaganda, Culture and the Cold War* (New York: St. Martin's Griffin, 1997), pp. 25–27.
10. "Overseas Information Programs of the United States," Report No. 406, Senate Foreign Relations Committee, 83rd Congress, 1st session, June 15, 1953, pp. 6–13.
11. Reorganization Plan No. 8 of 1953, 18 Federal Register 4542, June 1, 1953, p. 1.
12. Interview with Henry Loomis, p. 24.
13. Robert R. Bowie, "President Eisenhower Establishes His National Security Process," in David Abshire (ed.), *Triumphs and Tragedies of the Modern Presidency* (Washington, D.C.: Center for the Study of the Presidency, July 2000), pp. 152–157.

14. Secretary Dulles's attitudes on the subject are discussed in: "The Loneliest Man in Washington," *The Reporter,* October 18, 1956, pp. 11–16; Arthur Krock, "Why Are We Losing the Psychological War?" *New York Times Magazine,* December 8, 1957, p. 12.

15. James Marcio, "The Planning Coordination Group: Bureaucratic Casualty in the Cold War Campaign to Exploit Soviet-Bloc Vulnerabilities," *Journal of Cold War Studies* 4, no. 4, fall 2002, pp. 3–28.

16. The Bogart study was not released at the time. A one-volume version of the report was published twenty-two years later. Leo Bogart, *Promises for Propaganda: The United States Information Agency's Operating Assumptions in the Cold War* (Boston: Free Press, 1976). Another useful study of agency policies and actions in assessing overseas public opinion in the early stages of the Cold War is Oren Stephens, *Facts to a Candid World* (Stanford, Calif.: Stanford University Press, 1955).

17. "New Information Unit Has Some Big Plans," *New York Times,* November 1, 1953, p. 34.

18. "Russians Hearing Moderate 'Voice,'" *New York Times,* September 13, 1959, p. 22.

19. "Who Is Conover? Only We Ask," *New York Times Magazine,* September 13, 1959, p. 22.

20. J. D. Ratcliff, "The USA Goes to the Fair," in Urban G. Whitaker (ed.), *Propaganda and International Relations,* Chandler Studies in International and Intercultural Relations (San Francisco: Chandler Publishing Co., 1960), pp. 62–66.

21. "Industry Communications Programs in Support of U.S. Foreign Policy," *Department of State Bulletin,* vol. 46, no. 1180, February 5, 1967, pp. 213–215.

22. "USIA Would Man Cinerama Ship," *New York Herald-Tribune,* July 3, 1955, p. 12.

23. "U.S. Magazine Appears in Moscow," *New York Times,* July 24, 1956. p. 12.

24. Hixson, *Parting the Curtain,* p. 104.

25. Ibid., p. 105.

26. "Cultural Exchanges as the Soviets Use It," *The Reporter,* April 7, 1966, pp. 20–25.

27. Marilyn S. Kushner, "Exhibiting Art at the American National Exhibition in Moscow, 1959: Domestic Politics and Cultural Diplomacy," *Journal of Cold War Studies* 4, no. 1, winter 2002, pp. 6–26.

28. Hans N. Tuch, *Communicating with the World: U.S. Public Diplomacy Overseas* (New York: St. Martin's Press, 1990), pp. 63–64.

29. Hixson, *Parting the Curtain,* p. 191.

30. For background on Soviet radio jamming and U.S. attempts to stop it, see: David F. Krugler, *The Voice of America and the Domestic Propaganda Battles 1945–1953* (Columbia: University of Missouri Press, 2000), pp. 102–105.

31. Sorensen, *The Word War,* pp. 94–99.

32. "Newsmaker: George V. Allen of USIA," *Newsweek,* October 28, 1957, p. 16.

33. Howard R. Simpson, *Bush Hat, Black Tie: Adventures of a Foreign Service Officer* (London: Brassey's Books, 1998), p. 7.

34. Report of the President's Commission on Information Activities Abroad. Reprinted in: *Department of State Bulletin*, vol. 44, no. 1128, February 8, 1961, pp. 182–195.

5

The Murrow Years

IN 1960, NATIONAL attention focused on the presidential race between Vice President Richard Nixon and his challenger, Senator John F. Kennedy. Although better known than Kennedy, Nixon had stood in Dwight Eisenhower's shadow for eight years. Kennedy brought a fresh face and new attitudes to the campaign. In Congress, he had played the traditionally assigned role of a junior senator, largely content to serve his Massachusetts constituency and go along with his party's legislative agenda. This reticence was about to change dramatically as he prepared to take on presidential responsibilities.

The election campaign was marked by high-level rhetoric and low-level political tactics. The foreign policy debate centered on charges and countercharges about which candidate was best qualified to stand up to the Soviet Union. USIA became involved in the debate when Kennedy challenged Nixon's claim that U.S. prestige overseas was never higher, thanks to Republican policies in the Eisenhower years. Kennedy campaign managers had gotten access to classified USIA overseas polling data that tended to prove otherwise. The result was a standoff, with the Nixon campaign charging that Kennedy supporters within the agency had manipulated the polling results.

After its narrow electoral victory, the Kennedy White House faced a long agenda of foreign policy decisions. These included the continuing threat of Soviet and Chinese military buildups, disarmament negotiations, the impact of the *Sputnik* space achievement, and unrest in Eastern Europe, among other issues. But the subject that seized their attention was one that would have a major effect on USIA's operations during the Kennedy years and beyond—the U.S. response to the doctrine of "wars of national liberation" proclaimed by Soviet premier Nikita

Khrushchev in the late 1950s. In essence, Khrushchev offered Moscow's support (including money and weapons) to dissident groups in newly independent countries, particularly in Asia and Africa, for the ostensible purpose of resisting U.S. political and economic pressures. More specifically, it meant Soviet backing of communist and left-wing guerrilla movements to gain control of fragile third-world governments.

This Khrushchev challenge dominated the thinking of Kennedy foreign policy advisers as the new administration took over. Their attempts to cobble together a strategy for dealing with the problem drew heavily on research produced at academic think tanks, particularly at MIT, Columbia, and Harvard. Although the studies differed in details, they agreed on the essentials of what came to be known as modernization theory. The general idea was that the United States should develop an integrated strategy of political, economic, and psychological operations in the threatened countries. The overall aim, as defined by MIT scholar Daniel Lerner, was to reinforce potentially democratic groups in the third world who were, in Lerner's phrase, on a forced march to modernity.[1]

Modernization was an appealing doctrine, fitting easily into American's latent missionary impulses. It also served as an ideological counterweight to Marxist-Leninist theories about imperialist attempts to dominate the new nations of Asia, Africa, and Latin America. Equally important, it provided a policy framework for Kennedy initiatives such as the Peace Corps, the Alliance for Progress in Latin America, and, less successfully, the decision to step up direct U.S. involvement in the French government's attempt to maintain its political control over Vietnam.

These initiatives brought about major changes in how USIA carried out its mission, particularly in shifting its program focus more directly onto third-world concerns. The agency's operations in Europe and Japan were steadily scaled back in favor of programs in newly independent countries. In 1959, USIA had twenty-four posts in thirteen African countries, ten of them newly independent. Four years later, the agency had operations at fifty-five posts in thirty-three African countries.

Meanwhile, Kennedy officials were reorganizing the White House policy structure to deal with international challenges, including third-world insurgencies. USIA's role in this structure was a minor but relevant part of their plans. The president's advisers were by and large agreed that the organization should remain an independent agency. They also recommended that it be given a larger role in policymaking at the National Security Council (NSC) level. This idea was rejected by Kennedy when he decided to abolish the Operations Coordinating Board, the one part of the NSC where USIA had a specific set of policy responsibilities.[2]

For a short time it appeared that the agency would not play a significant role in the new policy structure. This perception began to change with the White House announcement naming Edward R. Murrow, the veteran CBS news correspondent, as USIA director. Murrow had first come to national prominence with his live radio reportage of the German air assault on Britain in the early 1940s, identified by his signature opening line—"This (pause) is London"—as bombs burst in the background. In 1961, he had been at the height of his professional career as host of the CBS television programs *See It Now* and *CBS Reports*.

Murrow's appointment was welcomed by the general public and by his professional colleagues. James Reston, the *New York Times* chief political reporter, declared:

> Edward R. Murrow, the best left-handed putter in Christendom and the most influential reporter of his time, has been given the job of fixing his country's overseas propaganda. Considering the fix it's in, this is quite a job, for no country had a better story to tell, or failed so lamentably to tell it well as the United States since the end of the war. . . . No doubt Ed Murrow has the qualities to do the job. He has the poetry of the nation in his bones. He has the respect of reporters in all media here and abroad. He has style and ideas, and if he can hold his temper on Capitol Hill, which won't be easy, he may prove to be the best of Kennedy's excellent appointments.[3]

Murrow himself was nonplussed by the national interest surrounding his appointment. Asked why he took a 90 percent pay cut to accept a $23,000 job in the Kennedy administration, he replied: "I just figured that if this young man couldn't do it, no one could, and if he wants my help, I have an obligation to do it."[4]

The overseas propaganda program finally had a certified public personality as its head. Moreover, Murrow was someone who knew the media business and particularly the art of telling a story convincingly. Morale within the USIA staff soared, with an enthusiasm that rippled down the agency halls and out to the overseas posts. The new director moved into his government-issue office at 1776 Pennsylvania Avenue, bringing with him a breezy shirt-sleeve style, the famous low bass voice, and always a cigarette in his left hand, one from the two packs a day that were to kill him less than three years later.

Murrow quickly appointed two chief aides who formed what he called "the troika" to run USIA. His deputy, Donald Wilson, was a former *Time* magazine correspondent who had served in the Kennedy election campaign and on the White House foreign policy transition team. The other appointee was Tom Sorensen, a USIA Foreign Service officer with field experience, who knew the details of how the agency operated. He had the added advantage of being the brother of Ted Sorensen, the president's chief policy adviser. Both Wilson and Sorensen proved to be adept at helping their new boss learn the bureaucratic ropes.

This did not prevent Murrow from making a major blunder in his early days at USIA. One of his last CBS television programs had been a documentary, "Harvest of Shame," detailing the primitive working conditions of migrant farm labor in the South. It was a compelling report on an underside of American life. Without informing his USIA staff, Murrow called the director of the British Broadcasting Corporation, which had already contracted with CBS to run the program, and asked him not to air it. The director, an old friend of Murrow's, demurred, but the incident became public. The new USIA director looked like a government censor. He was chagrined, and he let it be known that he had made a wrong move.

In those early days at the agency, Murrow spent a lot of time meeting with the staff, aware of stories about the alleged incompetence of the organization's personnel. He was surprised by the depth of talent he found. "I could staff any commercial media outlet in the country with people from this agency," he later remarked, "and it would be as good or better than any of its competitors."[5]

However, he had also spotted some misfits. At one Friday staff meeting, he asked his administrative officer, Ben Posner, how he could get rid of the deadweight. Posner replied that there were strict procedures to be followed. He presented Murrow with a volume of government rules on the subject. Murrow promised to read the regulations over the weekend. At the Monday staff meeting, he turned to Posner and said: "I've been through the firing regulations and I've concluded that the only way to get rid of anyone in the government is to discover them with a sheep in Lafayette Park." Despite the obstacles, he managed to ease a number of top-level agency officers out of their jobs.

The key to understanding Murrow's directorship, as with that of his predecessors and successors, lay in his relationship with the White House. Initially there were mixed feelings among the Kennedy staff on how to handle the man who was the best-known public figure in the new administration. Their fears that he might upstage the president were quickly laid to rest. By nature reticent, Murrow proved to be a valuable member of the White House team. McGeorge Bundy, the White House foreign policy adviser, later noted: "Murrow never once asked to go to a meeting. In time he never had to ask. President Kennedy increasingly said: 'Let's find out what Ed thinks' or 'Be sure Murrow is here.'"[6] The USIA director was granted the ultimate Washington perk: a direct telephone line to the president's office. Murrow called it "the blower," and he seldom used it.[7]

When he did, he was effective. That was the case in August 1961 when the Soviet Union abruptly announced the resumption of atmospheric nuclear testing, breaking an unwritten agreement against such tests that had been in effect for several years. In Washington, Kennedy administration officials drafted a statement proposing U.S. resumption of such testing. Ed Murrow protested: "If we issue the statement, we destroy the advantages of the greatest propaganda gift we have had in a long time."[8] He recommended that the decision to resume testing be postponed to allow USIA time to mount a worldwide campaign, focused on the threat to peace and to the earth's environment represented by the Soviet decision.

The president agreed. Murrow took direct charge in orchestrating a media blitz attacking Moscow's resumption of nuclear testing. An agency survey of foreign press and radio comment later recorded the strongest surge of anti-Soviet sentiment since Moscow's armed repression of a popular uprising against Soviet domination of Hungary in 1956.

The biggest test of Murrow's relations with the Kennedy White House occurred during the Cuban missile crisis in 1962. Beginning in the closing months of the Eisenhower administration, the United States had conducted a covert program, Operation Mongoose, to overthrow Fidel Castro. It ranged from plans to contaminate Cuban sugar fields to plots to assassinate Castro. Another project inherited by Kennedy from the Eisenhower White House was an invasion of the island at the Bay of Pigs by a CIA-trained exile group, a venture that ended in failure.

Cuba became a dangerous flashpoint in global politics in October 1962 with the discovery on the island of Soviet missile sites capable of launching nuclear-tipped rockets at the U.S. mainland. It was the most serious crisis in the forty-year Cold War standoff between the Soviet Union and the United States, involving the direct prospect of mutual nuclear annihilation. The crisis called for cool heads and sober advice by the leadership of both countries.

In Washington, Ed Murrow helped provide both. In the months since he had joined USIA, he had been reinforced in his belief that the agency should persuade, not just inform. Moreover, he saw the need to take an aggressive role in advising the White House on the importance of overseas public opinion in making foreign policy decisions.

The discovery of Soviet missiles in Cuba gave Murrow a decisive opportunity to make his point. In September 1962, a month before the crisis unfolded, Murrow had personally drafted the U.S. government's response to a statement by TASS, the Soviet news agency, alleging that the United States was preparing to invade Cuba. "The Soviet statement reflects a lust for power and a disrespect for truth," he wrote. "The government of the United States threatens no nation and no people. . . . The [Soviet statement] appears to say 'Stop doing what you have no intention of doing, or terrible things will happen to you.'"[9]

In fact, terrible things were about to happen. On October 14, a high-flying U-2 surveillance plane, managed by the CIA, photographed what appeared to be a medium-range missile site in western Cuba. When its existence was confirmed by later flights, a special "Ex Com" (for executive committee) was set up in the White House to deal with the crisis. USIA was not included in Ex Com's initial membership. This changed two days later when it became clear that public communications, and particularly international opinion, would play a vital role in any successful resolution of the crisis. Murrow was invited to join Ex Com, but he was confined to a hospital bed with pneumonia. Donald Wilson, his deputy, represented the agency in the group.[10]

In the tense days before the Soviets agreed to dismantle the missile sites, Ex Com gave high priority to the role of overseas public opinion in defusing the crisis. One decision involved whether the surveillance-plane photographs should be released. CIA and Pentagon officials were opposed, on the grounds that declassifying the pictures would compromise the operation. USIA's Wilson successfully argued for releasing them. The photos were used with stunning effect by Adlai Stevenson, the U.S. ambassador to the United Nations, during the Security Council debate on the crisis. "The full extent of the menace which Cuba has become is dramatically expressed by the American photographs," the London *Daily Express* declared in a typical comment. "They enormously strengthen the American case."

Radio played a critical role in USIA's information strategy, given its ability to reach multiple audiences with a message on the global implications of the Soviet missiles. Cuban listeners were made the primary target, followed by Soviet-bloc citizens, and then the rest of the world. Broadcasting to Cuba—only 90 miles away from Florida—presented special problems. Voice of America facilities in the region were designed primarily to reach shortwave listeners, of whom there were very few in Cuba.

At the White House, the Ex Com approved a plan to commandeer eight private medium-wave stations with signals capable of reaching

Cuba from the U.S. mainland. The stations' owners readily agreed to cooperate, but there is interesting evidence that the White House had already made contingency arrangements with officials of the American Telephone & Telegraph Co. to have engineers enter the stations on the pretext of making technical adjustments. When the station owners asked for instructions on how to readjust their transmitter coverage to reach Cuba, they were told that the adjustments already had been made.[11]

The commercial stations blanketed Cuba with round-the-clock coverage. Their programming was reinforced by hastily arranged VOA medium-wave transmissions. An air-transportable mobile station being built in Texas under a USIA contract was sent to Marathon in the Florida Keys. A similar transmitter was installed by the navy on Tortuga Key. This combination of government and commercial programming assured that the Cuban public knew about the danger they had been exposed to by Fidel Castro's decision to permit the Soviet missile base.

Meanwhile, VOA's thirty-five language services were broadcasting news and commentary on the crisis to global audiences, particularly those in the Soviet bloc. All in all, fifty-two transmitters were involved in the effort. This massive concentration of transmitter power was particularly useful in breaking through Soviet jamming efforts.

Other USIA media were brought into play. Fifty thousand prints of the surveillance-plane photographs were airshipped to overseas posts, together with plastic plates that could be used for printing them on even the most primitive presses. In Pakistan, the USIS post's weekly magazine was turned into a daily, and its circulation increased eightfold for the duration of the crisis. Agency-supplied film footage of the missile bases was aired by hundreds of television stations abroad. President Kennedy's speech announcing the existence of the Soviet missiles was transmitted live to European audiences by Telstar, the first U.S. communications satellite, which had been launched a few months earlier. It was the first time that such satellites had been used for explicitly political purposes.[12]

USIA's operational performance during the Cuban missile episode was a case-study example of how the overseas information program could provide operational support in a major crisis. More significant was the agency's contribution at the policy level as a result of Donald Wilson's participation in the Ex Com. His advice (and that of Ed Murrow from his hospital sickbed) made a positive difference at a crucial turning point in U.S. foreign policy. This had never happened before at such a direct level nor, regrettably, since. Forty years later, the agency's policy role in the Cuban missile crisis, emphasizing the power of global public opinion, has lessons for contemporary U.S. diplomacy in a more complex international setting.[13]

With the resolution of the missile crisis, the agency resumed normal operations. Murrow was back at his desk after his bout with pneumonia, but his staff noticed that he appeared weaker and that his cigarette-induced coughing was worsening. Nevertheless, he was clearly in charge.

At Attorney General Robert Kennedy's suggestion, Murrow shifted agency resources to put more emphasis on reaching younger audiences abroad, particularly university student leaders, who were susceptible to anti-American appeals. They were a primary target for Soviet propaganda efforts, which included, among other projects, all-expense-paid trips to Moscow-sponsored "World Youth Festivals" in Vienna, Helsinki, and other capitals. Moreover, their sheer numbers made them important: at the time, two-thirds of the populations of India, Pakistan, Brazil, Egypt, and Indonesia were under thirty. "Youth officers" were assigned to agency posts abroad to work with this hitherto ignored audience. Appropriately, these officers tended to be younger, with language skills and a penchant for connecting with local student groups. A typical example was Rudolph Aggrey, a black officer who was the first director of the Rue Dragon Center in Paris, a USIS library and cultural center that served the large contingent of African students studying there. Aggrey later had a distinguished career as a U.S. ambassador.

Ed Murrow's relations with Congress were ambivalent. The legislators tended to be somewhat deferential to such a popular public figure. On the other hand, old suspicions about the information program remained. When Senator Allen Ellender, a Louisiana Democrat and perennial critic of the information program, told Murrow that he should make USIA more effective or get rid of it, Murrow agreed, adding that the organization's effectiveness depended, in part, on adequate congressional funding.[14] USIA budget appropriations zigzagged up and down during the Murrow years, although the overall trend was up.

Murrow was particularly skillful in fielding questions during his many appearances before congressional committees. During one committee discussion on the use of global communications satellites, a technology then being developed by U.S. researchers, he supported the Kennedy administration's decision to make the satellites available to all countries. A congressman challenged him, asking whether the policy included "equal time for Red China, financed at the U.S. taxpayer's expense." Murrow replied: "This would be a two-way street. If the Chinese were prepared to say we could get words and pictures from the satellites to their sets, I would have no doubt where the advantage would lie at the end of the day."[15] The congressman backed off.

Murrow was intrigued by communications satellites, and particularly by their ability to provide television and other media connections between any two points on earth. He lobbied successfully to have USIA represented on the interagency committee that drafted the congressional legislation governing the use of the satellites. He also proposed that the agency be given free use of the satellites, arguing that the federal government had funded much of the research that made them possible. His request was turned down in favor of setting up a congressionally chartered corporation modeled on private-enterprise lines. Once the global network began operations, USIA made extensive use of its facilities to provide television programming to overseas stations.

Meanwhile, the agency was being drawn deeper into third-world problems. As noted earlier, the Kennedy administration came into office with deep forebodings about Soviet plans to support so-called wars of national liberation in the new nations of Asia, Africa, and Latin America. Modernization and counterinsurgency theories, nurtured at MIT and other East Coast study centers, were being transformed into policy decisions in Washington.

The modernization project's driving force was Attorney General Robert F. Kennedy. With his brother's support, he took personal charge of counterinsurgency operations policy. His program included a mandatory training course in counterinsurgency doctrine for all senior officers in the State Department, USIA, and the defense and intelligence agencies assigned to so-called underdeveloped regions. The lectures were conducted in a large auditorium at the Foreign Service Institute, the State Department's training facility. The room's walls were festooned with dozens of large posters, each describing the insurgency situation in a third-world country. The course usually ended with an evangelical talk by the attorney general, exhorting the assembled bureaucrats to fight the good counterinsurgency fight with all the resources at their agencies' command.[16] USIA was brought into the counterinsurgency project at an early stage. This reflected Robert Kennedy's conviction, confirmed on his overseas trips to Asia, Africa, and Latin America, that ideological operations ranked with military and economic programs in promoting stable governments in these regions. He argued for treating third-world countries as potential allies, despite their tendency to adopt a neutral role in the East-West conflict.

In this Kennedy had the support of Ed Murrow. When a conference of seventy nonaligned countries was held in Belgrade in 1961, the State Department cautioned against sending a presidential message to the meeting expressing sympathetic interest in third-world political and economic problems. Murrow spoke in favor of the proposed message, pointing out that U.S. views needed to be heard if only as a counterweight to appeals from the Soviet Union and other Communist countries supporting the conference. Murrow prevailed.[17]

Meanwhile, USIA expanded its activities in Asian and African countries, focusing particularly on those threatened with insurgencies. Thailand, the Philippines, Laos, and the Congo were high on the list. Increasingly, however, Vietnam dominated the agency's efforts. Following the French withdrawal from its Southeast Asian colonies in the late 1950s, the United States became more involved in active collaboration with the South Vietnamese government, headed by Ngo Dinh Diem, to turn back Communist-led guerrilla advances. A USIA officer was assigned to Diem's staff as press adviser.[18] John Mecklin, a well-known *Time* correspondent, was put in charge of an expanded U.S. Information Service operation, whose activities increasingly involved producing and distributing propaganda materials in the name of the Diem government.

Another part of Mecklin's mission was to brief the expanding U.S. press corps in Saigon, a group that was reporting the failures of the Diem regime and, by extension, the inability of U.S. efforts to bring about needed reforms. Although Diem was overthrown in November 1963 in a coup in which the U.S. government was involved, the basic issues around the Communist insurgency remained largely unchanged. Increasingly, USIA, along with other Washington agencies, was drawn deeper into the Vietnam quagmire as U.S. policy and operational emphasis shifted away from reliance on ideological and economic programs to plans for a military solution.

USIA had more success in helping other third-world countries deal with guerrilla warfare, notably Thailand and the Philippines. Africa presented a special problem. There Soviet-sponsored guerrillas were secondary to tribal political tensions as a disruptive force. During the Murrow years, agency posts in Africa increased from thirteen countries to thirty-three, in large part due to the rush to decolonization within the continent in the early 1960s.[19]

Colonial authorities in Africa had resisted U.S. Information Service operations during the years leading up to independence. At one point, Belgian officials warned U.S. authorities against opening a USIS library in the Belgian Congo, arguing that the local population would not be capable of using such a facility for fifty years. In South Africa, officials resisted plans for a similar library in Johannesburg after learning that it would be available to both black and white users. The library was opened, creating a small but symbolic breach in the apartheid laws.

The new libraries in Africa were crowded as soon as they opened their doors. The idea of having books freely available on open shelves, and for circulation, was a new experience for almost all cardholders. In Morocco, library attendance was so heavy that the USIS librarian issued cards in seven different colors, restricting the patron to entry once a week, the day designated by his or her card color. An extensive book translation program was set up in African countries, with low-cost books in English, French, and local languages. A USIA-produced newsreel, *Africa Today,* was seen by 30 million moviegoers monthly.

These were important assets, but USIA had a tough sell in Africa. The early 1960s saw the quickening of the U.S. civil rights movement, together with often violent opposition to it. A defining event was the massive August 1963 civil rights march on Washington, culminating in Martin Luther King's "I have a dream" speech. Continuing incidents of racial violence were grist for the Soviet propaganda mill. The Washington march, declared the TASS news agency, showed the world "the sores of American society . . . and the exploitation of 20 million American Negroes."[20]

Putting civil rights developments into perspective became the information agency's most challenging policy problem. Its position, stated in one of its reports to Congress, was that "the facts could not be denied but they could be placed in perspective." Nevertheless, overseas opinion on the issue generally ranged from skepticism to hostility, particularly in Asia and Africa.

Despite setbacks in the civil rights area, the agency thrived under Ed Murrow's leadership. One of his constant admonitions to his staff was the importance of encouraging other people to tell the American story. This included foreign correspondents stationed in the United States, a group that had been generally ignored by the White House, the State Department, and other Washington agencies.

Murrow turned this around. His first move was to authorize a Foreign Press Center in New York, a few blocks from United Nations headquarters. It was an instant success, with a reference library, news teletypes, and special press conferences and briefings by U.S. officials.[21] A similar center was later opened in Washington. (Both the New York and Washington centers have remained active.) In a related initiative, Murrow successfully lobbied the White House to add a USIA officer to its press-briefing office to assist the large foreign press corps.

The agency's biggest asset in the Murrow years was the image of a vigorous young president who spoke about new frontiers, economic growth, and reaching out to conquer outer space. Kennedy's predecessor, Dwight Eisenhower, had set a new global pattern of presidential influence with, among other events, his groundbreaking trip around the world in 1959. The Kennedy White House built on this initial success with a series of overseas trips, most notably the president's June 1963 trip to Europe that included his commitment to West Berliners to protect their city from Soviet encroachment, confirmed by his famous quip, "*Ich bin ein Berliner.*"

The president's wife, Jacqueline, attracted equal attention when she accompanied her husband, projecting the image of a confident, talented American woman. Her solo visit to South Asia in 1962 took on the trappings of a royal procession as she passed by millions of onlookers in India and Pakistan. These trips by Kennedy and his wife were carefully orchestrated, with considerable USIA help, to project not only the Kennedy aura but also the foreign policy purposes behind the trips.

The Kennedy presidency ended abruptly on November 22, 1963. The Dallas assassination was an event shared instantaneously by people around the globe. Newly available communications-satellite resources relayed live video coverage of the three days leading up to Kennedy's funeral. Thanks to the satellites and other new transmission links, few other events in modern times had triggered such a universal reaction.

USIA was a major channel for information about the president's death and the events that followed. Governments and public opinion reacted sympathetically to the loss of a popular world leader. The exceptions were in China and the Soviet Union. The government-controlled Chinese media all but ignored the event. After a short period of conventional condolences, Soviet propaganda spoke of right-wing plots and capitalist conspiracies as the cause of the assassination.[22]

In the weeks following the assassination, USIA was assigned the task of collecting and sorting the huge volume of international tributes, most of them sent to U.S. embassies overseas. These included official statements, scrawled letters from schoolchildren, poems, and thousands of drawings, paintings, and sculptures of the fallen president. Eventually, most of these tributes were acknowledged by an engraved card sent under Jacqueline Kennedy's name. Others were referred to her for more formal acknowledgment, such as a Dutch request to name a new grammar school after the president.[23]

One project stood out in USIA's coverage of the Kennedy assassination. It was a documentary film, *John F. Kennedy: Years of Lightning, Day of Drums*. Written and directed by a young Hollywood producer, Bruce Herschenson, and narrated by actor Gregory Peck, the film was the most widely praised documentary produced and distributed by the agency over its forty-five-year history. "A magnificent motion-picture tribute to President Kennedy," the *New York Times* declared.²⁴ *Years of Lightning* was distributed commercially in over sixty countries abroad. USIS posts arranged other special screenings. Following one screening, the speaker of Iceland's parliament declared: "This is the only picture I have ever seen during which I wanted to cry."²⁵

The film also attracted considerable domestic attention, leading to requests that it be made available to the public. The obstacle was a long-standing congressional restriction against distributing the agency's media output within the United States. The Senate quickly passed a resolution permitting the film's domestic distribution, but the House, caught in a rush to recess for a holiday, did not. There were objections, in and out of Congress, about the Senate's action. "USIA is frankly a propaganda agency," the *New York Herald Tribune* cautioned. "This is frankly a propaganda film." The issue was settled in a compromise that made the film a one-time exception to the no-domestic-distribution rule. Six prints of the film for domestic release were given to the committee organizing the proposed Kennedy cultural center in Washington, with the stipulation that the box-office receipts would be used to help finance the center.

Meanwhile, USIA turned its attention to acquainting the rest of the world with Kennedy's successor, Lyndon Johnson. Despite his long political career, notably as Senate majority leader in the Eisenhower years, Johnson was little known abroad, remaining largely in the shadow of the glamorous Kennedys. It was an unfair position: among other duties, Johnson had carried out important overseas missions for the Kennedy White House, including visits to Vietnam and to Berlin, where he delivered a powerful warning to the Soviet Union about interfering in the city's independence.

In addition to these substantive achievements, Johnson's overseas trips added to the agency's lore about the care and handling of junketing public officials. One of his quirks was insisting that he be photographed from the left side. He could not control commercial news photographers, but he would dress down any government photographer, including those from USIA, who inadvertently found themselves on the wrong side of the vice-presidential profile. His foreign audiences were intrigued by his glad-handing style as he waded into crowds. He and his family sometimes handed out LBJ-inscribed pencils, each with a plastic flower sprouting from the top. ("Regarding those pencils, Mr. Vice President," one Copenhagen paper commented, "the Marshall Plan is over.")

While visiting Pakistan in May 1961, Johnson was greeting a street crowd in Karachi when, on an impulse, he invited an illiterate camel driver, Bashir Ahmad, to visit him at his Texas ranch. His USIS interpreter, Roy Bisbee, whispered to Johnson that such an invitation would be taken seriously by Pakistanis. Bisbee was waved off, and the local USIS post was left with the problem of assuring that a camel driver's voyage to the United States was not a public relations disaster. In fact, Bashir's visit was a big success. He turned out to be something of a folksy philosopher whose advice to the vice president and other Americans he met was gleefully reported by both the U.S. and Pakistani media. He returned to Karachi a hero, with a gift pickup truck, Texas-tooled boots, and enough money to hire an assistant to take care of his camel.[26]

Johnson's relations with USIA had been somewhat prickly before the assassination, in part because he felt that the agency was ignoring him. He regarded USIA, with some justification, as a haven of Kennedy supporters who viewed him as a boorish Texas intruder into Camelot. The agency mounted a major media campaign, including pamphlets, books, films, and posters, to publicize Johnson abroad. Its research unit carefully tracked the largely favorable overseas reaction to the new president.

Ed Murrow turned in his resignation soon after the assassination, but Johnson persuaded him to stay on. By that time, Murrow was clearly in the terminal stages of lung cancer. He resigned several months later, retiring to his farm in Pawling, New York, where he died in April 1965. In a typical tribute, historian and Kennedy assistant Arthur Schlesinger Jr., who had worked with Murrow, noted: "He revitalized USIA, imbued it with his own bravery and honesty, and directed its efforts especially to the developing nations. . . . When his fatal illness began, he must have had the consolation, after those glittering years of meaningless success, that at the end he had fulfilled himself as never before."[27] Among the continuing legacies of Murrow's USIA career is the Murrow Center for Public Diplomacy at Tufts University, one of the few research institutes in the country dedicated to propaganda studies. Several years after his death, a small park across the street from USIA headquarters was dedicated to him.

Johnson chose a former newspaperman, Carl Rowan, to replace Murrow. Public attention focused on the fact that Rowan was the first African American to run a large federal agency. It was an important precedent, but it obscured the fact that Rowan had been a highly competent reporter and foreign correspondent for the Minneapolis *Tribune*. Moreover, he had previously served as the State Department's chief press spokesman and as ambassador to Finland.

Rowan had come up from a hardscrabble childhood in Tennessee. He attended Oberlin College and the University of Minnesota and was commissioned one of the first black officers in the U.S. Navy. Behind a deceptively soft drawl, he had a direct approach that turned away all attempts at condescension. In one of his sly stories, he was mowing the lawn at his home in an all-white Chevy Chase neighborhood when a passerby called to him: "Hey, boy. How much do you charge to cut the grass?" Rowan replied: "Well, the lady of the house lets me sleep with her."

One of the new director's early problems was to gain the confidence of his top officials, almost all of whom were still under the Murrow spell. He called them (including this author) into his office one day and announced that he was setting up a Bureaucrats Bowling League and that he would like them to report to a recently desegregated local bowling alley the following Monday evening. At the alley Rowan proceeded to outbowl them all. The assembled bureaucrats then informed him that they would arrange to have the alley resegregated if he continued to humiliate them so badly. He loved it, and the bowling sessions became weekly events that helped establish a strong bond between the new director and his staff.[28]

Critical issues dominated the agency's agenda, notably the worsening political situation in Vietnam. Theories about a neat, balanced counterinsurgency strategy of long-range political, economic, and psychological efforts went by the boards as U.S. military involvement expanded. USIA was increasingly caught up in the new escalation. Its limited U.S. Information Service operation in Saigon was transformed into a Joint U.S. Public Affairs Office (JUSPAO) in April 1965, with a mandate to coordinate all psychological operations in the conflict.[29] The new unit's staff was expanded from 150 to over 200 officers—more than ten times the size of any other USIA post. JUSPAO's budget was increased to $10 million, an unprecedented sum for a country operation.

Equally important, JUSPAO was given a strong leader in the person of Barry Zorthian, a tough former Marine with long experience as a Voice of America newsman. Zorthian was quickly tagged with the nickname "Zorro" by his staff and by the embassy, military, and economic aid officials he cajoled into dealing with the problem of convincing a fractious South Vietnamese population to support the war. The large contingent of U.S. media correspondents in Saigon were suspicious of JUSPAO's daily press briefings on the war, which became known as the Five O'Clock Follies. However, the newsmen came to respect Zorthian for resisting attempts by his superiors to censor or cover up bad news.

Despite the infusion of more staff and other resources, JUSPAO's efforts to rally South Vietnamese public opinion fell short. Increasingly, the unit became a surrogate propaganda ministry for the Vietnamese government, producing vast quantities of magazines, films, pamphlets, and radio and television programs in the name of the Vietnamese Information Service (VIS), a government agency run by inept officials. (One of the last VIS directors had been a druggist in private life.)

Whatever his misgivings about this strategy, Carl Rowan dutifully followed President Johnson's lead in expanding USIA's operations in Vietnam, though he was clearly frustrated. He finally turned in his resignation in July 1965 and was replaced by Washington lawyer Leonard H. Marks.[30]

The new director represented a distinct change in the agency's operational and management style. Marks was a highly successful attorney whose clients included many of the leading U.S. media industries. One of these clients was the president's wife, Lady Bird, who managed the family's extensive broadcasting properties in Texas. Marks's discreet use of his connections with the Johnsons proved to be useful in advancing USIA's interests during his directorship.

Marks also brought to the agency particular expertise in the new communications technologies, including his experience as one of the founding directors of the Communications Satellite Corporation, which managed the international satellite network authorized by Congress in 1962. His most lasting contribution to USIA was to focus it for the first time on the role that advanced communications technologies could play in its future operations.

The agency's immediate concerns continued to be defined by the imperatives of the expanded military effort in Vietnam. The task became an increasingly frustrating one, beset by contending U.S. bureaucracies in Saigon and by the incompetence or outright corrupt activities of many Vietnamese officials. The January 1968 Tet Offensive, which ended in heavy losses for the Viet Cong insurgents, was turned into a U.S. psychological defeat, largely on the basis of press reports that highlighted, among other details, the Viet Cong's temporary takeover of the U.S. embassy compound in Saigon.[31]

JUSPAO operations continued for six years after the Tet Offensive. The unit's activities were gradually cut back as part of the new Nixon administration's decision to withdraw U.S. troops and other resources. This change eventually allowed USIA to get a better balance in its overseas operations. The agency increased its presence in Asia and Africa as it shifted resources from Vietnam and from its European posts.

The information program's long-term prospects also had been enhanced by a strong lobbying effort by Leonard Marks to give USIA officers permanent career status within the Foreign Service. (Previously they had been reserve officers, subject to dismissal at the end of their limited contracts.) Congressional legislation supporting the change was passed in August 1968. This action gave USIA a firmer personnel base with which to implement its programs. It also helped revitalize the agency as it approached bureaucratic middle age. As with men and women, such a turning point often leads to an attraction for the routine, a reluctance to resist the rising vapors of complacency, and a willingness to settle into easy assumptions about purposes and goals.

Despite these dangers, there were signs that USIA's best days were ahead of it at the beginning of the 1970s. The agency was growing more confident in its ability to reach out effectively to foreign audiences. Its staff included a large proportion of seasoned officers, many with service that reached back to Office of War Information days.

Moreover, it had a new agenda of positive messages to deal with, including those related to the national space program that had resulted in the 1969 landing on the moon.[32] Perhaps its greatest gain from its past years of successes and failures was a deeper recognition that quick-fix solutions designed to influence overseas public opinion almost never worked. In effect, the organization had settled down to the realization that any significant progress would be the result of steady long-term efforts. This attitude was to dominate most of its activities in the final decades of its existence. In those years, new challenges for U.S. strategic interests included the growing influence of third-world countries, the global spread of American pop culture, the emergence of China from isolation, and the collapse of the Soviet Union.

Notes

1. Michael E. Latham, *Modernization as Ideology: American Social Science and 'Nation Building' in the Kennedy Era* (Chapel Hill: University of North Carolina Press, 2000). One of the most influential early studies of modernization was: Ithiel de Sola Pool and Donald Blackmer (eds.), *The Emerging Nations* (Cambridge, Mass.: MIT Press, 1962).

2. Thomas C. Sorensen, *The Word War: The Story of American Propaganda* (New York: Harper & Row, 1967), p. 120.

3. "Policy and Propaganda: Murrow's Appointment," *New York Times*, January 31, 1961, p. 31.

4. Quoted in Sorensen, *The Word War*, p. 123.

5. Ibid., p. 134.

6. "A Startlingly Decent Man: He Symbolized Integrity," *Washington Star*, April 28, 1965, p. 1.

7. Murrow's relationship with Kennedy is described in: "John F. Kennedy, USIA and World Opinion," *Diplomatic History* 25, no. 1, winter 2001, pp. 63–84.

8. Sorensen, *The Word War*, p. 147.

9. "USIA Commentary on TASS Statement," USIA press release No. 46, September 12, 1962. For background, see: Sorensen, *The Word War*, pp. 197–198.

10. The story of Ex Com's role in the Cuban missile crisis is documented in: Michael Beshchloss, *The Crisis Years* (New York: HarperCollins, 1991), pp. 450–470.

11. Interview with Clifford Gross, a senior VOA official who played a key role in the Voice's operations during the Cuban missile crisis. Association for Diplomatic Studies and Training Foreign Affairs Oral History Program, February 8, 1988, p. 6.

12. "Cuba: Challenge and Recoil," in *18th Review of Operations*, July 1–December 31, 1962, U.S. Information Agency, pp. 5–12.

13. Wilson's Ex Com experience is described in: "Interview with Donald M. Wilson, Vice President, Time Inc.," Oral History Interview Project, John F. Kennedy Presidential Library, November 17, 1970, pp. 16–21.

14. "Give USIA a New Look or Junk It," *Variety*, June 28, 1961, p. 44.

15. "Congress Debates Satellite Arrangements," *New York Times*, July 15, 1961, p. 12.

16. Robert Kennedy's role in counterinsurgency policy and operations is described in: Latham, *Modernization as Ideology*, pp. 166–167.

17. Sorensen, *The Word War*, pp. 162–163.

18. Howard Simpson, *Bush Hat, Black Tie* (Washington, D.C.: Brassey, 1998), p. 7.

19. *19th Review of Operations, July 1–December 31, 1963*, U.S. Information Agency, p. 13.

20. "Africans' Views on March Vary; Approval Sought in Arab Lands," *New York Times*, August 30, 1963, p. 10.

21. "U.S. News Center Helps Foreign Press," *Editor & Publisher*, December 22, 1961, p. 11.

22. A counterpoint to these Soviet comments was the public reaction in Poland and other Eastern European countries. See: "Public and Propaganda Reactions to the Kennedy Assassination in Poland," Report No. M-429-63, December 18, 1963, Office of Research, U.S. Information Agency.

23. "Items on Kennedy Pour into Office," *New York Times*, January 5, 1964, p. 14.

24. "The Screen: A Tribute to a President," *New York Times*, November 27, 1964, p. 47.

25. Sorensen, *The Word War*, p. 257.

26. "Life Is Altered for Camel Driver," *New York Times*, January 9, 1962, p. 32.

27. Arthur M. Schlesinger Jr., *A Thousand Days: John F. Kennedy in the White House* (Boston: Houghton Mifflin, 1965), p. 612.

28. Rowan's personal account of his USIA experience is contained in his autobiography, *Breaking Barriers: A Memoir* (New York: HarperCollins, 1992).

29. The details of this arrangement are described in: C. K. Hausman, "Levels of Command Conducting Psyops Planning," in *The Art and Science of Psychological Operations: Case Studies of Military Applications*, Department of the Army Pamphlet No. 525-7-1, Department of Defense, April 1976, pp. 181–185.

30. "Marks Confident He Can Run USIA," *New York Times,* August 15, 1965, p. 14.

31. The background of Viet Cong successes in Vietnam is analyzed in: Douglas Pike, *Viet Cong: The Organization and Techniques of the National Liberation Front of South Vietnam* (Cambridge, Mass.: MIT Press, 1966). Pike, a USIA officer, was assigned to MIT to write the book. He later established a major archive on the Vietnam War at Texas Tech University.

32. "A Space Age USIA," *Foreign Service Journal*, March 1968, pp. 30–32.

6

High Summer

BY 1970, THE U.S. Information Agency had entered the high summer of its bureaucratic life. It was increasingly secure of its place within the Washington foreign policy community. Although the agency had not been accorded status as a strategic policy adviser (notably in the National Security Council), it was effectively engaged at the middle and lower rungs of the policy ladder where its advice on public-opinion factors had an impact. Overseas, the agency had completed a decade of expansion that created a network of posts in over 175 countries, including many new ones in Asia and Africa. Most of its European posts were gradually downsized to accommodate this redistribution of resources to third-world nations.

These shifts reflected the emergence of new political forces. Developing countries were becoming more assertive in their claims for a larger share of political and economic power. By 1970 more than a hundred of them had organized themselves into a so-called nonaligned movement to press their grievances against the United States and other advanced industrialized nations. Changes in communications patterns also affected the North-South balance as satellites and other advanced technologies opened up new electronic information links between the regions.

In the early 1970s, these events increasingly influenced U.S. strategic policy and, by extension, USIA's role in implementing it. With the hindsight of three decades, two other developments stand out in defining turning points in Cold War politics. One was the long-simmering ideological confrontation between the Soviet Union and China over leadership of the world communist movement. The second was the 1968 election of Richard M. Nixon. The conjunction of these events set the tone and thrust of U.S. Information Agency operations for the remainder of the Cold War.

Richard Nixon moved into the White House in 1969 with more on-the-job training in foreign affairs than any chief executive before or since. During his twenty-four years as U.S. representative, senator, and vice president, he had traveled to all parts of the world, familiarizing himself with postwar politics and politicians. His career had been marked by policy positions that reflected conventional Republican views, including blaming the Democrats for being, in the then-current phrase, "soft on communism." He entered the White House convinced that he could break the Cold War deadlock in the United States' favor. His self-confidence was reinforced by theories on the strategic use of power espoused by Harvard professor Henry Kissinger, who became his national security adviser and, later, secretary of state.

Armed with high strategic purpose and a considerable amount of tactical improvisation, Nixon and Kissinger changed the Cold War balance. A critical part of their plans called for exploiting the doctrinal tensions that had emerged in the 1950s between the Soviet and Chinese Communist Parties over their competing claims to be the true heir of Lenin and Marx in leading the world revolution.

It was high-stakes ideological warfare. By the 1950s, the Soviet Union had assumed the mantle of "senior brother" in its alliance with the new Communist government in Beijing. The Chinese had to be satisfied with the role of junior partner. By the end of the decade, they had discarded this distinction as ideologically incorrect. The Soviet Union, they declared, was merely the "temporary majority" in the world communist movement. These semantic games masked the hard reality that underlay the political and ideological differences between the two regimes. The eventual open split marked the end of the myth of a monolithic communist threat to the United States and its allies.

The Nixon-Kissinger strategy combined political, economic, and military moves at the base of which lay the exploitation of doctrinal differences between the two communist powers. (In the parlance of the times, this strategy became known as "playing the China card.") It involved an intricate game of both bilateral and multilateral negotiations with the Soviet Union and China, trading on their ideological differences.[1]

In dealing with Moscow, President Nixon moved toward a more structured détente than had been attempted by any previous postwar president. This "Nixon thaw" was a mix of initiatives, including negotiations that eventually resulted in a groundbreaking agreement on strategic arms limitation (SALT I). The White House strategy also called for relaxing Soviet information barriers to the outside world. This led to a 1973 agreement between the two countries that put cultural exchanges on a long-term basis.[2] (Earlier agreements had to be renewed every few years.) In general, however, the Soviet leaders resisted any significant commitment to relaxing information and cultural exchanges.

Their stubbornness on this point was challenged by the United States, Canada, and the West European democracies, who called for wider negotiations to lower East-West tensions. The Helsinki Accords—more officially, the final acts of the Conference on Security and Cooperation in Europe, signed in April 1975 after three years of negotiations—marked the success of that challenge. The agreements included an important concession sought by the Soviet leadership: implicit recognition of the territorial changes it had imposed in Eastern Europe after World War II. In exchange, Moscow agreed to limited cooperation with the West on a series of military, economic, and information issues.

The negotiators bundled these issues into three "baskets." The first two covered political and economic subjects. The third dealt with information issues, broadly defined as cultural, educational, and person-to-person contacts. "Basket Three" emerged as the most sensitive part of the negotiations, as the Soviets attempted to limit the scope of such contacts. The Western countries stood firm, making third-basket issues the key to their acceptance of the provisions of the other two baskets. As one British diplomat summed up the Western position at the time: "If we don't lay eggs in the third basket, there will be none in the other ones either."

Faced with the prospect of losing important political concessions, Soviet negotiators agreed to increased East-West information and cultural exchanges. They also accepted a proposal for follow-on meetings to monitor compliance with all three basket agreements. Despite these concessions, the Kremlin moved slowly in implementing the Helsinki Accords, in particular the Basket Three provisions on opening up information channels. Among other factors, the Kremlin leadership had to deal for the first time with significant support by Soviet citizens for greater access to foreign information and cultural resources.

At the center of this movement was the Helsinki Monitoring Group, formed by Soviet dissidents in Moscow shortly after the Helsinki Accords were signed. Although some of its leaders received long prison sentences for their activities, the group flourished. Similar initiatives were undertaken in Eastern Europe, notably Prague's Charter 77, whose organizers included Vaclav Havel, later the first president of postcommunist Czechoslovakia.[3]

The Helsinki agreements opened up new prospects for USIA to reach out to audiences in the Soviet Union and Eastern Europe. Agency officials had played an important policy role on the U.S. negotiating team, particularly in defining the details of a proposal for ending Soviet jamming of the Voice of America and other Western radio stations.

The Kremlin's practice had been to reduce jamming of individual Western transmissions for limited times, a tactic it used as a barometer to signal the state of its relations with the United States and its European allies. Although Soviet negotiators balked at making a specific commitment to end all jamming in the Basket Three agreement, there was a slow but steady cutback in their jamming efforts following the Helsinki Final Acts, making Western broadcasts more accessible to millions of listeners in the Soviet Union and Eastern Europe after 1975.

Together with other areas covered by the Helsinki agreements, the limited Soviet concessions on information flow had a powerful cumulative effect. As historian Richard Davy has noted:

> The Final Act as it emerged was almost the opposite of what the Soviet Union had wanted. Instead of endorsing the status quo it was a charter for change. Instead of legitimizing the Soviet sphere of influence it legitimized Western intrusion into it. Instead of making frontiers immutable it specifically affirmed the principle of peaceful change. Instead of putting contacts under official control it emphasized the role of the individual.[4]

U.S. information and cultural contacts with the Soviet Union continued to be constrained after the Helsinki Accords, but the agreement provided a benchmark for further negotiations.

By contrast, China remained closed to the rest of the world, a modern-day extension of the country's Middle Kingdom past. Telephone and telegraph connections with North America and Europe had effectively been closed down for over two decades after the 1949 Communist takeover in China. When phone traffic resumed in 1971, it was limited to six circuits open for only three hours a day.[5]

Despite Beijing's general intransigence in dealing with the West, Nixon and Kissinger decided to make an offer to normalize relations with Beijing. In particular, they wanted to take advantage of the widening political and ideological split between Beijing and Moscow, a development that had led to a massive troop buildup and occasional skirmishes along their common border by the late 1960s. The White House strategy represented a bold gamble. The Chinese could reject the U.S.

initiative outright in the interests of ideological purity. Moreover, there was strong opposition in Washington, particularly among Republican Party conservatives, to any retreat from hard-line opposition to the Chinese Communist regime.

Diplomatic relations between China and the United States had been broken off two decades earlier, following the People's Liberation Army's victory over Chiang Kai-shek's Nationalist forces. One narrow channel for maintaining contacts between the two countries existed, however. In a brief moment of détente, they had agreed in 1955 to meet every six months at the ambassadorial level to discuss current issues. The meetings, held in Warsaw, were generally used as forums for trading charges and countercharges about each other's perfidious behavior.[6]

Nixon and Kissinger decided to make a direct approach to the Chinese, using the Warsaw connection to propose resumption of full diplomatic relations. Because the periodic talks were in recess at the time, the contact was made in December 1969 to a group of startled Chinese diplomats in an improbable setting—a Warsaw night club during a Yugoslav embassy fashion show, to the beat of a rock-and-roll band. (In the confusion, embassy press officer Edward Harper and I made the first contact.) A few days later, the Chinese responded in a telephone call to the U.S. embassy, tentatively agreeing to meet. Thus began a series of negotiations that culminated in the formal exchange of ambassadors in January 1979, almost a decade after that first contact in Warsaw.

The opening to China, together with the détente negotiations with Moscow, resulted in subtle but significant changes in the Cold War's ideological balance, both at the highest levels of strategic policy and in its implications for USIA's role in dealing with its major operational challenge—reaching out to audiences in communist-dominated areas.

The bilateral negotiations with Moscow, together with the Helsinki Accords, led to slow but steady progress in expanding information and cultural contacts within the Soviet bloc. The Chinese meanwhile showed almost no interest in lowering their ideological guard during the talks that led to restoration of formal relations with the United States—with some exceptions. The Beijing government adroitly used its version of cultural exchanges, notably ping-pong players and circus performers, to signal their intentions during the long negotiations.[7] Their interest in resuming student exchanges showed their clear intent to draw upon U.S. technical expertise to improve their economy. From a standing start in the 1970s, Chinese students and academicians represented by the turn of the century the largest single group of students from overseas in U.S. colleges and universities.

The slow but steady opening of information channels to China and the Soviet Union in the 1970s strongly influenced the pattern of USIA's policies and operations for the next twenty-five years. Media and cultural relations with the two major Communist powers, however limited, set a new tone for the agency's role in U.S. global strategy. Nevertheless, the Nixon administration stayed cautious in accommodating to the shift.

This was apparent in its choice of Frank Shakespeare as the new agency director after the 1968 elections. A CBS network executive who had served as television adviser to the Nixon presidential election campaign, Shakespeare was young, energetic, and self-assured. He was also the first USIA chief to wear his political ideology prominently on his sleeve, displaying a deeply conservative bent, with a dark view of the communist menace that anticipated by a decade Ronald Reagan's characterization of the Soviet Union as an evil empire. Although Shakespeare never publicly questioned the Nixon White House's strategy of détente with the Soviets or the decision to negotiate with the Chinese, he quickly became identified as a leading advocate within the administration of a cautious approach to both initiatives.[8]

The new director surrounded himself with a coterie of advisers who shared his political credo. They included William Buckley, the guru of American mainstream conservatism, who joined the agency's advisory board; Edward (Teddy) Weintal, a former Polish diplomat, who reinforced Shakespeare's anticommunist views; and Kenneth Towery, a conservative Pulitzer Prize–winning Texas editor, named to head the agency's policy unit.

Shakespeare was something of an enigma to agency staff, who were unaccustomed to such sharply ideological attitudes from its leaders. Inevitably he and his associates ran into difficulties with the Washington power structure. Early in his directorship, the State Department objected to what it regarded as inappropriate Voice of America commentaries at a time when it was negotiating with the Soviet Union on sensitive Middle East issues.[9] In another incident, a Shakespeare appointee, film producer Bruce Herschensohn, made the unforgivable bureaucratic mistake of publicly attacking a member of Congress when he characterized as "naïve and stupid" the foreign policy views of Senator J. William Fulbright, head of the Foreign Relations Committee. Herschensohn resigned when it became clear that the committee would cut back the agency's budget in retaliation for his remarks.[10]

The 1972 Watergate affair presented USIA with its biggest credibility challenge during the Nixon years. Originally dismissed by the White

House as a "third-rate burglary," the thwarted attempt by Republican Party operatives to steal documents from the Democratic National Committee offices in the Watergate building soon took on the trappings of a serious political event.

At first there was little interest abroad in the Watergate incident. This changed when it became clear that the head of the world's oldest constitutional democracy could be driven from office as the result of a botched attempt to play dirty politics. Suddenly other factors came into play, including USIA's role in reporting the unfolding scandal. Given the Nixon White House's attempt to manipulate the story in the U.S. press, there were suspicions, originally reported in the *Washington Post,* that the administration was also censoring the agency's Watergate coverage.[11] In fact, this never happened: USIA media outlets, in Washington and overseas, were told to play the story straight, up to and including Nixon's dramatic resignation in August 1974.

This policy was vigorously enforced by James Keogh, the *Time* magazine executive who replaced Frank Shakespeare as agency director in December 1973.[12] A watch group of agency officials was formed to check all VOA scripts and agency newsfile stories for balance and accuracy. (The author was in charge of the panel.) These precautions paid off, particularly after the *Wall Street Journal* assigned a team of reporters to examine the agency's coverage of Watergate developments by the Voice of America. The paper's investigation resulted in a front-page story, headlined: "At Voice of America, There's No Cover-up on Watergate News."[13] Overall, the agency was given high marks for reporting a story that dramatized, as few events could, the resilience of the U.S. democratic process.

Watergate tested the USIA's ability to live up to its congressionally designated mission of presenting a full and fair picture of the United States to foreign audiences. Other events presented similar challenges to the agency. Among the many issues it dealt with over the decades, four stand out: the Apollo space program, the 1976 celebration marking the country's bicentennial, the U.S. civil rights revolution, and the complex array of issues involved in the threat of nuclear warfare. This eclectic mix of subjects mirrored both the opportunities and difficulties in presenting U.S. purposes and actions to overseas audiences. It is useful to take a closer look at the special role each played in the middle years of USIA's organizational life.

The Apollo space program was the biggest single story covered by the agency during its forty-five-year history. Over and above its technical achievement, the successful first landing on the moon in 1969 was a watershed event in modern history, with direct implications for the outcome of the Cold War. Perhaps more than any other single event, it tipped the world's perception in favor of the United States in the Cold War years. The moon landing was only one part of the emergence of "big science" as a factor in the Cold War mobilization of resources by the two superpowers.[14] Both the United States and the Soviet Union brought enormous technological resources to this effort. Eventually, it became clear that the United States had a decisive advantage in the overall range of its accomplishments in science and technology, from computers to medical research.

This perception of U.S. scientific leadership was rudely shaken in 1957 when the Soviet Union successfully launched *Sputnik,* the first space satellite to orbit the earth. It followed this achievement with a more spectacular event, the 1961 launch of cosmonaut Yuri Gagarin into global orbit and his retrieval.[15] Despite attempts by some U.S. officials to denigrate *Sputnik* and the Gagarin space ride, these accomplishments had an immediate impact on world opinion, bolstering perceptions of Soviet technical prowess and, by extension, Moscow's overall claims to superpower status.

The Soviet successes overwhelmed the relatively modest achievements of the U.S. space program at the time. The failure of several U.S. space experiments in the months after *Sputnik*'s orbit reinforced the image of Soviet technical strength. This in turn provoked a strong U.S. reaction, reflected in public opinion polls, declaring catching up to the Russians in space a national priority. A massive, if occasionally overwrought, effort to speed up U.S. space efforts ensued. In fact, the outcome was never really in doubt. Despite its early setbacks, the U.S. space effort was more comprehensive and scientifically advanced than its Soviet counterpart. But it took a decade to prove it.

Meanwhile, USIA had to deal with the propaganda edge Moscow had gained from the *Sputnik* and Gagarin achievements. The Soviets had a special advantage in their ability to control most of the information about their space program, including suppression of its failures. U.S. officials took the only course open to them, namely full disclosure of their space projects, including the failures. Slowly, this policy paid off in a rising level of credibility about U.S. space accomplishments among overseas audiences.

USIA's involvement in publicizing the space program moved into high gear following President John Kennedy's dramatic 1963 proposal to send and return a manned mission to the moon by the end of the decade. The challenge added a powerful political dimension to the so-called space race.

Publicity played a prominent role in what became known as the Apollo project. A special public relations task force was set up at NASA headquarters in Washington to plan and carry out media programs for the man-on-the-moon operation. Headed by Julian Scheer, a Charlotte, North Carolina, journalist, the group's focus was primarily on reaching domestic audiences, in particular the taxpayers footing the bill for this extremely expensive project. Special attention was given to the team of astronauts being trained for the Apollo missions. They were accorded movie-star treatment, including extensive personal appearance tours, to underscore that they had what came to be known as "the right stuff" for reaching the moon.

Few details were missed by Scheer and his associates in their public relations planning. They spent months debating the wording on the plaque that would be left on the moon by the Apollo astronauts. Should the United Nations be mentioned? Should God be invoked? The White House let it be known that President Nixon favored a reference to God, but not to the United Nations. After a series of delicate negotiations, God was dropped from the plaque inscription and the UN's role was downgraded to a project in which small flags of its member nations would be taken to the moon and then returned for presentation to each country's leader.

The UN flag decision reflected NASA's increasing concern for the international dimension of the Apollo missions. USIA was assigned the primary role in managing this aspect of the Apollo publicity effort; agency officers were assigned to NASA to work directly with Scheer's group. This attention to overseas public opinion was largely driven by intelligence reports indicating that the Soviets were making an all-out effort to put men on the moon before the Americans did. By 1966, the Russians had landed an unmanned craft on the moon's surface and sent back photographs as well as data about the lunar soil. They followed this up with a spacecraft that circled the moon with turtles aboard, returning the craft and its living cargo to earth.[16]

Despite these successes, Moscow authorities denied they were in a space race with the United States, meanwhile hedging their bets by describing the Apollo project as a jerry-built exercise designed for military purposes. Soviet commentators professed to worry about the dangers faced by the U.S. astronauts, in contrast (as a Radio Moscow commentary put it) to the "peaceful, safe and scientifically sound Soviet approach."[17] As it turned out, Moscow's effort to be first to the moon was set back in 1969 by what was later identified as a technical glitch in the capsule that would shuttle Soviet cosmonauts from their spaceship to the moon's surface.

According to reports published since then, NASA offered to include a Soviet cosmonaut in the *Apollo XI* mission, the first in a series of moon probes that actually put a man on the lunar surface. The Soviets declined the offer, and the moon landing in July 1969 was an all-American show. Astronauts Neil Armstrong, Edmund "Buzz" Aldrin, and Michael Collins were immediately accorded the status of international celebrities. Over and above its scientific purposes, their achievement largely erased the propaganda gains that the Soviet Union had made with its space achievements, beginning with *Sputnik* twelve years earlier.

Working with Julian Scheer's NASA publicity team, USIA had been preparing to exploit the Apollo events for over five years. The basic theme of the publicity campaign was that the moon landing be portrayed as a human achievement rather than a political one. Inevitably, U.S. triumphalism was the strong subtext. Books, pamphlets, and press packets were prepared to record the project's progress. Novelist John Dos Passos was commissioned to write a leaflet about the moon venture. Films, photographs, exhibits, and tens of millions of Apollo lapel buttons were produced in anticipation of a successful moon landing.

Television was the defining medium in all of these plans. By 1969, the new technology of communications satellites was transmitting video images to dozens of countries on all continents. In the year before the *Apollo XI* launch, USIA negotiated arrangements with overseas television stations abroad for live coverage of the moon landing. Delayed coverage was arranged for stations in countries that did not have direct access to the satellite transmissions. As a result, billions of people watched the event in real or close-to-real time at home or in public gatherings. Thousands of Koreans followed the moon flight via satellite on a giant TV screen set up by the U.S. embassy on Namsam Hill in Seoul.

The televised moon landing was, according to the *Melbourne Age,* "the climactic moment of a communications revolution. . . . The fact that two men have walked on the moon and found it, in Neil Armstrong's words, 'starkly beautiful' is no more amazing than the fact that their earthbound fellows heard every word, watched their movements and knew their blood pressures."

The only major countries that did not provide live coverage of the event were China and the Soviet Union. The Chinese media ignored the moon landing. Soviet television reported it as the fifth item in its nightly national news program, following a salute to Soviet metalworkers and a description of ceremonies marking Poland's national day. Polish television, on the other hand, provided extensive live coverage of the moon landing, viewed by most of the country's population during the early hours of the morning. The Polish network's coverage used spaceship models, charts, and other visual materials supplied by the local USIS post. Television stations in other Soviet-dominated countries in Eastern Europe provided similar coverage.[18]

Following that first moon landing, USIA posts around the world turned to the job of dealing with the intense interest in the event. This involved managing a twenty-two-country tour by the *Apollo XI* astronauts that included meetings with the queen of England, the pope, and the emperor of Japan, together with triumphal parades. NASA loaned the agency seven moon rocks brought back by the astronauts—ordinary-looking stones that were viewed with awe by tens of millions of spectators who lined up for hours to pass before them. Moscow authorities eased their general ban on Apollo events to permit one rock to be displayed in an "Education USA" exhibit then touring the Soviet Union. Czech officials made a similar concession, authorizing a moon-rock display at the Prague planetarium. A half-sized model of the *Apollo* lunar capsule, set in front of the U.S. Embassy in Warsaw, was blanketed with floral tributes as if it were a shrine.

There were similar unusual reactions in other countries. The U.S. embassy in Brazil was inundated with sixty thousand congratulatory letters in the first days after the moon landing. In Stockholm, a chain of clothing stores offered a suit to every man named Armstrong, Aldrin, or Collins. (Fifteen men walked away with a free suit.)

In the weeks after the moon landing, Apollo euphoria seemed to sweep the earth. Everyone seemingly understood the significance of the event, with some exceptions. An enterprising *Washington Post* correspondent, Henry Aubin, reported on a poll he took in Moroccan villages after the moon landing. Almost 90 percent of the respondents had heard about the event, but a large majority (63 percent) thought it was a hoax or had other doubts about it. Some of the villagers characterized televised images of the moon landing as Hollywood fakes. "The moon never stands still," one old man declared. "How are you going to land on it?" Another respondent cited Koranic warnings against believing things that you have not seen firsthand with your own eyes: "It is like believing false prophets, and you lose 40 days prayer." Twenty percent of those queried thought that it was the Russians who had landed on the moon.[19]

Despite the Moroccan villagers' doubts, public opinion worldwide generally agreed that the Apollo project was, in Neil Armstrong's moon-landing phrase, a giant leap for mankind and that it was an American who had taken it. Within a few months, overseas interest in the *Apollo XI* achievement began to subside. Five other manned missions to the moon attracted relatively little attention before the entire project ended in 1975. The Apollo project did, however, succeed in ending general doubts about the United States' technological edge in the Cold War balance of power, according to opinions polls conducted by USIA's research unit.

As the Apollo missions wound down, the agency found itself engaged in another event that offered a special opportunity to project American ideas and accomplishments abroad. It was the two-hundredth anniversary of the Declaration of Independence in 1976. The bicentennial celebration was originally envisioned primarily as a domestic event, with limited interest expected abroad. This attitude was not shared within USIA, which began planning for overseas coverage of the event more than a decade before the July 4, 1976, culmination of bicentennial activities.[20]

In March 1966, the agency sent a detailed proposal outlining its bicentennial proposals to its overseas posts for their comment. At the same time, it set up a planning group for the event, headed by an experienced officer, Margo Cutter. Cutter and her team recommended that the agency's theme for the bicentennial should be the relevance of the U.S. experiment in democracy to that of other countries. By and large, this guideline was maintained throughout the decade leading up to the 1976 bicentennial year.

Operationally, USIA planners saw the bicentennial as a special opportunity to reinforce a critical but often neglected program goal, the promotion of American studies in universities and research institutes abroad. Aside from Britain and a few other European countries, such studies were weak or nonexistent in most colleges, universities, and other research centers abroad. The few study programs that did exist depended on Fulbright research grants, where a U.S. professor or researcher would be assigned for an academic year before returning to his or her stateside job. There was little organizational structure for maintaining continuity once the Fulbright scholar had left. Although USIA sponsored many lightweight media projects for marking the bicentennial, it maintained a strong focus on strengthening American studies programs abroad.[21]

As bicentennial planning progressed, USIA found itself involved in larger Washington controversies that arose once the political establishment saw the value of getting on the bicentennial bandwagon. An American Revolution Bicentennial Commission (ARBC) had been set up by the Johnson White House in 1966 whose membership was an eclectic combination of leading scholars and others chosen primarily because they were deserving Democrats. The commission did virtually nothing for three years. In 1969, the new Nixon administration reorganized the commission, dropping many of the Johnson appointees and adding deserving Republicans. The Democratic National Committee in turn accused the White House of "stealing the American Revolution."

The bicentennial commission began to take its duties seriously for the first time, in part as a result of the efforts of a White House official, Daniel Patrick Moynihan, whose duties included overseeing the ARBC. Moynihan, on leave from a Harvard professorship, brought a large measure of organizational order and intellectual rigor to the commission's activities. USIA managed to avoid most of the bureaucratic squabbling surrounding bicentennial plans, primarily because the White House and the ARBC were only mildly interested in the event's impact abroad. By April 1970, the agency had drafted an $11 million operational plan for the 1976 celebration.

A critical decision in implementing the plan involved how, when, and where to begin the bicentennial celebration abroad. Burnett Anderson, the agency's public affairs officer in Paris, argued that the initial event should take place in France, the United States' most important revolutionary ally. He got his wish, with unintended help from the Soviet Union. In 1970, the Soviet government had pressured French officials to sponsor a large exhibit marking the centennial of Lenin's birth in the Grand Palais, the most prestigious exhibition space in Paris.

The French agreed to the Soviet request but were unhappy about what turned out to be a blatant propaganda show. They welcomed Anderson's proposal for a large bicentennial exhibit as a good opportunity to restore the prestige of the Grand Palais. The exhibit, "The World of Franklin and Jefferson," was funded by IBM and the renamed American Revolution Bicentennial Administration. It featured valuable artifacts and other memorabilia that highlighted the role the two men played in the revolution, including their close associations with France. The exhibit was a major success when it opened in January 1975, drawing the largest attendance ever recorded for such an event in France. The show then moved on to Warsaw and London, where it attracted even larger audiences.

The success of the Franklin-Jefferson exhibit energized the agency's overall bicentennial planning. As noted above, encouragement of American studies abroad was a key priority. A distinguished Yale scholar, Robin Winks, was recruited to develop an extensive program that included convocations of scholars in all parts of the world to discuss the relevance of the American Revolution in their own societies. Meanwhile, the project to expand American studies was vigorously pursued. The result was to give permanent status to such studies for the first time at scores of universities and other academic institutions abroad.

As July 4, 1976, approached, other bicentennial events went into high gear. The most striking element was the degree to which foreign governments and private institutions became involved in the celebration. Denmark and Venezuela each declared a national holiday. Four thousand events took place in Germany, financed in part by a $3 million government fund. Antique-car enthusiasts sponsored a 6,000-mile round-the-world race in honor of the bicentennial.[22]

Popular enthusiasm for the bicentennial abroad was especially strong in Japan. "Few people can walk anywhere in Tokyo without encountering signs, seals, stickers, stationery and songs proclaiming 'Happy birthday, America,'" a *New York Times* correspondent reported.[23] The USIA post in Tokyo assigned one of its officers, Hugh Ivory, to monitor local bicentennial events as well as to determine which would get the embassy's support. A "Bicentennial Food Fair" by local grocers and a promotion campaign by Dunkin' Donuts stores passed the test, but not the topless "Viva America" revue at Tokyo's Las Vegas nightclub, which featured (as one observer put it) "bicycle acrobats waving American flags and statuesque American and Japanese dancers, wearing three-colored hats, among other little pieces of costuming."

The bicentennial was largely ignored in Communist-bloc countries. The Chinese media barely mentioned it. After long negotiations, Soviet authorities allowed USIA to mount an exhibit in Moscow, "USA—Two Hundred Years," as part of an exchange arrangement in which the Soviets put on a similar-sized exhibit in Los Angeles marking the sixtieth anniversary of the Russian Revolution. The Los Angeles exhibit attracted sparse crowds. The U.S. show in Moscow averaged ten thousand visitors daily, each of whom was given a colorful plastic bag containing a bicentennial button, a short history of the United States, a recording of American music, and translated copies of the Declaration of Independence and the Constitution.[24]

Overseas interest in the bicentennial peaked in July 1976. Mexico City's *El Universal* declared that "after Christianity, the American revolution constituted the most important event in world history." Britain's *Economist* suggested in a spoof editorial that Britain should agree to become the fifty-first state. A London newspaper, the *Daily Mail,* declared: "The greatest of all the gifts the Americans have given us is hope. We shall continue to be dragged along in their wake, fascinated, often alarmed, but when the chips are down, unambiguously grateful. . . . We were lucky George the Third lost."[25]

Other comments, particularly in third-world media, were less enthusiastic. A columnist in Tanzania's *Sunday News* acknowledged the American Revolution's role in world political thinking, adding that "now America is a land of shame, a wounded giant who in an attempt to save democracy has been a party to the destruction of democracy in many parts of the world. Many progressive Americans know this, but a great portion of the Americans still live with the Spirit of '76, unaware that their corrupt system has made them a hateful nation whenever people talk of real freedom."[26]

The dramatic bicentennial and Apollo moon landing episodes offered unique opportunities to project a strong, confident United States. Other events offered a more troubled view of U.S. policies and actions. Two of these stood out as the most complex issues USIA dealt with during the Cold War decades: the threat of nuclear war and the domestic civil rights revolution. Each tested the agency's legislative mandate to present a full and fair picture of the United States.

Nuclear issues presented a special problem. Except for a small group of policy mandarins, few people understood the political and technical complexities of the subject. Popular feelings were reflected in generalized fears of atomic annihilation. Most informed foreigners knew that the United States had first used atomic bombs. However valid the strategic purposes for the 1945 decision that ended World War II, overseas perceptions of the event were dominated by images of two large Japanese cities, Hiroshima and Nagasaki, reduced to moonscape devastation in a few seconds, bringing death to tens of thousands of men, women, and children.

Arms control and other nuclear issues became more complex in the late 1940s when the Soviet Union announced that it also possessed atomic-bomb capabilities. Among the many outcomes of the early atomic age was a propaganda cat-and-mouse game, primarily involving the U.S. and Soviet governments, in which each attempted to shift the responsibility for threatening apocalyptic nuclear destruction to the other. Nuclear weapons, and particularly international attempts to control their spread, became an important part of USIA's policy agenda as Washington and Moscow vied to establish their peaceful nuclear credentials.[27]

The United States bore the psychological burden of dealing with overseas public attitudes on nuclear issues throughout the Cold War. The first substantive U.S. proposals addressing fears of atomic annihilation came in 1954 in the form of President Eisenhower's "atoms for peace" initiative, which proposed to divert nuclear resources to medical, industrial, and other nonmilitary uses, an idea immediately rejected by the Soviet leadership. USIA mounted a worldwide media campaign to support the Eisenhower plan. The effort fell short of blunting a Soviet countercampaign that relied heavily on repetition of U.S. statements, official and otherwise, about maintaining the nuclear deterrent.[28]

The first break in this confrontation look place in 1958, when both Washington and Moscow agreed to a cessation of nuclear testing in the atmosphere. The unwritten agreement was broken unilaterally in 1961, when the Soviet Union resumed atmospheric testing, citing "feverish preparations" for war by the United States and its NATO allies. USIA played a useful role in the aftermath of the Soviet action when Edward R. Murrow convinced President Kennedy to postpone resumption of U.S. testing until the agency could mount a worldwide campaign to indict the Soviets for their action. The result was to shift the onus of nuclear irresponsibility, temporarily at least, to the Kremlin leadership.[29]

Murrow's intervention was an exception to USIA's normally slight impact on overall arms control policy in the Cold War decades. Its primary channel of influence was the Arms Control and Disarmament Agency (ACDA), a unit set up within the State Department during the Kennedy administration to deal with nuclear issues. Ned Nordness, a USIA officer, was assigned to ACDA, where he became an acknowledged expert, in and out of government, on the public-diplomacy aspects of nuclear policy.[30]

In the 1960s, USIA officials proposed programs for advancing understanding of U.S. nuclear disarmament proposals that would target a relatively small number of overseas leaders concerned with nuclear policy. In part, this initiative resulted from a conference, "Pacem in Terris," which drew several hundred world leaders, including Soviet representatives, to New York in February 1965 to discuss disarmament proposals advanced by, among others, Pope John XXIII. The conference ended with an exemplary statement of both realism and hope for defusing nuclear threats.[31]

Following the New York conference, USIA took the initiative in forming an interagency policy group to study ways of providing high-level continuous briefings on arms control realities to overseas policymakers, academicians, and media leaders. (I was the USIA member of the group.) The project would be managed by a small group of U.S. universities involved in arms control research and studies.[32] The proposal was treated respectfully by the Washington policy hierarchy, but it did not survive the bureaucratic rigors of getting high-level support for budget and personnel resources. Although USIA continued to publicize U.S. arms control and disarmament policies abroad, it was never influential in the formation of these policies.

U.S. policies and actions on civil rights were another critical issue the agency found it difficult to explain abroad. The subject was a politically and emotionally sensitive one in U.S. society. Partisan politics played a role in the treatment of racial issues in government information programs. As early as 1943, segregationist congressmen forced the Office of War Information to withdraw allegedly provocative media materials showing whites and blacks working together.

Internationally, U.S. civil rights ideals clashed with domestic realities. The UN Universal Declaration of Human Rights, initiated by the United States in the late 1940s, was the first document of its kind to identify racial justice as a global issue.[33] It did so against a backdrop of embedded violations of this principle in almost all countries, including the United States. American attitudes on racial issues slowly began to change in the postwar years, with important implications for the overseas information program. But the discrepancies between new civil rights policies and old practices were fodder for Soviet propaganda efforts, particularly those aimed at the new nations of Asia and Africa.

Harry Truman, the first postwar president, led the way in identifying the global implications of the issue. Assembling the first national commission on civil rights, he announced in a mixed-metaphor statement that "the top dog in a world which is over half colored ought to clean his own house."[34] The most immediate outcome of the commission's work was the 1948 Truman decision to desegregate the armed forces.

The Eisenhower administration was, in the words of one historian, supremely ambivalent about civil rights, particularly in the wake of a 1954 Supreme Court decision to declare segregation unconstitutional. Domestically, the Republican Party was aggressively courting Southern white voters, most of whom opposed racial desegregation. Reluctantly, the White House also had to face the international implications of civil rights disturbances, particularly after President Eisenhower called out federal troops to enforce a court order mandating the enrollment of black children at a previously white Little Rock high school in 1957. Images of nine black youngsters walking to school protected by burly soldiers were prominently displayed on overseas television screens and in publications.

The State Department had been generally unresponsive to warnings about the overseas impact of Little Rock and other civil rights events, reflecting the attitudes of Secretary John Foster Dulles. Among other actions, Dulles had turned down a 1954 request from the embassy in South Africa that proposed inviting several local black leaders to its annual Fourth of July reception. The Little Rock crisis forced Dulles to reconsider his general reluctance to see the civil rights movement as a foreign policy issue. Referring to the 1956 Soviet suppression of a populist uprising of Hungarians against their Communist government, he declared that Little Rock "is ruining our foreign policy. The effect of this in Asia and Africa will be worse for us than Hungary was for the Russians."[35] His comments were triggered by a USIA public-opinion survey of the negative impact of the Little Rock events on overseas public opinion.

USIA meanwhile struggled to give greater attention to civil rights issues. A special minorities affairs unit was set up, headed by a former newspaperman, William Gaussman, who had strong contacts with civil rights organizations. Among other activities, he supplied a steady stream of reports on overseas reaction to civil rights events to a White House subcabinet group concerned with overall policy on the subject. Within USIA, Gaussman monitored the thrust and content of agency media's handling of civil rights developments. One project was a documentary film (*Nine from Little Rock*) that won an Oscar for its sensitive portrayal of desegregation in a Deep South school.

By the early 1960s, enough progress had been made on civil rights issues to give the agency an increasingly positive story to tell abroad. Further events, in particular the passage of the Civil Rights Act of 1964, led to a series of small but perceptible changes in overseas views of U.S. progress toward resolving the country's most sensitive vulnerability as a democratic world leader.

USIA's ability to deal with a wide range of sensitive issues like the civil rights revolution was strengthened by its credibility as a foreign policy asset within the Washington bureaucracy. By 1970, it was involved with dozens of other agencies, many of them not normally associated with international policy. In the next chapter, we will look at the three agencies that had a direct continuing impact on USIA's policy and operational activities—the State and Defense Departments and the Central Intelligence Agency.

Notes

1. Henry M Kissinger (ed.), *Kissinger Transcripts: The Top Secret Talks with Beijing and Moscow* (New York: New Press, 1999).

2. "Nixon and Brezhnev See Signing of 4 New Accords," *New York Times*, June 19, 1973, p. 4.

3. The long-term impact of the Helsinki Final Acts is described in: Daniel C. Thomas, *The Helsinki Effect: International Norms, Human Rights and the Demise of Communism* (Princeton, N.J.: Princeton University Press, 2001).

4. Richard Davy, *European Détente: A Reappraisal* (London: Royal Institute of International Affairs, 1992), p. 19.

5. "British-Chinese Phone Link to Open After 22 Years," *New York Times*, April 15, 1971, p. 6.

6. Alfred D. Wilhelm, *The Chinese at the Negotiating Table* (Washington, D.C.: National Defense University Press, 1991), pp. 79–82.

7. The role of ping-pong in Chinese diplomacy during the negotiations is described in "The Ping Heard Round the World," *Time*, April 26, 1971, pp. 17–28.

8. "Thinking Positive at USIA," *Time*, December 5, 1969; "New USIA Head Talks Conservatively but He Vows to Seek 'Balance,'" *Wall Street Journal*, December 23, 1969, p. 1.

9. "Tough USIA Line Drew a Complaint from Rogers," *New York Times*, October 25, 1970, p. 7.

10. "USIA Sends Apology for Fulbright Insult," *Washington Post*, March 31, 1972, p. 1.

11. "Voice of America Curbed on Broadcasts of Watergate Story," *Washington Post*, June 7, 1973, p. 7.

12. "Muted Voice of America," *Time*, December 16, 1974, p. 80.

13. "At Voice of America, There's No Cover-up on Watergate News," *Wall Street Journal*, May 16, 1974, p. 1. See also: "Voice of America Coverage of Watergate Tells It Like It Is," *Washington Post*, May 6, 1974, p. F-16.

14. Walter A. McDougall, "The Cold War Excursion into Science," *Diplomatic History* 21, no. 1, winter 2000, pp. 117–127.

15. *Sputnik*'s propaganda impact is described in: Paul Dickson, *Sputnik: The Shock of the Century* (New York: Walker & Co, 2001).

16. "Vasily Mishin," *Economist* (London), November 10, 2001, p. 81. Soviet attempts to reach the moon first are described in: "Eclipsed," *New York Times Magazine*, June 27, 1999, pp. 28–66.

17. "Soviet Propaganda About the U.S. Space Program," Report M-142–66, USIA Office of Research, March 23, 1966, p. 21.

18. "Worldwide Treatment of Current Issues: Apollo XI," No. 11, USIA Office of Research, July 22, 1969, p. 11. See also the more extensive report on global reactions to *Apollo XI:* "Effect of the Moon Landing on Opinions in Six Countries," USIA Office of Research, Report R-10–69, September 12, 1969.

19. "Neil Armstrong, Did You Really Go There?" *USIA Communicator*, January 1973, p. 36.

20. USIA's coverage of the U.S. bicentennial was thoroughly documented in an 189-page report prepared by Richard C. Wooten, the agency officer who managed the project from its early days. It is the most thorough description of a single agency operation ever recorded. The report, "The United States Information Agency and the American Revolution Bicentennial," is undated but it was issued in spring 1977.

21. Wooten, "The United States Information Agency," pp. 107–116.

22. "Frankfurt Hails U.S. Bicentennial," *New York Times*, May 16, 1976, p. 1.

23 "Japanese Mark U.S. Bicentennial with Signs, Shirts, Shows, Songs," *New York Times,* May 18, 1976, p. 6.

24. "Americana Boffo in Moscow," *Washington Post,* December 3, 1976, p. B-1.

25. "Foreign Media Reaction: The Bicentennial," USIA Office of Research, July 9, 1976, p. 4.

26. Ibid., p. 22.

27. For an analysis of this confrontation in the early arms control period, see: John W. Spanier and Joseph L. Nogel, *The Politics of Disarmament* (New York: Praeger Publishers, 1962). See also: Wilson P. Dizard. "Propaganda Objectives for an Arms Control Period." Publication C/63/50, Arms Control Project, Center for International Studies, Massachusetts Institute of Technology, November 1963.

28. "Information Unit Shows High Score," *New York Times,* September 6, 1955, p. 5.

29. For the propaganda aspects of the 1961 nuclear testing crisis, see: "Cessation of Nuclear Testing: A Case Study in Propaganda of the Word," in Urban G. Whitaker (ed.), *Propaganda and International Relations* (San Francisco, Calif.: Chandler Publishing Co., 1962), pp. 179–217.

30. Thomas C. Sorensen, *The Word War: The Story of American Propaganda* (New York: Harper & Row, 1967), p. 147.

31. "When the World's People Talked Peace," special supplement in *Saturday Review,* May 1, 1965.

32. "World Security and Arms Control: Closing the Communications Gap," Office of Policy, U.S. Information Agency, April 1965.

33. For an overview of these early human rights initiatives, see: Mary Ann Glendon, *A World Made New: Eleanor Roosevelt and the Universal Declaration of Human Rights* (New York: Random House, 2001).

34. Azza Salama Layton, "The International Context of U.S. Civil Rights Politics." Paper presented at the American Political Science Association annual meeting, Washington, D.C., August 1997. See also: Thomas Borstelman, *The Cold War and the Color Line: Race Relations and American Foreign Policy* (Cambridge, Mass.: Harvard University Press, 2002); Mary L. Dudziak, *Cold War Civil Rights: Race and the Image of American Democracy* (Princeton, N.J.: Princeton University Press, 2002).

35. Borstelman, *The Cold War,* p. 126.

Edward R. Murrow, USIA director during the Kennedy administration, converses with his two senior deputies, Donald Wilson (left) and Thomas Sorensen (right).

Turkish visitors view a USIA display of American fashions at an international trade fair in Izmir in 1952.

USIA's Russian-language magazine, *Ameryka*, was popular with Soviet citizens in Moscow during the Cold War decades. The magazine, originally distributed during World War II but suspended after the war, was revived in 1956 under a bilateral cultural exchange agreement negotiated by the Eisenhower administration.

Laotions watch a live television show sponsored by the USIA post in Luang Prabang in the 1950s. The agency's posts were often the first to demonstrate the possibilities of the new medium, particularly in developing countries.

Primary-school teachers attend a two-week English-teaching seminar in Lomé, the capital of Togo, during the 1970s. The sessions were part of a USIA program to improve the quality of English teaching in Africa and other developing areas.

News Review, a biweekly USIA newsmagazine edited and produced in Beirut for distribution in Arabic and English, was distributed to opinion leaders throughout the Middle East. It combined news articles with commentaries on U.S. foreign policy actions affecting the region.

CÁC BẠN TRONG HÀNG NGŨ CỘNG SẢN

— Các bạn đã làm đường lạc lối theo chủ nghĩa Cộng sản
— Các bạn đang sống đơn độc trong các mật khu hay lén lút lẩn trốn tại các vùng ven biên.
— Các bạn đã thấy rõ cộng sản xảo trá, vô lương tâm đã lừa gạt các bạn vào vòng tội lỗi đã gây nên biết bao cảnh chết chóc, tàn phá cho đồng bào vô tội.

Nhân Dân Tự Vệ chúng tôi sẵn sàng giúp đỡ và đón tiếp các bạn trở về với chính nghĩa quốc gia và với sự khoan hồng của Chính phủ.

Nhân Dân Tự Vệ chúng tôi mở rộng vòng tay để đón nhận các bạn quay về với tình thương Dân Tộc và với hàng ngũ nhân dân chiến đấu chống cộng.

Nhân Dân Tự Vệ chúng tôi tự nguyện làm nhịp cầu thông cảm để các bạn sớm trở về dưới mái gia đình thân yêu của các bạn.

Chúng ta sẽ cùng nhau xây dựng quê hương xứ sở trong thanh bình và thịnh vượng.

3942

FRIENDS IN THE COMMUNIST RANKS

—You have been misguided by the Communist doctrines.
—You are living a lonely life at secret bases along the border areas.
—You have seen the Communist duplicity and ruthlessness deceive you into committing crimes of death and destruction to innocent compatriots.

We, the members of the PSDF, are ready to help and welcome you back to the national fold with clemency from the government.

We, the members of the PSDF, stretch out our arms to welcome your return to the people of the anti-communist civilian ranks.

We, the members of the PSDF, volunteer to serve as the bridge of understanding to help you rejoin your families and loved ones just as soon as possible.

Together we will reconstruct our country in peace and prosperity.

Surrender leaflets were an important part of USIA's operations in South Vietnam. This leaflet, typical of the tens of millions dropped from U.S. Air Force planes, was attributed to the Vietnamese government's Popular Self Defense Forces.

Jacqueline Kennedy was the object of major interest abroad during the Kennedy presidency, particularly among women. This USIA brochure, translated into dozens of languages, was widely distributed around the world.

Helen Hayes, a popular stage and screen actress, appeared regularly on the Voice of America English-language service program *Have You a Question?* where she answered queries about the United States sent to her by overseas listeners.

During the Cold War years, the master control board at Voice of America studios in Washington handled twenty-six programs simultaneously, feeding them to thirty domestic transmitters.

Dancers from the San Francisco Ballet pose for a USIS publicity shot in front of the royal palace in Athens during their successful 1959 tour of Europe.

"Working the cocktail circuit" was part of a USIS officer's chores, even when (as in this case) there was no hard liquor served in deference to Muslim customs in Pakistan. Here the author (left) and his wife converse with Chief Justice S. M. Murshad and his wife.

As television stations proliferated abroad during the 1960s, USIA made heavy use of the medium to sponsor a *Let's Learn English* series that attracted large audiences. Ann Wood was the television teacher for the program on a Lisbon station.

Argentinians examine American books at an international book fair in Buenos Aires in the 1970s. The display, sponsored by the local USIA post, included works in Spanish produced by the agency's book-translation program.

A USIA cameraman shoots a scene in Bolivia for an agency-produced weekly newsreel, *Panorama Panamericano*, in the 1960s. The newsreel, featuring economic aid projects sponsored by the Kennedy administration's Alliance for Progress, was shown on television and in movie theaters in eighteen Latin American countries.

Over 350 specially designed Jeeps, known as mobile units, were used by USIS posts throughout the world to deliver films and other media materials to remote areas. Here the author navigates one of the units across a rickety bridge in the Chittagong Hill Tracts along the Burmese-Pakistan border in the 1960s.

7

Playing Bureaucratic Games

TO THE EXTENT that the U.S. public knew about its activities, USIA was "the Voice of America radio" during the Cold War years. In this role, the agency was alternately praised and damned for its performance in providing world audiences with, in the words of its congressional charter, a full and fair picture of the United States.

But USIA was only one member of a noisy chorus of American voices. The agency's operations overlapped activities of many domestic public and private organizations, each with its own particular messages aimed at overseas audiences. This included the big U.S. media companies, many of whom had begun a massive expansion into global markets in the early Cold War decades. Collectively, these firms were the loudest voice of America after World War II. Hollywood films led the way in shaping the world's perception of a far-off land. Commercial television, radio, music, and print publications added their own distinctive influences.

U.S. media organizations maintained a generally arm's-length relationship with USIA throughout the postwar years. They were inclined to regard the agency as the thin edge of growing government involvement in media activities that might restrict their freedom to operate. They also feared that the agency's overseas media programs might compete with their own export ventures. At the same time, U.S. media companies also cooperated with agency programs that promoted the overseas expansion of their products through trade fairs and other export programs. This was particularly true in Asia, Africa, and Latin America, where U.S. media products were largely unknown in the early years after World War II.

The international impact of U.S. commercial media has been well documented in recent years.[1] Less known, because it was less visible, was the fact that USIA was only one of many federal agencies in the business of influencing foreign audiences. The field was crowded, with a dozen major bureaucracies involved, along with scores of smaller organizations. The Rural Electrification Administration (REA), concerned with providing electrical power to U.S. farms, might seem an unlikely candidate for foreign information operations. However the REA had an international staff that provided consultant services to developing countries on how to organize rural cooperatives. As such, it played a special, if modest, role in influencing foreign officials about one aspect of the American experience.

Collectively, these agencies had budgets, staffs, and other resources for reaching overseas audiences that were many times greater than any USIA could match. Among the bigger players were the Departments of Defense, Commerce, and Agriculture. Smaller agencies such as the Library of Congress, the Smithsonian Institution, and the National Science Foundation reached out to influential constituencies abroad, often in cooperative projects with USIA.[2]

This chapter will focus on the three Washington agencies whose overseas activities most directly affected USIA operations: the Defense Department, the Central Intelligence Agency, and the State Department. USIA's relations with each involved a melding of policies and operations at times cooperative and at other times contentious.

Of the three agencies, the Defense Department had a special impact on the information agency's overseas operations. The department dealt with overseas opinion at many levels, bringing massive resources to the task. During the Cold War, it ran the largest federal program for bringing foreign visitors to the United States, most of them military personnel being trained at defense installations throughout the country.

The Pentagon's training programs involved many separate projects in different military services, making it difficult to get an accurate picture of its exchange activities during the Cold War years. Many of these visitors were involved with classified projects and thus not usually listed in official statistics. In 1963, the Pentagon made public the fact that it had funded travel grants for 180,000 visitors, both military and civilian, over the previous fifteen-year period. At that time, there were 18,000 foreigners enrolled in military training programs.[3]

Although occupied largely with training duties, most of these military visitors spent enough time in the United States to get a good overall impression of American life and attitudes. A small but significant number of them returned to become leaders in their own societies.

Other Defense Department activities had a wider daily impact on foreign audiences. The most important of these was the Armed Forces

Network (AFN), the department's global radio and television broadcasts for troops stationed abroad. From its beginnings in 1942 with one small station in England, the network spread, following military units as they advanced in Europe and the Pacific. During the Cold War decades, AFN's radio operations continued to expand, with local stations installed in countries where U.S. units were stationed. In the 1960s, AFN added television stations to the network, serviced by communications satellites.[4]

AFN's primary mission was to provide information and entertainment programming for soldiers, sailors, and airmen stationed abroad. However, the network also attracted a large "shadow" audience of foreign listeners. In effect, AFN was an alternative Voice of America. The Defense Department has always played down this aspect of AFN's influence, primarily because the network's official purpose (and the justification for its congressional budgets) was to serve its own troops. Nevertheless, a mass of anecdotal evidence, bolstered by overseas listener polls, has underscored AFN's considerable impact on local audiences abroad. A 1962 congressional report cited what it called ample evidence that AFN had a substantial foreign drop-in audience "many times that of the Voice of America broadcasts in English, if estimates are credible."[5]

Local AFN stations had some built-in advantages over VOA transmissions, primarily that AFN programs were transmitted locally on medium-wave frequencies and easy to find on the dial. Voice of America programs were generally available only on hard-to-tune shortwave bands and were often inaudible due to atmospheric disturbances. In addition, AFN stations usually broadcast around the clock, whereas most VOA transmissions, particularly in local languages, were limited to an hour or two a day in most areas.

By the 1960s, AFN officials claimed an audience of over 20 million Europeans.[6] This drop-in listenership often had special characteristics: a 1967 survey of Munich radio listeners indicated that AFN had four times as many listeners among car drivers during the morning and evening rush hours as the local Bavarian radio station.[7]

Young listeners dominated AFN's foreign audiences. In large part, this reflected the network's heavy emphasis on "Top Forty" pop music, which accounted for over half its programming schedule. Another attraction for young people was that AFN programs were a convenient way of honing their English-language skills. What they heard from AFN announcers was distinctly different from the stilted (and often outdated) English-language textbooks they used at school. It was colloquial, fast-paced, and often mystifying. As reported by a *New York Times* correspondent, an AFN disk jockey in Japan once opened his program with a crudely misdirected attempt at humor. "Stay tuned, folks," he declared, "because in a few minutes we'll be auctioning off a pair of hot pants once worn by Joan of Arc."[8]

That AFN targeted U.S. troops rather than foreign audiences added to the network's credibility, particularly for younger listeners. AFN was a U.S. station broadcasting to Americans, most of whom were their own age, with similar tastes. This credibility extended in particular to AFN news broadcasts. The network had free access to news reports of the Associated Press and other U.S. media agencies on condition that the text of these reports be broadcast without editorial changes.[9] This did not prevent periodic attempts by AFN authorities to censor material, particularly in their selection of which commercial news reports to air. Overall, however, AFN played the news straight.

USIA had an arm's-length relationship with AFN during the Cold War decades. The only direct connection involved sharing shortwave transmission facilities, most of which had been built for Voice of America programming. Various proposals to incorporate some VOA programs into AFN schedules were periodically debated and then dropped.

The most active collaboration between USIA and the Defense Department took place in other areas. One of these involved what the Pentagon called community relations, aimed at minimizing the often strained contacts between U.S. military personnel and local citizens abroad. These relations were generally covered in so-called status-of-forces agreements negotiated with countries where U.S. troops were stationed. Community relations programs were designed primarily to reduce the day-to-day irritants, from jet plane noises to traffic accidents, that annoyed local communities near U.S. bases.

In the military view, community relations also had a political aspect, including attempts to point up, usually with folksy overtones, American values, as opposed to those of the communists. As one 1957 air force community relations manual put it: "The basic difference between ourselves and the communists provides our greatest long-run community relations asset. The air force shared with others the task of making this difference known to people with which it came in contact."[10]

Military-inspired community activities ranged widely, from band concerts to "friendship week" ceremonies. In Europe, an annual air force "Operation Kinderlift" brought thousands of Berlin children to summer camps in western Germany. The air force at one point mandated that all of its installations in Europe begin soccer training so that airmen could compete in local leagues. At Wheelus Field in Libya, an agreement was reached with the local community to suspend all jet flights during Friday Muslim prayer services. At times, these activities took on a more directly political tone. On one occasion, the military stepped up community relations programs in northern Italy in a pointed effort to counter local Communist Party influence.[11]

USIA's overseas posts supported Defense Department commanders in planning and carrying out their community relations projects, particularly in Europe. A standing committee of military and USIA representatives oversaw community relations policy and operations in over a dozen countries throughout the region.

The most extensive area of USIA/Defense Department cooperation, however, was in psychological-warfare operations. This connection had roots in World War II, when USIA's predecessor, the Office of War Information, became directly involved in tactical psywar projects with the military. This collaboration ended with the Japanese surrender in August 1945, but Pentagon officials continued to build on their newfound enthusiasm for psychological operations. A Psychological Warfare School was set up at Ft. Leavenworth, Kansas. The first army units specifically created for psywar operations had their headquarters and training facilities at Ft. Bragg, North Carolina. In the process, the phrase "psychological warfare" was dropped in favor of "psychological operations," on the theory that it reflected a wider view encompassing both battlefield and civilian operations.[12]

The Korean War (1950–1953) provided the Pentagon with a major test of its new psyops resources. The emphasis was on relatively simple operations such as leaflet drops and loudspeaker surrender appeals to enemy soldiers. The USIA's predecessor organization, the International Information Administration, played a direct role, through its USIS post in Korea, in planning and carrying out these operations. However, these efforts were marred by some heavy-handed psyops projects, including an offer to pay an enemy pilot $100,000 if he would defect with a Russian-built MIG jet. The proposal was roundly criticized in the U.S. press and was withdrawn.[13]

When USIA was created in 1953, it reduced the level of its involvement in Defense Department psyops planning and operations. The agency actively opposed the efforts of military planners to extend their psychological operations to civilian audiences abroad. In the mid-1950s, a Defense Department project called "Militant Liberty: A Program of Evaluation and Reassessment of Freedom" aimed to put Pentagon resources behind a massive campaign to educate overseas public opinion about the dangers of communism. Among other impacts, the project had the potential of overshadowing USIA's overseas programs, given the military's access to massive budgets and other resources.

A Defense Department statement supporting Militant Liberty, issued by the Joint Chiefs of Staff, criticized USIA by declaring that current U.S. government programs "lacked the verbal ability to explain or defend completely what liberty is, and thereby have forfeited the field to the Communists. . . . Communist ideology can only be supported by a stronger *dynamic* ideology." The Militant Liberty proposal, which had been developed by John Broger, a consultant to the Joint Chiefs, was given the department's imprimatur, along with that of a group of prominent businessmen and other civilians assembled at the Pentagon to support the idea.[14] Despite these efforts, the Militant Liberty project was quietly dropped, largely because of a series of bureaucratic challenges by civilian agencies, including USIA.

The most intensive cooperation in psychological operations between USIA and the Pentagon took place during the Vietnam conflict. Begun on a low-key basis in the mid-1950s, this relationship increased as U.S. involvement in the war escalated. By the mid-1960s, the Defense Department had six psyops battalions in place throughout the country, with a full array of radio stations, printing plants, and tactical units supporting troop operations. What was lacking was adequate coordination between the military and the civil agencies, including USIA, operating in Vietnam. The April 1965 decision to assign coordinating responsibilities to the Joint U.S. Public Affairs Office (JUSPAO) led to a definite improvement in coordination between the agencies involved, particularly in establishing a consistent set of messages among headquarters and field units.[15] Under Barry Zorthian, the experienced USIA officer who headed JUSPAO, the office was also charged with responsibility for psyops support for the Vietnamese government.

As the military situation deteriorated after 1970, these coordinating arrangements became unraveled. In the end, all the sophisticated resources the U.S. government could muster for this effort could not overcome the inefficiencies of the South Vietnamese government or the simple appeals, couched largely in nationalist terms, of the opposing Communist forces. Psychological operations now have a permanent role in U.S. military strategy. They were used effectively in the 1991 Gulf war, the 2001 Afghan campaign, and in the 2003 invasion and occupation of Iraq.[16] By and large, Defense Department psychological operations are now limited to battlefield situations.

Indications that the Defense Department would like to extend its psyops influence to civilian audiences linger, however. This became apparent in February 2002 when the *New York Times* and the *Washington Post* revealed a proposal for an "Office of Strategic Influence" in the department. Among the new office's purported activities were plans to mount "disinformation" campaigns, feeding false reports to the civilian press both in the United States and abroad as part of an effort to confuse current or potential enemies. In the ensuing public uproar, the Defense Department was forced to cancel plans for the new office.[17]

USIA had a complex relationship with the Central Intelligence Agency during the Cold War years. The CIA is only one part of what its officials prefer to call the Washington intelligence community. It is in some ways a junior member, normally accounting for only about a tenth of the federal government's estimated $30 billion annual intelligence budget. (Most of the budget funds high-tech military surveillance projects.)

The CIA had a special role in USIA's history, however, because it operated overseas information and cultural programs that paralleled much of what the information agency was doing. But USIA activities were, with a few exceptions, publicly identified as U.S. government activities. The CIA, again with some exceptions, operated its ideological program through surrogate organizations. A key distinction between these two arrangements was "deniability." The CIA could disclaim any connection with its covert operations, even when the connection became known. USIA put its name on almost all of its output. In the relatively few instances where it issued materials without explicit attribution, it acknowledged its role when it became public knowledge.

The different approaches toward attribution taken by USIA and the CIA had their origins in the 1940s, when the initial decisions about the relationship between overt and covert ideological programs were made. As noted in Chapter 2, the Office of War Information (OWI) was designated the overt propaganda agency while the Office of Strategic Services (OSS) handled covert operations. The OWI evolved into the U.S. Information Agency, and OSS ideological activities were eventually lodged in the CIA's Directorate of Operations. The names had changed but the original missions remained essentially the same. However, the distinctions between the two operations were never fully clarified. A wary relationship prevailed between the two agencies, particularly when their missions crossed the bureaucratic barriers designed to keep them separated.

The CIA's covert ideological activities during the Cold War have been extensively documented.[18] Many of them affected the parallel activities of the U.S. Information Agency. The CIA had played a generally benign role in the decision to transfer overseas information operations from the State Department in 1953 to the U.S. Information Agency. One of the key players in negotiating the move, Henry Loomis, a former CIA official, served as a quiet contact with the agency's headquarters in Langley, Virginia, during the transition and in his later role as director of the USIA research service.

Throughout its forty-five years, USIA maintained links with Langley that became useful when operational problems between the two organizations arose, as they often did. The USIA director's office designated one person as the CIA liaison. In general, however, there was relatively little day-to-day contact between the two agencies at lower levels, either in Washington or in the field. USIA personnel routinely referred to the CIA as "the other agency," or with such wry acronymic twists as the Cigar Institute of America and Christians in Action.

Despite the studied public indifference between the two agencies, the relationship was not always smooth. USIA officials often went unbriefed on CIA operations that affected their programs. This included the activities of the many organizations that the CIA covertly funded, primarily to match the Soviet Union's vast worldwide network of front organizations. Moscow's strategy involved direct assistance to Communist parties throughout the world, as well as to local "friendship societies" and a wide assortment of cultural and academic organizations. To match these Soviet efforts, the CIA set up a mirror-image network of similar groups. Among the organizations the CIA supported were the European-based Congress of Cultural Freedom, the Asia Foundation, the New York–based National Students Union, and a string of smaller organizations, many of them created for short-term political operations.[19]

The CIA was particularly active in recruiting U.S. academics to support programs directed at overseas intellectuals. Among other activities, agency funds helped support two influential intellectual journals, *Encounter* and *Der Monat,* in England and West Germany respectively.[20] Although USIA often publicized the activities of CIA-supported projects in its own media output, it generally maintained an arm's-length relationship with them.

The most confusion between the CIA and USIA took place in their respective mass-media operations. The CIA operated a covert network of media projects abroad that at times paralleled USIA's public programs. It included newspapers, magazines, books, and news agencies as well as radio, film, and television operations. The CIA also subsidized some U.S. and foreign journalists and their publications to report news that was slanted and at times false.[21] Other publications, notably *Reader's*

Digest, were used as pass-throughs for editorial materials supporting CIA themes.[22]

At times these "disinformation" reports were unwittingly picked up by U.S. media organizations, including USIA. During a 1977 congressional hearing on its propaganda activities, the CIA acknowledged that this happened routinely. Under pressure, the CIA said that it would no longer hire full-time writers to prepare such reports. This was only a partial retreat; three years later the agency admitted that it still had about thirty U.S. free-lance writers and other part-time foreign reporters under contract.[23]

The CIA was also involved in covert book-publishing projects. During the 1977 congressional investigations, the agency admitted that it had sponsored over a thousand books in both English and foreign languages, some of which were sold in the United States. To avoid accusations that it was propagandizing the U.S. public, the agency agreed to stop distributing its covertly sponsored books, magazines, and newspapers in the United States.[24]

Although the precise costs of the CIA's covert media operations throughout the Cold War will probably never be known, they were much larger than USIA's media budgets, probably by a factor of five or six. As with most of its information operations, these activities were carried out by surrogates. The only publication openly attributed to the CIA during the Cold War decades was a daily roundup of news and editorial opinion broadcast by foreign radio stations. Produced by the agency's Foreign Broadcast Information Service (FBIS), each day's output often ran to over a hundred pages, divided into regional editions. In addition to being distributed throughout the Washington foreign policy community, the publication was made available by subscription to libraries and other research facilities throughout the country and overseas. The FBIS series is a primary documentary resource for students of post–World War II history.

Where USIA and CIA operations most overlapped (and occasionally clashed) was in radio broadcasting. The complementary role of the two agencies in broadcasting had its roots in World War II, when the Office of Strategic Services, as noted in Chapter 2, set up a series of black radio operations in Europe and Asia designed to undermine morale in enemy military units and among civilians. The stations often masqueraded as local resistance operations, broadcasting news and other materials not available through government-controlled media in enemy countries. Trading on their reputation for accurate reporting, black-station broadcasters included selected disinformation items designed to confuse their listeners. The stations were, in effect, the dark face of the OWI's Voice of America, whose credibility with foreign audiences rested on its reputation for providing straight news.

In the early postwar years, Soviet authorities had steadily expanded their overseas broadcasting facilities, from the Radio Moscow transmissions to those of a series of black stations. The CIA undertook to match these Soviet efforts. The project's focus was on reaching audiences in the Soviet Union and its client-states in Eastern Europe, where U.S. and other Western information channels had been cut off or were greatly reduced.

The CIA's most important broadcasting projects involved the creation of two radio networks in the late 1940s—Radio Free Europe (RFE) and Radio Liberation (RL). RFE broadcasts were targeted to Eastern Europe, RL's to the Soviet Union. The "Radios," as they were known in the Washington foreign policy community, were ostensibly funded by public contributions solicited by a New York–based National Committee for a Free Europe. The very expensive costs of building and operating the two networks were, in fact, largely underwritten by the CIA.[25]

The decision to create the two Radios stemmed partly from criticisms by Cold War hard-liners in Washington that the Voice of America was not aggressive enough in attacking the Soviet Union. Although the VOA had at times shifted from its original mandate of presenting a "full and fair" picture of the United States to include more direct criticism of Soviet policies and actions, the change did not satisfy the hard-liners. They saw the RFE/RL stations as surrogate voices within the Soviet bloc, providing listeners with information denied them by their own governments. Typically, RFE/RL broadcasts to Eastern European countries began each morning with the local weather report, followed by news bulletins that, among other purposes, corrected distortions in local Communist media output, particularly those involving political developments.

The Radios' ability to present a coherent message to their audiences was complicated by the fact that their broadcasting staffs consisted largely of Russian and East European émigrés, many with contrasting political views on how to present the news. The result was a steady pattern of internal bickering within RFE/RL as each faction tried to press its agenda over the others. In one 1960 incident, eighteen Czech Service broadcasters were dismissed by their boss as a result of such a dispute. A month later, the political dynamics changed: the eighteen were rehired and their boss was fired.[26]

RFE and RL played a critical role in U.S. ideological operations throughout the Cold War. Their influence in Soviet-bloc countries was roughly evidenced by the consistent jamming of their transmissions within the region, even after such electronic interference was relaxed for VOA, BBC, and other Western broadcasts in the 1980s. Surveys of foreign radio listenership within the Soviet bloc were based largely on anecdotal evidence; both RFE and RL were generally ranked below the VOA and BBC in these surveys. Although their audiences were smaller, the Radios had a markedly higher listenership among political dissidents and other disaffected groups. This factor was later acknowledged by Lech Walesa, founder of Poland's Solidarity Movement: "In Poland, as in other communist countries, we listened to Radio Free Europe and other Western broadcasting stations despite the continual interference. From these broadcasting stations, we gleaned our lessons of independent thinking and solidarity action."[27]

The Radios' credibility depended heavily on the accuracy of their reports on Soviet-bloc developments. They relied on documentation prepared by RFE/RL research units, which in turn had access to information from the CIA and other intelligence sources. Many of these reports were given wide public distribution to Western academics and others interested in communist developments. They were (and are) a major resource for historians of the Cold War decades.

The RFE/RL role in covert propaganda operations changed dramatically in the early 1970s. (By that time, Radio Liberation had been renamed Radio Liberty.) Media investigations of the CIA's connection to the Radios led to calls for changing the ways in which they were operated.[28] When more details about the CIA's involvement became available, Congress finally acted. Legislation was introduced to reorganize the Radios. In debates on the bill, the most powerful voice for closing down the stations was that of Senator J. William Fulbright, chairman of the Foreign Relations Committee.[29] In a February 1972 floor speech, he declared: "I submit these Radios should be given the opportunity to take their rightful place in the graveyard of Cold War relics."[30] Given Fulbright's standing as a leading foreign policy spokesman in Congress, it became clear that the Radios' future was precarious.

The State Department and USIA did not want the Radios shut down, but neither was prepared to assume responsibility for the stations. Both agencies were primarily concerned with protecting the Voice of America's separate role as a credible source of news and information. Soviet propaganda outlets had consistently muddied the distinction between USIA and CIA information operations, including radio broadcasting. This theme was often picked up by noncommunist commentators abroad. In a typical example, the French newspaper *Le Quotidien de Paris,* in a 1975 series on U.S. cultural imperialism, described USIA and its overseas posts as affiliates of the CIA.[31]

A bureaucratic solution to determining the Radios' future was worked out in the months after Senator Fulbright's attack. The Nixon administration set up a special commission, headed by Milton Eisenhower, president of Johns Hopkins University. The group's report, issued in February 1972, recommended ending the CIA's connection with the two stations and creating an independent Board for International Broadcasting (BIB) composed of private citizens to oversee RFE/RL operations. Open congressional appropriations, managed by the new board, would replace the intelligence agency's covert funding. The BIB's principal role, the Eisenhower report declared, would be to assure "the professional independence" of the Radios in promoting a free flow of information to Soviet-bloc audiences.[32]

The BIB proposal was accepted by Congress, effectively ending the long-running dispute about RFE/RL's role in U.S. ideological operations.[33] Under the board's management, the Radios lost some of their strident propaganda edge, but they gained greater credibility among Soviet and East European audiences, particularly in their reports on political, economic, and social events within the region.

A half-century after they began operations, RFE/RL continued to broadcast, although their activities (and their influence) had been reduced from their Cold War levels. The Radios' primary audiences continued to be in the former Soviet-bloc countries, where, with some notable exceptions, the mass media still faced government harassment and controls. The Board for International Broadcasting was reorganized in 1999 to include supervision of the Voice of America, RFE/RL, and several smaller overseas government networks.

The transfer of RFE/RL activities to the BIB in 1972 eased, but did not end, USIA's somewhat prickly relations with the CIA, and particularly with the intelligence agency's covert information activities. Both agencies tripped each other up on numerous occasions in their parallel efforts to influence foreign audiences. Attempts to get better coordination between the two generally faltered on the CIA's reluctance to reveal what it was up to. Mixed signals and, often, public embarrassment for the United States resulted. Overall, however, the number of such incidents declined in the later Cold War decades.

The Department of State was USIA's most important intragovernment link during the Cold War years. USIA's role as the government's overseas information voice was bracketed by the program's early tenure within State between 1945 and 1953 and its eventual return to the department in 1999. USIA's organizational charter, as originally defined by the Eisenhower administration, made clear its responsibility to follow State's policy guidelines both in Washington and at overseas embassies.

Nevertheless, the relationship between the two agencies was often uneasy, based on differing bureaucratic cultures. State Department officials traditionally regarded themselves as part of an elite enterprise, one that was averse to sharing its thoughts with the outside world except under closely controlled circumstances. USIA's staff consisted largely of media professionals trained to produce information for public use. It took a long time for many Foreign Service officers to adjust to the information agency's mission of describing the details of U.S. foreign policy on a round-the-clock basis—and to foreigners at that. The preferred voice of America for many of them was a department spokesman reading a prepared script that had been carefully vetted throughout the bureaucracy. The major characteristic of the resulting policy declarations was, as a State official once famously declared, constructive ambiguity. This did not make it easier for USIA policy officers, who needed to know what to say about a given foreign policy issue in the next Voice of America broadcast.

The State Department's responsibilities in overseeing USIA's activities focused on two policy areas—public media operations and cultural relations, both traditionally neglected by the department throughout its history. Until the 1940s, the department's idea of media relations was an informal off-the-record review of the day's issues for reporters covering the diplomatic beat. The department's press officer before World War II was a genial Irishman, Mike McDermott, whose principal job was to keep "the press boys" happy. His small office also prepared a daily news digest that was sent by navy wireless-telegraph transmitters to embassies and legations around the world.[34]

This relaxed attitude toward the media changed dramatically after Pearl Harbor. A new office, the Bureau of Public Affairs, was created. Special attention was paid to the hitherto-neglected role of radio as an important news source for Americans. For the first time, the State Department had an adequate public voice for describing foreign policy developments. The new bureau also took on a stronger advocacy role in explaining the department's policy agenda. In 1944, it made its first major effort in this direction with a campaign to publicize the Roosevelt administration's plans for a postwar United Nations organization. The new public affairs bureau issued two million copies of a pamphlet describing the United Nations proposal. It also assigned senior department officers to explain the proposal in radio interviews—an unprecedented step for an agency that had been historically reluctant to get involved in mass-media discussion of its policies.[35]

Department officials originally saw the public affairs bureau primarily as an information channel to the U.S. public. However, they were soon faced with the challenging prospect of dealing with overseas public opinion following the creation of the Office of War Information in the spring of 1942. The OWI was an independent agency whose charter specified that it should take policy guidance from the State Department in its overseas media output. It was the beginning of a mixed cycle of cooperation and confusion between the department and the overseas information program that extended into the Cold War decades.

During the early postwar years, coordination problems lessened, primarily because the remnants of the OWI organization had been transferred to the State Department. The policy guidance issue was raised again in 1953 with the Eisenhower administration's decision to centralize overseas propaganda activities in an independent U.S. Information Agency. USIA took two steps to ensure adequate policy coordination with State. The first was to set up a centralized policy office of its own. A veteran Associated Press correspondent, Andrew Berding, who was well known to State Department officials, was recruited to assure adequate coordination with State on major policy issues. The new agency was organized along lines that matched the department's bureaucracy with geographic bureaus responsible for policy in various parts of the world, plus so-called functional bureaus dealing with economic, military, and other specific policy areas. This arrangement permitted USIA officials to operate laterally in their policy dealings with their opposite numbers at State.

Overall, the system worked. USIA officers were usually able to make their points at the lower levels of the policy chain—particularly in discussions with the department's so-called country desks, where the original drafting of policy positions usually took place. The agency's contribution in these discussions included assessments of the overseas public attitudes on a given policy initiative, whether it involved an arms control treaty or restrictions on textile imports from Africa. Over the years, this arrangement played an increasingly larger role in assuring that overseas public opinion received due recognition in the U.S. foreign policy process.

The next step in the process for USIA officers was the daily task of passing on State Department guidelines to the Voice of America and other agency media offices. A shorthand language was developed internally to cover the day's menu of guidelines. One legendary example was a State Department request that the Voice of America should give low-key coverage to a U.S.-sponsored Miss World contest in which a contestant from India was to appear for the first time. Her presence at the contest had sparked riotous protests by Indian religious zealots. The guidance to agency media went out: "Lay off Miss India."

By and large, USIA and State developed good working-level relations on policy guidance. The weakness in this arrangement was a general lack of coordination at higher policy levels, notably the question of USIA's representation (or lack of it) at the National Security Council in the White House. Edward R. Murrow, the agency's best-known director, often said that his organization needed to be in on the policy takeoffs as well as the landings at the White House level. For a long time, this did not happen. "We were occasionally let into the room," one agency officer pointed out, "like poor relatives visiting their betters."

USIA's role in high-level policy formation was improved markedly in 1966 when President Lyndon Johnson ordered the creation of a Senior Interdepartmental Group (SIG), headed by the deputy secretary of state, to oversee interagency policy coordination. The USIA director was made a full member of the group from the start. The SIG arrangement underwent some bureaucratic changes over the years, but it gave agency officials a stronger role in policymaking.[36]

State and USIA interests intersected in important ways also in managing overseas educational and cultural programs. The United States was the last of the major powers to officially promote its cultural wares in other societies. The French had their *mission civilisatrice,* heavily subsidized by the government. The Germans practiced *Kulturpolitik.* The Soviet government relied on VOKS, a government program to support international exchanges. British official policy on overseas cultural relations had been somewhat reticent, but in 1934 the government created a special organization, the British Council, to manage a wide-ranging program of academic and artistic exchanges.[37]

The United States had a checkered history in this area until the middle of the last century. A good part of the reason was what political scientist Seymour Martin Lipset calls "American exceptionalism," an attitude that includes a curious measure of cultural isolationism. Before World War II, educational and artistic exports were largely limited to Western Europe. Private groups financed almost all of these activities, with some small exceptions. The best-known of these was a congressionally approved arrangement in the 1920s that allowed Finland to repay its World War I war debt to the United States by funding a special academic exchange program between the two countries.

The interwar period saw a few isolated attempts to involve the U.S. government in cultural programs. The Institute of International Education was formed in New York to coordinate student and teacher exchange programs, using private funds.[38] The institute's exchange programs were small and scattered, and its attempts to get the State Department interested in the subject were largely ignored. The break came in 1936 when, as part of the Roosevelt administration's newly proclaimed Good Neighbor policy in Latin America, the United States signed the Buenos Aires Convention. The document contained a provision committing the signatories to expanding international cultural exchanges within the region. The United States' initial response was to create a Division of Cultural Relations in the State Department in 1938.[39] Its mission was to implement the Buenos Aires agreement, but it was underfunded and otherwise generally ignored by the department's leadership.

This situation changed in 1940 with the arrival of Nelson A. Rockefeller in the department to head the effort to combat German political and economic penetration in Latin America. As coordinator for inter-American affairs, he saw expanded cultural relations as part of his mission. Using State Department funds, he set up programs for academic and cultural exchanges throughout the region. Most important, he encouraged the development of binational centers—U.S. cultural institutes in major cities that provided a base for carrying out these activities.

It was a small beginning for an overseas cultural initiative that is now embedded in the Washington bureaucracy. Rockefeller's cultural programs were largely suspended during World War II, but they were revived in the early postwar years and expanded beyond Latin America to the rest of the world. The U.S. Congress, traditionally skeptical of funding cultural activities, gave the effort a major boost in 1947 when it approved the Fulbright scholarship program, in which funds from the sale of surplus war equipment abroad would be used to finance academic exchanges between U.S. and foreign institutions. A year later, Congress approved the Smith-Mundt Act, which gave its imprimatur to a permanent role for cultural programs in U.S. diplomacy.

In the early postwar years, overseas information and cultural operations were lodged in the State Department. This changed in 1953 when the Eisenhower administration decided to split bureaucratic responsibilities for the Cold War ideological campaign. Information operations were transferred to the new U.S. Information Agency; cultural programs would remain in the State Department. In part, this responded to congressional concerns that high-minded cultural operations would be tainted by association with the USIA's propaganda operations, a point made in an influential Senate Foreign Relations Committee report on the future of the information program.[40] In particular, the leading Democrat on the committee, Senator Fulbright, wanted to shield overseas cultural operations, and particularly his namesake scholarship program, from any hint of low political motives.

The other pressure on the White House to split the information and cultural programs came from Secretary of State John Foster Dulles's insistence that the department should not be saddled with propaganda operations that did not fit his ideas about high diplomacy. He had no objections, however, to keeping the more genteel-sounding cultural exchange programs under the department's protective wing. By and large, this was bureaucratic legerdemain: although State's cultural division had overall supervision of cultural operations, the planning and execution of these operations was largely carried out by USIA at home and abroad.

This bureaucratic split between information and cultural programs was ended in 1979 when State's cultural office was eliminated and its activities transferred to USIA. It was a latter-day acknowledgment that information and cultural programs were complementary parts of an effective overseas ideological strategy. When USIA was closed down in 1999, its information and cultural operations were moved as a single unit to a new State Department bureau, headed by an under secretary for public diplomacy.[41]

Notes

1. For the early postwar expansion of U.S. commercial media abroad, see: William Read, *America's Mass Media Merchants* (Baltimore, Md.: Johns Hopkins University Press, 1976); Reinhold Wagnleitner and Elaine Tyler May, *Here, There and Everywhere: The Foreign Politics of American Culture* (Hanover, N.H.: University Press of New England, 2000).

2. The most comprehensive description of the overseas information and cultural activities of other federal agencies in the Cold War decades is contained in: "The U.S. Ideological Effort: Government Agencies and Programs," a sixty-five-page addendum to "Winning the Cold War: The U.S. Ideological Offensive." Hearings before the Subcommittee on International Organizations and Movements, Committee on Foreign Affairs, March 1963–February 1964. House of Representatives, 88th Congress, 1st and 2nd sessions, vol. 2, Appendix A.

3. Ibid., p. 36. See also: "Thousands of Military Men Studying in the U.S.," *New York Times,* January 11, 1970, p. 8.

4. For a summary of AFN's postwar expansion, see: Donald R. Browne, "The World in the Pentagon's Shadow," *Educational Broadcasting Review* 5, no. 2, April 1971, pp. 31–48.

5. "Overseas Military Information Programs," Report 646, Committee on Government Operations, House of Representatives, 88th Congress, 2nd session, 1962, p. 5.

6. "A Voice That Europe Trusts," *New York Times,* April 17, 1966, p. C-32.

7. Ovid Bayless, "The American Forces Network–Europe," *Journal of Broadcasting* 12, no. 2, spring 1968, p. 163.

8. "For Japan, a Window on U.S. Life," *New York Times,* March 30, 1976, p. 8.

9. Browne, "The World in the Pentagon's Shadow," p. 36.

10. "The USAFE Community Relations Story," U.S. Air Force (Europe) pamphlet. USAFE public information office, Wiesbaden, Germany, June 1957, p. 5.

11. "The U.S. Ideological Effort: Government Agencies and Programs," Addendum to Hearings (see note 2), p. 39.

12. For a useful summary of postwar Department of Defense psychological operations, see: William Daugherty, "Psyops in Perspective," in *The Art and Science of Psychological Operations: Case Studies in Military Applications,* Report No. 525-7-1, Department of the Army, April 1976, pp. 81–85. See also: Roy A. Gallant, "More Psycho Than Logical," *The Reporter,* March 31, 1953, pp. 17–19.

13. "Paying Red Pilots for MIGs Is Declared Morally Wrong," *Washington Post,* May 30, 1953, p. B-5.

14. "Militant Liberty and the Pentagon," *The Reporter,* February 9, 1956, pp. 30–34.

15. The details of the agreement are given in: "Psyops in Vietnam: A Many-Splintered Thing," in *The Art and Science of Psychological Operations: Case Studies in Military Applications,* Report No. 525-7-1, Department of the Army, April 1976, pp. 225–228.

16. "When Bombs Are Not Enough," *Washington Post,* December 10, 2001, p. C-1.

17. "Rumsfeld Kills Pentagon Propaganda Unit," *Washington Post,* February 27, 2002, p. A-21.

18. Academic probes into the CIA's covert ideological activities are a specialized cottage industry within the larger field of foreign policy scholarship. A useful summary of this research is contained in Tony Shaw: "The Politics of Cold War Culture," *Journal of Cold War Studies* 3, no. 3, fall 2001, pp. 59–76. Some of the most impressive investigatory work on this subject was done during the 1960s and 1970s by the *New York Times* and by *Ramparts,* a left-wing California magazine.

19. Peter Coleman, *The Liberal Conspiracy: The Congress of Cultural Freedom and the Struggle for the Mind of Postwar Europe* (New York: New Press, 2000); Volker R. Bergahn, *America and the Intellectual Cold Wars in Europe* (Princeton, N.J.: Princeton University Press, 2001).

20. This effort to reach intellectuals is recorded in: Francis Stone Sanders, *The Cultural Cold War: The CIA and the World of Arts and Letters* (New York: New Press, 2000); Robin W. Winks, *Cloak and Gown: Scholars in the Secret War 1939–1962* (New York: Quill Publishers, 1987).

21. The CIA's activities in suborning newsmen were revealed in a three-part *New York Times* series, "CIA: Secret Shaper of Public Opinion," December 19, 26, and 27, 1977.

22. The *Digest*'s role is discussed in a book about DeWitt and Lila Wallace, the magazine's founders: Peter Canning, *American Dreamers* (New York: Simon & Schuster, 1996).

23. "Panel Monitors CIA News Plants," *Washington Post*, January 17, 1976, p. 9.

24. "Congressman Says CIA Pledges to Stop Sponsoring English-Language Books," *New York Times*, May 5, 1977, p. 14.

25. The origins and later history of the two stations are described in: Michael Nelson, *War of the Black Heavens: The Battles of Western Broadcasting in the Cold War* (Syracuse, N.Y.: Syracuse University Press, 1997).

26. Ibid., p. 98.

27. Ibid., p. 102.

28. The first substantive details of the connection between the CIA and the Radios were published in a series of reports in the *New York Times* between February 14 and February 21, 1967.

29. "The Station That Fulbright Wants to Shut Down," *New York Times Magazine*, March 26, 1972, p. 36.

30. *Congressional Record*, 92nd Congress, 2nd session, vol. 118, p. 21.

31. *Media Reaction Digest*, USIA Office of Research, July 13, 1975, p. 1.

32. "The Right to Know: Report of the Presidential Study Commission on International Broadcasting," U.S. Government Printing Office, Washington D.C., 1973, pp. A3–4.

33. Under the BIB's direction, the Radios were eventually reorganized as a single operation, RFE/RL Inc., in 1976. Nelson, *War of the Black Heavens*, p. 148.

34. "How Cordell Hull Handled the Press," *State Magazine*, May 1987, pp. 28–29.

35. Jonathan Soffer, "All for One or All for All," *Diplomatic History* 21, no. 1, winter 1997, p. 45.

36. The SIG was authorized in National Security Action Memorandum 341, March 8, 1966. Keith Clark and Laurence Legere (eds.), *The President and the Management of National Security* (New York: Praeger Publishers, 1969), p. 93.

37. Emily S. Rosenberg, *Spreading the American Dream: American Economic and Cultural Expansion 1890–1939* (New York: Hill and Wang, 1982), pp. 108–121; Philip M. Taylor, *The Projection of Britain: British Overseas Publicity and Propaganda* (London: Cambridge University Press, 1981), pp. 125–128.

38. Akira Iriye, *Cultural Internationalism and World Order* (Baltimore, Md.: Johns Hopkins University Press, 1997), pp. 73–74.

39. Rosenberg, *Spreading the American Dream*, p. 205.

40. "Overseas Information Programs of the United States," Report No. 406, Senate Committee on Foreign Relations, 83rd Congress, 1st session, June 15, 1953, p. 2.

41. "USIA-State Integration: A Work in Progress," *State Magazine,* December 2000, pp. 23–27.

8

A Stone's Throw from the University

USIA WAS A government agency with all the bureaucratic baggage that phrase implies. Its unique distinction among Washington agencies was that it could not operate in the United States, a congressional restriction designed to head off the creation of an all-encompassing government propaganda bureau.

Between 1953 and 1999, the information agency's working territory included almost three hundred cities and towns, from Tromso, 200 miles north of the Arctic Circle in Norway, to Barisal, a Bangladesh river port surrounded by steamy jungle. This geographic reach has never been matched by any other U.S. government agency then or since. The agency's overseas posts constituted the U.S. Information Service, known locally as USIS. This acronym became a familiar word in scores of languages overseas.

USIS was in many ways the public face of the United States in cities and towns across the globe. This was particularly true in the more than one hundred new nations created out of former European colonies after World War II, most of which had little or no previous contact with Americans or their cultural products before the war. The USIS center was usually located in the center of town on a main street. Its most prominent feature was a library available to all comers. These libraries had open shelves where patrons could browse in the stacks, select books, and borrow them to take home, something without precedent in most cities where USIS operated.[1]

Throughout the postwar decades, the USIS library network was the most extensive of its kind in the world. Among many accomplishments, it played a special role in encouraging local open-shelf public libraries, particularly in Asia, Africa, and Latin America. In part, this was the result of a special USIA project that trained tens of thousands of overseas librarians in modern library practices.

USIS libraries were usually crowded with students and other readers throughout the day. Attendance was so heavy in many of them that patrons had to reserve a time to be admitted. One of these was the Calcutta library, located near one of the city's major universities. It had large plate-glass windows facing the street. As with other USIS libraries, the windows were a tempting target for anti-American demonstrations, often led by the very students who were the libraries' patrons. The windows suffered as a result, leading to the wry observation among USIS officers that their libraries were just a stone's throw from the university. A *New Yorker* cartoon in the 1960s depicted a USIA training class where the staff was being taught window glazing.

Aside from their accessibility, USIS posts were distinct among U.S. operations abroad in the people who ran them. One of these distinctions was that most had little or no specific training for their duties. Though they were de facto propagandists, there was almost no provision to prepare them for their trade. Most other large countries had information and cultural ministries manned by professionals who could be assigned to overseas embassies to run propaganda operations. Their USIS counterparts had no such experience, aside from occasional briefings and lectures by a small USIA training division.

The Americans who operated USIS posts overseas were, by and large, part of a pickup crew that was trained on the job. Beginning with the wartime Office of War Information, the program's information and cultural staffs were drawn largely from commercial media companies or from academia. Most of them came into the service with the idea of spending a few years overseas before returning to their old jobs. Reinforcing this attitude was the fact that their Foreign Service appointments were limited to a few years. In the early postwar decades, a USIS job was not one you planned to retire from. This began to change after 1965, when agency officers were integrated into the regular Foreign Service career system with permanent appointments and other perks.[2]

Nevertheless, the pattern of a learn-as-you-go officer corps dominated USIA's overseas operations throughout the agency's existence. Overall, this group had an oddball quality to it. One reason was that the agency attracted more than the normal share of misfits, most of whom resigned or were pushed out early in their careers. Those who were left represented a new breed of Foreign Service officer, particularly in the early postwar years when U.S. diplomacy was still dominated by a tradition of protective elitism. USIS officers did not fit this mold, either by training or inclination.

They were an eclectic group. Steve Dachi was a Hungarian dentist who fled his country after the failed popular uprising against Soviet occupation forces in 1956. Gene Karst was a press agent for the St. Louis Cardinals. John Maddux was a former Jesuit. Patricia Van Delden served in the anti-Nazi underground, later returning to Europe to run the USIS post in Holland. Stepney Kibble was a featured player in Hollywood's *Our Gang* films. Arthur Hummel, born in China, escaped from a Japanese concentration camp, joined a Chinese guerrilla group, and then took a job with USIS in Tokyo after the war.

Men and women like these brought new viewpoints to the Foreign Service. This involved a certain brashness, combined with an edgy impatience with traditional service practices and attitudes. By and large, the information service did not encourage bureaucratic shrinking violets. One freewheeling officer, a former Hollywood press agent who ran a USIS post in Asia, once enraged the State Department by some breach of orthodox protocol. A telegram was sent from Washington informing him, somewhat colorfully, that he had raped the program. No, not rape, the officer declared in a return telegram, just a quick feel in the subway. It was not the kind of response that endeared the information program to department officials.

Despite such incidents, USIA officers generally adapted to conventional Foreign Service practices. A few sank into bureaucratic conformity. The rest brought a new kind of energy to the diplomatic process, particularly in dealing with the public. Ed Murrow, the agency's best-known director, would tell them that the critical distance in communications was the last three feet between one person and another. This, he said, is where agency officers should focus their efforts.

John McKnight, a talented officer assigned to the USIS post in Rome, once underscored this point in a congressional appropriations committee hearing. If you only had $15 in your post budget for the year, a congressman asked him, how would you spend it? McKnight replied that he would take the minister of education to lunch and try to convince him to create more American studies programs in Italian universities.[3]

The importance of getting out and mingling with the locals set up another distinction between USIA officers and their embassy counterparts. The latter's contacts outside the embassy were usually limited to a small group of elite circles, both public and private. USIS officers operated in a much wider field, which included a lot of travel outside the big cities.

They were in effect circuit riders, touring the outback and meeting with local opinion makers, from newspaper editors to college professors. This could involve formal conferences or simply an opportunity to talk things over at a coffee shop in the town square. A favorite mode of travel, particularly in developing countries, was in Jeeps, which could navigate backwoods roads and ford streams. Accommodations were often primitive. Phil Carroll, an information officer in India, remembered one frequent overnight stop on his provincial trips at a fleabag inn with the wonderfully contradictory name of the Spartan Luxury.

USIS posts were only one part of the official U.S. presence in each country. The postwar years had witnessed a massive expansion of federal agencies into overseas operations. Before the war, U.S. embassies were staffed almost exclusively by the State Department. By 1960, State employees were usually in the minority, as dozens of agencies claimed the right to be represented in overseas missions.

The result was often administrative and policy chaos, undercutting the ambassador's authority as (in the traditional diplomatic phrase) the "extraordinary and plenipotentiary" representative of the U.S. president. In the early 1960s, the Kennedy White House took strong steps to reassert ambassadorial authority. The order was aimed particularly at the Defense Department and the CIA, both heavily represented in embassies. The Kennedy initiative created what came to be called the "country team," whose meetings, presided over by the ambassador, usually resulted in better coordination of policy and operations within the mission and with Washington. USIS posts benefited from the country team process, because it gave the post director, known as the public affairs officer, a direct voice in influencing the embassy's policy mission.[4]

Over and above the country team system, USIS effectiveness within the embassy depended heavily on the ambassador's interest in information and cultural operations. Some old-line ambassadors regarded USIS as an administrative and policy burden. Others welcomed its role. The strongest ambassadorial advocates were often political appointees who owed their jobs to their loyalty to the party occupying the White House. They were usually business executives who had a better understanding of the value of public relations than many career ambassadors. Chester Bowles, a New York advertising executive who was twice ambassador to India, gave strong support to the embassy's information operations, even writing a regular column in *American Reporter,* the USIS newspaper.[5]

Another USIS supporter was Shirley Temple Black, ambassador to Ghana in the 1970s. When she was appointed, some critics suggested that the embassy in Accra be renamed the Good Ship Lollypop, after one of her film songs. In fact, Ambassador Black was a successful envoy, in part through her support of the embassy's information and cultural programs. Claire Booth Luce, the playwright and author who served as ambassador in Rome, was equally attentive to USIS activities, including participating in public speaking tours. She made a brave attempt to learn Italian, which she flourished with good humor, disarming her audiences by declaring, "I am going to speak in a language which is not mine, and by the time I finish you may be wondering whether it is yours."

Ambassadors were important to USIS because they could give authoritative voice to U.S. government policies at the local level, influencing the public tone and direction of U.S. interests in their country of assignment. An ambassador willing to meet with influential media and cultural leaders was a potent asset for any USIS operation. Two postwar ambassadors to Japan, Edwin Reischauer and Mike Mansfield, were outstanding examples. Born in Japan of missionary parents, Reischauer was fluent in Japanese. He was also a leading scholar of the country's history at Harvard before taking on his embassy post in 1961.[6] Mike Mansfield had a more eclectic career as a mining engineer, political science professor, and U.S. senator from Montana, before serving an unprecedented dozen years as ambassador in Tokyo from 1977 to 1989.

Mansfield became known for his informal on-the-record press conferences. He ended each session with a gentle admonition to the assembled reporters. "Tap 'er light, boys," he would tell them. "Tap 'er light." One day, a *New York Times* correspondent asked Mansfield what this meant. "Well," he replied, "when I was a young fellow I used to work in the copper mines in eastern Montana. As a miner pounded that stick of dynamite into the shaft walls, you'd holler down the line: 'tap 'er light, tap 'er light'—and that's what we've got to do here in Japan. . . . We don't want to tap 'er too strong. Let's see if we can do it without raising the decibel count."[7]

Tapping 'er light was also a useful guideline for USIS operations when dealing with U.S. policy positions, particularly those where local opinion differed sharply with Washington decisions. Invariably the problem was to present the U.S. viewpoint clearly and forcefully in ways that reflected understanding of contrary opinions.

That was the challenge every day as USIS posts opened their doors across twelve time zones around the world. There was no cookie-cutter standard for organizing posts. They came in all sizes and shapes, determined primarily by the importance of the host country to U.S. policy interests. By 1970, USIA had established posts in over 150 countries. The average capital-city USIS staff at the time generally consisted of four to six officers. In larger, strategically important countries these big-city posts were augmented by smaller operations in provincial towns, usually run by a single U.S. officer with a small staff of local employees. The resident officer had to be a jack-of-all-trades, carrying out information and cultural operations with limited program resources.

Lee Dinsmore, a former YMCA secretary who joined the information agency in the early 1950s, was typical of the breed. His first overseas assignment was to set up a USIS post in Kirkuk, the largest city in the Kurdish-dominated region of northern Iraq. It was the first official U.S. presence in a remote area that has since played a critical role in Middle Eastern politics. Dinsmore operated out of a modest house with a small library in the front room. He learned Kurdish and traveled around the region in a Land Rover—or by horse or mule when the roads were impassable—meeting with local leaders and recruiting the first groups of young Kurds sent to U.S. universities as exchange students.[8]

Dinsmore's experience was replicated in over one hundred provincial cities around the world where small USIS outposts operated. As in Kirkuk, they were often the first U.S. presence in the region. The posts also served as a learning-by-immersion training experience for young USIA officers, many of whom later became senior managers in the service.

Most USIS posts had similar daily routines. Work was divided roughly between "information" and "cultural" operations. The two often overlapped, but it is still a useful distinction in describing the pattern of USIS activities abroad. The first order of business each morning for the public affairs officer and his information staff was to deal with a news file that had been transmitted electronically overnight from Washington headquarters. The file was the oldest overseas information service provided by the U.S. government, dating from 1935. President Roosevelt personally authorized the operation after hearing complaints from his ambassadors that they needed a reliable way to get current news affecting U.S. policy at their overseas posts. A press summary was prepared by the State Department and sent by navy shortwave wireless transmitters to a small group of overseas diplomatic missions.[9]

The service became known as the "Wireless File," a name that stuck long after high-speed cables and satellites replaced shortwave reception. In 1994, the File became an Internet web site, servicing embassies and other U.S. missions on a round-the-clock basis. As a result, the File is now available to anyone anywhere with a computer and Internet access. (The daily edition of the File can be viewed at www.usinfo.state.gov.)

The USIA Wireless File was the most widely distributed news service in the world, eclipsing the Associated Press and other commercial agencies. Its contents differed from those of the private services. The basic daily File, edited at USIA headquarters, averaged eight-to-ten thousand words, heavily weighted toward U.S. government official texts. The File also included news stories of direct regional or local interest to USIS posts, such as the Washington visit of a foreign minister or a report on congressional legislation affecting the host country.

The Wireless File was originally transmitted only in English. In the 1950s, its contents were split into five geographic editions, which allowed for customizing its contents more directly to regional interests. French and Spanish translation versions were added later. Currently, the File is also distributed in Arabic, Russian, and Chinese versions.[10] In the USIA decades, the Wireless File was often the most direct source overseas embassies had for current guidance on U.S. policy. In effect, it set out the day-to-day policy agenda for U.S. overseas missions. At any USIS post, the priority audience for the File was the ambassador and his key aides. Copies of the overnight File were on their desks first thing in the morning. Other copies were often dispatched by messenger to the local foreign office and other ministries.

Meanwhile, USIS officers had an early-morning editorial meeting to determine which items in the overnight File should be included in a daily news bulletin for distribution to the local media—newspapers, radio, television—either in printed bulletin form or by teletype. Translation was a problem for posts where the File's editions in French, Spanish, and other languages were not relevant. In these instances, the File had to be translated locally every workday into as many as three dozen other languages—a time-consuming process.

The Wireless File was, in many ways, the bedrock product of local posts around the world in the USIA years. Its effectiveness depended primarily on its ability to supply immediate and authoritative full-text versions of U.S. policy statements. These were supplemented in the File by editorial analysis on such subjects as U.S. domestic politics, foreign policy, economics, culture, and scientific developments. These commentaries were prepared by a group of USIA editors, usually writing under a nom de plume for each of the specialized columns. A long-running commentary on economic developments was attributed for many years to a fictional Guy Sims Fitch, whose views were often cited authoritatively in overseas publications that ran his column as part of their editorial menu.

The Wireless File was a daily record of U.S. policies that affected individual foreign nations. It was accorded strong credibility by foreign governments and media outlets as a useful guide to current U.S. policy positions. Very often, File texts were used by overseas governments to reinforce their opposition to Washington actions: "As the American embassy news bulletin admits . . ."

The USIS local edition of the worldwide File also had a wider public impact. Thousands of newspapers and other publications printed its contents, often identifying them with a USIS credit line similar to those of the Associated Press or United Press International. Many of these publications did so because they could not afford the commercial services. Their only alternative was often a government-controlled press agency that was, more often than not, simply an outlet for self-congratulatory stories about the local regime.

The USIS daily bulletin also reported on U.S.-related events within the country. These were usually picked up by the local media, whatever their editorial attitudes on U.S. policy. A routine example would be an announcement of a prominent U.S. visitor. Once, when I was the press officer at the Athens embassy, I put out a notice about a distinguished Ivy League professor who was scheduled to give a talk on Benjamin Franklin at a local university. That night a reporter interrupted my sleep to ask for further details, specifically, what time Franklin's plane would arrive. Annoyed by the nocturnal intrusion and stretching my pledge to truth-in-propaganda, I informed him that Doctor Franklin had been grounded in Philadelphia.

Since 1999, when USIA was abolished, the Wireless File has been produced within the State Department. Its basic content remains the same, centered around full-text statements of U.S. policies and actions affecting other countries. As one Foreign Service diplomat noted in 2002, the File "is a primary tool. If we were cutting resources, it would be the last to be cut."[11]

The care and feeding of the local media was only one small part of a USIS post's daily activities. In addition to its media operations, the post dealt with a steady flow of visitors, such as American tourists who were inclined to drop into USIS for answers to their questions. The sign out front said it was a U.S. information service and they were taxpayers. They were accordingly given special deference, even if only to tell them where to find a cheap hotel.

U.S. visitors who came with some kind of official mandate from Washington were something else. At the top of this list were members of Congress and their staffs. They had a clear right to investigate any aspect of U.S. government activities, including embassies and other diplomatic missions. These congressional probings took place most often in such cosmopolitan centers as London, Paris, and Rome. However, many legislators had a taste for the exotic. It was a Foreign Service precept that any congressional delegation within an hour's airline flight of Istanbul would find a reason to spend a few days there. Their official purpose was to check out the local consulate's operations, a hurried duty often sandwiched between sightseeing and shopping trips.

By the mid-1990s, the American Foreign Service Association (AFSA), representing State and USIA officers, officially protested what it described as the requirement to baby-sit official delegations, in particular those from Congress. "We need official travel," the group's president, F. Allen "Tex" Harris, declared. "It serves the purposes of good government and good policy. What we don't need is official tourism." The AFSA statement, based on a survey of its members, chronicled one congressman's request for a cocaine fix. Another ordered several rooms of locally bought furniture shipped home at government expense. One ambassador declared that if one in ten congressional trips had any serious purpose, "it was happenstance."[12]

USIS posts were heavily involved in such visits, providing logistic support that included escorting members of Congress and their spouses around town. Some legislators took their roving duties more seriously, including investigating local USIS operations. One of these, Senator Allen Ellender, a Louisiana Democrat, was convinced that the information program was a global boondoggle. "It is obvious," he declared in one of his trip reports, "that our so-called information experts are determined to maintain a staff in each and every country where the American flag flies, whether it is needed or not." The evidences of waste and mismanagement he cited were often anecdotal and unproved, but he could be a shrewd investigator at times. A staunch conservative, he criticized mismanagement of USIS propaganda operations in South Vietnam as early as 1956, years before the program's shortcomings became evident to other observers.[13]

Visits by presidents and other high Washington officials rated a special category. Such events were a modern phenomenon. As late as the early 1950s, Secretary of State John Foster Dulles made his first trip to the Far East without fanfare on a Pan American commercial flight, accompanied by one aide. This informal pattern changed dramatically in 1959 with President Eisenhower's groundbreaking round-the-world tour, made possible by the introduction of intercontinental jet planes. The Eisenhower trip set a standard that has been followed, with variations, by every president since.

Over the years, a presidential trip became an increasingly complex operation, involving hundreds of government officials, including those in USIS. The event instantly became top priority on the post's agenda, with most other projects put on hold until the presidential party had departed. Elaborate scripts were prepared, describing every detail of each stop along the way.

USIS had special responsibility for shepherding the large contingent of U.S. media correspondents accompanying the presidential party.[14] (They traveled in a separate chartered aircraft that became known as the "zoo plane.") Large press facilities were set up, complete with video, voice, and print facilities, a briefing room, and an information desk to answer questions about local restaurants, where to get laundry done, and how to order a taxi. For all the frantic activity surrounding them, presidential visits were important, particularly in highlighting U.S. interest in the country visited. At times a trip underlined a vital strategic policy, such as John Kennedy's 1963 visit to West Berlin during which he affirmed the continuing U.S. commitment to defend the city.

Richard Nixon's 1969 visit to Romania—the first presidential visit to a Communist country—was another strategic project. The local propaganda ministry was totally unprepared to deal with the event. I had been assigned temporarily to Bucharest to handle media details for the visit. When I met with the chief of the Romanian foreign office's press bureau, he asked me how many media correspondents would be covering the event. A half dozen? A dozen? In the Romanian official's experience, such coverage normally involved the local correspondent from TASS, the Soviet press agency, together with a few Western newsmen stationed in Bucharest. When I informed him that we estimated there would by upwards of a hundred reporters accompanying Nixon, he blanched. After some polite chitchat, the meeting ended and I never saw him again. We proceeded to make our own media arrangements for the visit.

The government-controlled newspapers in Bucharest limited their announcement of the Nixon visit to a short notice buried in the back pages, with no details of the schedule. However, the Voice of America and other Western broadcasters provided full details in the days before the presidential party arrived. One result was that tens of thousands of Romanians lined the road from the airport to cheer the Nixon motorcade.

Dealing with VIPs, from presidents on down, was only one part of the USIS information section's daily schedule. Another more immediate duty involved the role of the embassy's spokesman—a duty usually assigned to the USIS press officer. Explaining U.S. foreign policy to impatient and usually skeptical news correspondents is a perilous exercise, particularly when the spokesperson is limited to saying little or nothing about a given policy. In these situations, press briefings became major exercises in circumlocution. Robert McCloskey, a well-respected State Department spokesman in the 1960s, described his role as practicing the art of constructive ambiguity. Secretary of State Colin Powell, who often has acted as his own press spokesman, has his own variation in this. When pressed, he declares: "Secrets of all hearts will be revealed in due course later."[15]

In addition to serving as embassy spokesmen, USIS press officers were often pressed into service to draft speeches and other statements, where constructive ambiguity also reigned. A more complex situation prevailed in Washington, where speech drafts were often vetted by a dozen or more officials before a final version emerged. I and a Foreign Service colleague, Monteagle Stearns, were once assigned by our State Department boss to write a short prayer for President Eisenhower to deliver at the lighting of the national Christmas tree. A draft complete with blandly appropriate sentiments was sent to the White House speech-writing office. When we tuned into the ceremony at the State Department, I said to my colleague: "Monty, I recognized one of our words—Amen!"

Secretary of State Dean Acheson was a master of English prose, but in the rush of business he had to rely on speech writers. One day, a young officer brought in a draft of a foreign policy address that included the statement that man's aspirations can no longer be satisfied within the narrow confines of national boundaries. "Young man," Acheson told him, "this is a bit overwrittten. Some of man's aspirations can be satisfied within the narrow confines of one small bedroom."

USIS had a group of press officers who were adept at the give-and-take of press conferences. One of them was Ben Bradlee, who later became executive editor of the *Washington Post*. Another was Bradlee's successor in Paris, Harold Kaplan, who brought political savvy (as well as a fluent command of French) to the job. Barry Zorthian, head of USIA operations in Vietnam in the 1960s, was a master of the "deep backgrounder," informal off-the-record briefings for U.S. correspondents in Saigon.

In between speech writing and dealing with media correspondents, USIS information officers in the Cold War years managed a global multimedia enterprise. Then as now, USIS media operations were statistically a small part of the U.S. information impact on the rest of the world. The postwar expansion of U.S. media products abroad is well documented.[16] Information goods and services were the last great U.S. industry, the London *Economist* declared at the turn of the century.[17] They are also the country's largest and most profitable export sector.

USIA played a small but useful role in this development. It was a significant purchaser of commercial information products, such as books, newspapers, films, and exhibits, for its own overseas operations. In particular, USIA familiarized large parts of Asia, Africa, and Latin America with U.S. media products through its own distribution channels. Previously, only Hollywood films had penetrated these regions, and then primarily in larger cities and towns.

USIA also gave direct support to commercial media expansion abroad by subsidizing the introduction of U.S. products in these regions. A book subsidy project, Franklin Publications, allowed U.S. publishers to make significant breakthroughs in a market previously dominated by British and French publishers. An Information Media Guaranty (IMG) program authorized by Congress and managed by USIA gave newspaper, magazine, and film companies access to overseas markets by guaranteeing the conversion of their foreign currency earnings into dollars, a critical point in the many soft-currency countries of Asia, Africa, and Latin America. Over $80 million in such transactions took place between 1952 and 1967, when the program was closed down after a congressional investigation belatedly discovered that IMG funds were used to subsidize the distribution of Tarzan comic books in Israel.[18]

The IMG program played an important role in increasing sales of leading U.S. publications abroad and proved especially useful in introducing American information and entertainment into Eastern European countries. By the mid-1960s, IMG had subsidized the sales of nearly $7 million worth of books, newspapers, magazines, and other media in Communist Poland. American TV programs, from *Robin Hood* to *Alfred Hitchcock Presents,* were the most popular half-dozen shows on Polish TV in the mid-1960s.[19] USIA also supplemented IMG support for overseas media sales by presenting newspaper subscriptions to key opinion leaders abroad. By the mid-1960s, this program involved over five thousand subscriptions each for the *New York Times* and the Paris-based *International Herald Tribune.*[20]

The agency's own operations relied heavily on commercial media products. Its posts carried out a multimedia effort on a global scale, predating by decades the strategy of such private-sector giants as Time Warner and Rupert Murdoch's News Corp. to develop synergistic operations in which individual media played off each other to deliver a common, profitable message. The supreme practitioner of this kind of product synergy was the Disney organization, which pioneered the technique in the 1930s, marketing books, toys, clothing, theme parks, and other products featuring Mickey Mouse and other denizens of its cartoon bestiary.[21]

USIA adopted this approach in ways that brought a range of integrated media resources to the staid field of promoting foreign policy. The process was governed by an annual "country plan" at each post that detailed the media activities it would pursue under each U.S. foreign policy objective for its host country. The plans were often overly ambitious in their goals, relying heavily on self-fulfilling prophecies of success. Overall, however, the country plan system helped to improve USIS programs in ways that distinguished U.S. overseas propaganda operations from those of its Cold War allies and enemies alike.

Among program resources available at USIS posts, print publications usually headed the list. USIA became the largest international periodical publisher in the world by the 1950s, certainly in the range of its print output, and probably also its volume. (The closest challenger would have been the *Reader's Digest,* with its dozens of foreign-language editions.) In 1960, the agency was producing fifty-seven magazines in twenty languages worldwide, together with twenty-two newspapers in fourteen languages. Their estimated total circulation at the time was 110 million copies.[22] Over two-thirds of these publications were produced overseas. Their contents were a mélange of local stories and articles, supplemented by material supplied by a central editorial unit in Washington.

Each was designed and edited for a particular constituency. One of the first overseas USIS publications was *American Reporter,* a newspaper published in New Delhi and targeted at an elite Indian audience. Its magazine counterpart, *Span,* was a glossy product similar to *Life* that consistently won local prizes for design and editorial content among Indian publications. Like many other USIS publications, *Span* had a significant readership of paid subscribers, creating a problem for the New Delhi USIS post because many of the copies it mailed were often stolen before they reached subscribers.[23]

World Today was a Chinese-language periodical produced in Hong Kong, distributed primarily to an overseas Chinese audience but with the clear (and often successful) intent that many of its copies would be smuggled into Communist China. Another USIS–Hong Kong publication, *Current Scene: Developments in Mainland China,* was a small-circulation newsletter analyzing Communist Chinese developments and distributed to media executives and scholars throughout the Far East.

When I was managing the USIS post in Dhaka, our premier publication was the Bengali-language *Markin Parikama* ("American Panorama"). It was the largest paid-circulation newspaper in what was then East Pakistan, with a total circulation of over 30,000 readers. The subscribers were devoted letter-to-the-editor writers, sending over five hundred letters a week to the USIS press office.

From a program standpoint, the single most influential publications produced by USIA were the magazines distributed in the Soviet Union and Eastern Europe, in particular the Russian and Polish editions of the *Life*-sized *America Illustrated*. Although their circulations were closely controlled by local Communist regimes, the magazines had an enormous pass-on readership. A common practice was to rent issues until they became too tattered to be read.[24] Another agency magazine published in Eastern Europe was *SAD*, whose somewhat startling name was the acronym spelling "USA" in Serbo-Croatian.

The largest single USIA publications effort took place in wartime Vietnam. In addition to numerous specialized magazines, the post's output included a monthly tabloid newspaper, delivered primarily by airdrops over enemy-controlled areas. The print run was 2 million copies. This was in addition to a massive continuing airdrop of leaflets (including surrender appeals) that in 1996 reached 115 million copies. The largest single airdrop that year involved 20 million leaflets with a message condemning the North Vietnamese government for rejecting peace offers.[25]

The consistently most influential USIA magazine throughout the Cold War decades was the small-circulation *Problems of Communism,* a scholarly review of trends and events in the Soviet Union, China, and their client states. *POC* was also the most independent of the agency's publications, thanks largely to New Yorker Abraham Brumberg, its maverick editor of many years. Brumberg was particularly averse to taking advice about the magazine's contents from USIA higher-ups, for the good reason that he knew more about communism and communists than they did. He once reviewed a sex guide to Soviet-bloc countries, complete with ideological analysis.

Brumberg heaped particular scorn on his bureaucratic betters when they decreed that Marx, Engels, and Lenin should not be mentioned in the publication. The prohibition was short-lived. As the London *Economist* once noted, *POC* was "one of a handful of serious Western guides to what was going on in the recesses of the Marxist-Leninist mind."[26] Plain in appearance, *POC* published heavily footnoted articles written by the small coterie of international scholars who tracked communist affairs.

The Soviet ideological journal, *World Marxist Review,* once described *POC*'s purpose as "the marshalling of the maximum of brain and energy to place anticommunism on some semblance of a scientific footing."[27] The description, minus the put-down, was a tribute to Abe Brumberg and the other editors of a unique and influential publication. When USIA stopped publishing *POC* in the early 1990s, it was replaced by a commercial edition, *Problems of Post-Communism,* edited at George Washington University and distributed by M. E. Sharpe, a New York publishing firm.

Beyond publications, the other medium heavily exploited by USIS was film. Arguably movies were the most potent mass media instrument developed in the twentieth century—and the United States led the world in exploiting it through Hollywood films. Josef Stalin once told a U.S. visitor: "If I could control the medium of American motion pictures, I would need nothing else to convert the entire world to Communism."[28]

Although dozens of countries had thriving film industries, they could not match the geographic reach and mass influence of Hollywood's products during the Cold War decades. Foreign moviemakers generally produced films that reflected local attitudes and conditions. By contrast, Hollywood took on the world, mastering the art of what came to be known as the international film.[29] The industry hired foreign actors, writers, and directors to make movies that attracted audiences across boundaries and cultures. André Malraux, the French writer, once described this approach as a process in which a Swedish actress playing a Russian heroine for an American director draws tears from the Chinese.

In the postwar decades, USIA played a small but useful role in this process. It produced only one feature-length film—*Years of Lightning, Day of Drums,* a retrospective on John F. Kennedy's career made after the president's assassination. The agency focused on short documentary films, and it made thousands of them in the United States and abroad. Documentaries suited USIA's advocacy purposes because of their ability to present a point of view quickly and dramatically. Such films have since gone out of style, in part because of television as well as Hollywood's postwar retreat from making what it called "short subjects" for screening in theaters before its feature films.

The information program's use of documentaries dates from 1941. The director of its first film was, improbably, Orson Welles. He was asked by Nelson Rockefeller, director of the State Department's propaganda program in Latin America, to go to Brazil to make a film that would demonstrate U.S. friendship with countries south of the border.

As it turned out, Welles's film had almost nothing to do with hemispheric solidarity. It had three sequences: the carnival in Rio de Janeiro, a farm boy and a bull, and a perilous 1,600-mile raft voyage by four fishermen to present their grievances to the government in Rio de Janeiro. What the production also had were some brilliant flashes of Orson Welles's film-making genius. For many reasons, including Welles's mercurial personality, the film was not released at the time. Its footage was recovered from a film archive in the 1990s and made available under the enigmatic title of *It's All True*.[30]

By the early 1950s, USIA had assembled the largest library of documentary films in the world, acquiring them from a variety of sources. About 40 percent of the films in its inventory were produced by U.S. film companies under contract to the agency. Other commercial films were acquired because they fitted the agency's program needs.[31] Most USIA films, however, were produced abroad by USIS posts, using local commercial facilities or, in a few large posts, the post's own film-production units.

The agency's film division in Washington oversaw production of a remarkable series of films covering a wide range of subjects. Some described general aspects of the American experience. *And Now, Miguel* portrayed life on a New Mexican sheep ranch, focusing on a family of Mexican descent. *The Numbers Begin at the River* was an evocative depiction of life in a small Iowa town. Over and above its stunning scenes of the American West, *American Cowboy* gave foreign audiences a factual corrective to the shoot-'em-up westerns produced by Hollywood.

Other films aimed to make a specific political point. One of these was *Nine from Little Rock*, which won an Oscar as best documentary in 1964 for its balanced portrayal of a racial crisis involving the admittance of nine black children to a previously all-white high school. The agency's Washington film division also made dozens of films on such themes as peaceful uses of atomic energy and U.S. disarmament efforts, as well as on anticommunist themes. *Poles Are Stubborn People*, produced in the 1980s, described popular resistance to Soviet domination in Poland.

At times, the agency overreached itself in its political films. The Vietnam War provided one example with films aimed at explaining the U.S. role in the war. The project's troubles started in 1965 when a U.S. correspondent in Vietnam came across a film crew faking a battle scene, using soldiers from a South Vietnamese army unit.[32] In the ensuing uproar, production was closed down. Despite later attempts to revive the project, the film, entitled *Vietnam, Vietnam,* was eventually shelved after $250,000 had been spent on it.[33]

Other efforts to use film for political messages enjoyed greater success. During the 1956 uprising of the Hungarians against Soviet occupation troops, the agency's film division produced a documentary on the event two days after the first newsreel footage of the revolt arrived in Washington. The division prepared twenty-seven different language versions of the film for shipment to overseas posts within seven days.[34]

USIA also went into the newsreel business. At the Washington level, this included a project, code-named "Kingfish," in which news clips selected by the agency were inserted unattributed into a Hearst Metrotone commercial newsreel distributed extensively abroad. The project was discontinued in 1967 after a long run. Meanwhile, local USIS posts in Greece, Iran, and other countries developed similar arrangements for providing news footage, most of it produced by the post, to local newsreel companies. These projects were phased out by the 1970s, primarily because television coverage of current events was displacing newsreels.

Many posts continued to produce their own documentary films, dealing with such local subjects as U.S. economic aid projects. USIS information officers found themselves in the unfamiliar role of film producers. Hundreds of such films were made, usually with makeshift equipment. What these productions lacked in Hollywood finesse, they made up in their popularity with local audience interested in seeing images of their own society.

USIS films were distributed in various ways. The most common outlet was the post's film-lending library, where individuals and organizations could simply check out the items they wanted. Other film requests were handled by mail. USIA documentaries were also shown in commercial movie houses abroad, particularly in Asia, Africa, and Latin America. Theater owners liked them because they were free and usually dubbed in the local language.

The most innovative distribution system involved film showings in outlying districts, often hundreds of miles from the USIS post. The delivery methods were varied. For years, USIS in Bangkok delivered films and other media products upcountry via an old-fashioned steam engine dubbed the Casey Jones Special.[35] Riverboat delivery was common in Asia, Africa, and Latin America. The most widely used distribution method in outlying areas was by Jeep. The Jeep Willys company developed a special model for this purpose in the late 1940s. The rugged vehicles, called mobile units, had a reinforced roof that could be used as a platform for a projectionist, elevating him and his projector above the heads of the audience in a town square at night. From there he could show the film on a wall or a portable screen. By the 1950s, over 350 USIA mobile units roamed the world's outbacks.[36]

At times, the only available area for showing films was an open field. I once set up a film show in a jungle clearing outside Banderban in the Chittagong Hill Tracts on the Burmese-Bangladesh border. The show drew an audience of five thousand Bohmong tribesmen, including their chief, Mong Shwe Prue, and his entourage of lesser tribal officials. When USIS officers were not showing films, they used the Jeeps to distribute publications, set up small exhibits, and make calls on local officials, as mentioned earlier.

USIA's global expansion in the Cold War decades coincided with that of a major new information medium—television. From the flickering black-and-white screens of the early 1950s to the satellite transmissions of the present day, TV emerged as a political force on a global scale. Its programs opened a window through which billions of people received their impressions of the outside world at large. The U.S. television industry led the way in setting the pace and content of television abroad. Its success in establishing the medium as a channel for commercial advertising overwhelmed the efforts of overseas governments to control local television broadcasting as they had done with radio. By 1980, television operations in most countries were either completely commercial or a mix of government-owned and private stations.

Moreover, TV programming abroad was heavily weighted in favor of popular U.S. programs, particularly in prime time. Hollywood and the New York networks were highly successful in marketing *I Love Lucy* and other lightweight productions overseas. This influence extended to news programming, particularly after the introduction of satellite-based international networks, beginning with CNN, in the 1980s.

Television was an orphan operation at USIA's Washington headquarters for many years. In part this was due to congressional reluctance to provide adequate funds for TV production. Bureaucratic disputes also stood in the way as the agency's film division sought control over television operations. This impasse ended in 1965 when then-director Leonard Marks gave equal status to television operations within a revamped film and TV division.[37] For the first time, studio facilities and production funds were available to produce made-for-television programs. Among the first productions were a series of half-hour documentaries, *Report from America*, which were shown on TV stations in over seventy countries overseas.

Agency TV producers followed this up with a Spanish-language soap opera, *Nuestro Barrio*, produced in Mexico City using well-known local actors. *Nuestro Barrio* ("Our Neighborhood") focused on a family in a poor district in an unnamed Latin American city. The series described the way the barrio dealt with its economic and social problems in ways that related subtly to U.S. policies in Latin America. The program featured good guys and bad guys—noble doctors and priests along with reactionary oligarchs opposed to change and opportunists with communist leanings who sought to exploit the barrio's inhabitants. It also contained a lot of emotional drama, including a muted touch of sex.[38]

Nuestro Barrio was a long-running success throughout the region. In Mexico, it ran on thirteen stations in prime time, capturing almost 90 percent of the audience. The program was later dubbed in Portuguese for showing in Brazil. USIA built on the show's success by creating a companion radio program along with a *Nuestro Barrio* comic book series.

Overseas, USIS post involvement in television was limited largely to placing Washington-produced products on local stations. However, a few posts successfully produced their own programs. In Morocco, USIS post director Ed Roberts, a former United Press foreign correspondent, persuaded the local station to run a children's prime-time show, *Uncle Awad's Friends Club*. Uncle Awad was Awad Hanna, an Arab-American living in Rabat, who dealt with such *Sesame Street* subjects as brushing your teeth and doing your homework. He also included many discreet but favorable references to contemporary life in the United States. Although the program was ostensibly aimed at children, it drew the largest adult listenership in its Saturday-night time slot.[39]

Uncle Awad's Friends Club was a somewhat offbeat example of how USIS information offices used media to reach local audiences around the world. Most of these efforts focused on current events, with an emphasis on those that affected U.S. strategic interests. Like Uncle Awad's TV show, other media programs emphasized positive images of contemporary American life and ideas. This task was expanded in the longer-range activities of cultural programs organized by USIA across the globe, the subject of the next chapter.

Notes

    1. Wilson Dizard, *The Strategy of Truth* (Washington, D.C.: Public Affairs Press, 1962), pp. 137–140.

    2. Fitzhugh Green, *American Propaganda Abroad* (New York: Hippocrene Books, 1988), p. 55.

    3. The incident, and its implications, is described in: Albert Bremel, "The Split Personality of USIA," *Harper's Magazine,* September 1965, p. 122.

    4. Dizard, *The Strategy of Truth*, p. 52.

    5. "Ambassador Does Column for USIS India Paper," *USIA Correspondent,* January 1967, p. 3.

    6. "U.S. Ambassador Is Closing the Gap with Japan," *New York Times,* March 31, 1962, p. C-3.

7. The incident is described in: Harry Kendall, *A Farm Boy in the Foreign Service: Telling America's Story to the World* (Berkeley, Calif.: Kendall Publications, 2003), p. 137.

8. Lee Dinsmore, "Communications: Kirkuk," *Foreign Service Journal,* January 1994, p. 60.

9. "The Wireless File—The Way We Were," *USIA World,* May 1983, p. 4.

10. "The Washington/Wireless File: Long Yet Alive," *State Magazine,* May 2002, pp. 15–19.

11. Ibid., p. 19.

12. "Shopping List of Undiplomatic Behavior," *Washington Post,* March 8, 1996, p. 1.

13. "Report of the Overseas Operations of the United States Government by Hon. Allen G. Ellender." U.S. Senate document No. 31, 85th Congress, 1st session, March 4, 1957, pp. 289–299.

14. Philomena Jurey, "With the Traveling White House Press Corps," *USIA World,* February 1978, p. 4.

15. "A Diplomatic Star with a Singular Style," *New York Times,* January 20, 2002, p. 6.

16. For the origins of this trend, see: William H. Read, *America's Mass Media Merchants* (Baltimore, Md.: Johns Hopkins University Press, 1976); Jeremy Tunstall (ed.), *The Media Are American,* Communications and Society Series (London: Constable, 1977).

17. "The Mass Media," *Economist* (London), February 29, 1992, p. 17.

18. "USIA's Media Guaranty Program Dies in Senate Anti-Aid Flare-up," *Washington Post,* June 13, 1967, p. A-19.

19. "Communist Notes," Report No. R-97-64, USIA Office of Research, July 16, 1964. The Polish magazine *Radio I Telewizja,* which published the information, also deplored the presence of American TV programs because, among other factors, they "imposed upon children the ideal of the American hero."

20. "USIA Press Budget Items Are Scrutinized," *Editor & Publisher,* April 13, 1957, p. 23.

21. Wilson P. Dizard, *Old Media, New Media,* 3rd ed. (New York: Longman, 2000), pp. 11–12.

22. "Telling America's Story Through Press and Publications," USIA Office of Public Information, 1960.

23. "The Magazine for India: Success That Continues," *USIA World,* October 1985, p. 13.

24. "Rent You a Copy of America Illustrated?" *USIA World,* November 1973, p. 4.

25. "115 Million Leaflets Dropped on North Vietnam," *USIA Correspondent,* March 1966, p. 9.

26. "Ex-Problems," *Economist* (London), May 16, 1992, p. 58.

27. Vladimir Osopov, "Problems That Occupy *Problems of Communism,*" *World Marxist Review* (Moscow), no 1, January 1973, pp. 95–102.

28. Dizard, *The Strategy of Truth,* p. 88. Stalin's visitor was Wendell Willkie, the 1940 Republican presidential candidate.

29. "Hollywood Flourishes, Its Colonies Languish," *Economist* (London), November 4, 1978, pp. 85–88.

30. The story of Welles's Latin American venture is told in: "Going South," *New Yorker,* November 1, 1993, pp. 122–125.

31. Roger W. Tubby, "Industry Communications Programs in Support of U.S. Foreign Policy," in Urban G. Whitaker (ed.), *Propaganda and International Relations,* Chandler Studies in International and Intercultural Relations (San Francisco, Calif.: Chandler Publishing Co., 1960), p. 68.

32. "USIA Bars Staged Battle Scenes for Vietnam Film," *New York Times,* January 14, 1965, p. 8.

33. "$250,000 USIA Film on Vietnam, 3 Years in Making, Being Shelved," *New York Times,* June 10, 1971, p. 6.

34. Dizard, *The Strategy of Truth,* p. 97.

35. "USIS Thailand Team Roughs It Aboard Casey Jones Special," *U.S. Information Agency News,* December 1956, p. 5.

36. "The Film Program of the United States Information Agency," USIA Office of Public Information, 1955, p. 9.

37. "Marks Combines Motion Picture, TV Services," *USIA Correspondent,* October 1965, p. 1.

38. "A Latin Audience for a USIA Drama," *Washington Post,* April 8, 1966, p. 19.

39. "Uncle Awad Aids U.S. in Morocco," *New York Times,* September 4, 1965, p. 8.

9

The Delicate Art of Exporting Culture

"IN THE FOUR QUARTERS of the globe, who reads an American book? Goes to an American play? Or looks at an American picture or statue? What does the world yet owe to American physicians or surgeons? What new substance have their chemists discovered?" Posed in 1820 by the English critic Sidney Smith,[1] these questions have long since been answered in the centrifugal explosion of U.S. arts and sciences across the globe.

This impact often unsettles intellectuals in older societies. As U.S. cultural influence surged after World War II, French writer Jean Paul Sartre warned his countrymen: "If France allows itself to be influenced by the whole of American culture, a living and livable situation there will come here and shatter our cultural traditions."[2] His concern reflected the potency of U.S. influence with which even Americans are reluctant to credit it. It also mirrored a sense of the inadequacy within traditional cultures in dealing with the current rush of global changes.

These attitudes deepened as the U.S. role in the arts and sciences spread. Overwhelmingly, this shift resulted from the overseas expansion of private organizations, led by the mass-media industries, corporations, and academia. A more recent influence has been the emergence of activist nongovernmental organizations (NGOs) with worldwide political agendas that range from defending human rights to protecting tropical forests. A 1999 United Nations survey identified almost thirty thousand NGOs involved in international issues, including a disproportionate representation by U.S. groups.[3]

USIA's small but special role in this expansion involved a subtle balancing act in presenting American society. At one level, the agency's mass-media programs often reflected the brash and flashy images of

American life as projected by Hollywood and other commercial media channels. At another level, it offered a more balanced view of U.S. society, one that went beyond the glitzy images often projected by the populist media.

These activities were identified within USIA as "cultural," as opposed to "informational." The distinction was never quite clear-cut. Both programs played off each other in agency programs overseas. In the early postwar years, information programs dominated. By 1950, so-called cultural programs came into their own, largely because of Cold War pressures, including a growing perception of the need to counter what was then seen as the attraction of Marxist-Leninist ideas, particularly within intellectual circles abroad. The 1948 Smith-Mundt Act, authorizing a permanent overseas ideological effort, acknowledged this by specifically identifying cultural operations as part of a strategy of presenting (in the bill's phrase) a full and fair picture of the United States.

Other factors figured in this decision. As cultural critic William H. White noted at the time: "No one ever puts it quite this boldly, but there lurks deep in some American breasts the feeling that there is a mystically beneficial quality in certain of our folkways and that if they were only exported the chasm in understanding would be bridged."[4] Our heavens-to-Betsy protestations about not wanting to impose our ideas on the rest of the world may convince us, but our foreign critics know better. No society ships trillions of dollars abroad, tens of millions of tourists, and thousands of Hollywood-style films without leaving a cultural mark, whether it intends to or not.

USIA faced special problems in providing a credible view of a vastly complex American scene. To begin with, no accepted dogma guided its cultural operations. Of all the world's nations, the United States was and is the most resistant to the idea of mandarins setting the cultural tone and direction of the whole society. The power of such cultural arbiters is eroding in the face of global pressures, but they remain a powerful force in many overseas cultures. The United States has its own self-appointed mandarin groups—thousands of them. Therein lies the rub: none have the final say.

Few things confuse foreign intellectuals about the American cultural community so much as its lack of coteries. Although U.S. academics and artists have their favorite cultural watering holes, they are usually widely dispersed and self-sufficient. "Even in New York," British writer C. P. Snow once noted, "distinguished literary figures show a cheerful unawareness of each other's existence." This absence of an elite network that sets the cultural rules explains why there are no rigidly defined "American schools" of painters, poets, philosophers, or musicians and other cultural groups.

As a result, the United States does not rely on a mandarin seal of approval to guide its overseas cultural efforts. In defending this approach, the U.S. rebuttal was often statistical, pointing out that we have more art galleries, libraries, opera houses, and community theaters than any other nation on earth, what cultural critic Sylvia Wright once called "the 659-symphonic groups approach to U.S. culture."[5]

USIA's mandate was to project a multilayered, pluralistic society, continually debating its shape and purpose. Inevitably, the agency fell short in this effort, in part because it lacked sufficient program resources to carry out its cultural mandate. More important, the agency was constantly embroiled in disputes about the way it went about this task, pressured by different groups pushing their particular views on national culture and purpose. This included a steady pattern of congressional criticism of USIA cultural operations, including attempts to control them through budgetary restrictions. The outsized example of this was the objection to agency-sponsored exhibits of modern art.

Despite these controversies, USIA mounted a complex range of programs that covered the spectrum of U.S. artistic and academic accomplishments. In doing so, it helped reverse a long tradition of discouraging official involvement in cultural matters, particularly at the international level. The subject received scant attention until 1938, when the State Department created a small Division of Cultural Relations. Its limited programs were suspended during World War II, with little chance of being revived at war's end. This prospect changed when Congress passed the Fulbright Act of 1946, authorizing an exchange-of-persons program funded by the sale of war surplus equipment to foreign governments. For the first time, cultural operations were on the foreign affairs agenda in a significant way.[6] The cultural division at the State Department was expanded and USIS posts overseas were assigned the job of managing Fulbright exchanges and other cultural projects.

This arrangement raised a problem. Most countries organized their international cultural and media operations separately, on the theory that cultural programs should not be tainted by political propaganda. The United States took a different approach, managing both aspects of its ideological operations—cultural and media—in a single embassy unit, the U.S. Information Service. In 1953, the Eisenhower administration chose to separate the two functions in Washington—USIA for mass media and other information programs and a new Bureau of Educational and Cultural Affairs in the State Department. The arrangement ended in

1979, when the State Department's cultural functions were transferred to USIA.[7]

The integration of information and cultural operations at USIS posts during the Cold War decades worked well. The public affairs officer could plan and deploy a full range of resources in pursuing an overall program strategy without considering largely artificial distinctions between "information" and "culture." In a typical post, the workload was divided pragmatically between information and cultural units, with a considerable amount of organizational incest between the two.

Cultural relations raise images of tweedy intellectuals and high thoughts. These were indeed part of the USIA style, but day-to-day its overseas cultural operations involved complex organizational projects. Their managers—usually identified in public as cultural attachés—were a varied group, drawn largely from academia. In the relatively short history of U.S.-government cultural operations abroad, no one ever identified precisely what they were supposed to do. The most effective thing the best of them did was to move around in local egghead circles, dealing (as a USIS cultural officer, John Brown, once noted) with "the most inconceivable variety of people . . . on the most inconceivable variety of subjects, from Etruscan archeology to Pop Art, from early U.S. coins to old age security. You're supposed to be an expert and interested in all of them. You're the Cultural Attaché, aren't you?"[8]

John Brown served as cultural officer in Paris in the postwar years. A writer with strong academic qualifications, he was an American readily accepted by otherwise skeptical French intellectuals. His credentials for the job were matched by many other cultural officers. Playwright Thornton Wilder served in Belgrade immediately after World War II. Frank Snowden Jr., chairman of Howard University's classics department, was cultural attaché in Rome in the mid-1960s. Duncan Emrich, who headed the folklore division at the Library of Congress, served in Greece and India. In Tokyo, Glen Shaw was inducted into the Japanese government's pantheon of "living cultural treasures," a tribute to his knowledge of the Japanese language and culture, including a flair for composing haiku verse.

Whatever their credentials, cultural officers were managers of a broad spectrum of projects offering insights into American life and ideas. Their responsibilities included USIS libraries, cultural centers, English courses, lecture series, book publishing, and exhibits. They were also key players in the most successful ideological project carried out by the U.S. government in the Cold War years—an exchange-of-persons program that involved the largest movement of academics, artists, and other professionals ever undertaken by one country to expand cultural relations with other societies.

In chronicling USIA cultural activities abroad, the library network played a special role. It was often the most visible presence of the United States in cities and towns on all continents. The agency operated more than two hundred libraries, either under its own sponsorship or in cooperative arrangements with local groups. The system's origins dated back to 1942, when the State Department established the Benjamin Franklin Library in Mexico City as a joint venture with the American Library Association. The Franklin Library continues to thrive six decades later. The library network spread rapidly in the early postwar years, particularly in Asia and Africa. It was often the first official U.S. presence in some Asian and African countries: the library in Nepal opened its doors six years before a U.S. embassy was established in Kathmandu.[9]

Accessibility accounted for the success of the USIS libraries. Unlike most foreign libraries, they had open shelves and the customers could take books home. This was a new idea in most overseas cities, particularly in the early postwar years. This transfer of U.S. library practices abroad not only spread American ideas, it also provided a working example of how a democratic society educates itself.

Credit for the effectiveness of the USIS libraries belongs to the talented group of professionals recruited to run them. Most were women, although their ranks included men like Jim Hulbert, a lean, lank Tennesseean who ran USIS libraries in France and Pakistan. (He was also one of the first African-American librarians in the service.) One librarian, Zelma Graham, was a legend in the business. In 1948, she opened the first USIS library in Burma, housed in a former British bank building in downtown Rangoon. Its brightly painted, light-filled rooms became as much a part of the city's life as its temples and canals. Reporting on Zelma Graham's library, a *New York Times* correspondent wrote: "Without fuss or fanfare, it has made thousands of friends for the United States in a part of the world where people automatically suspect and distrust the motives of the West. . . . It exemplifies the kind of aid which Asian countries really welcome."[10]

Another USIS librarian, Emily Dean, a gentle grandmotherly type, played a special role in introducing professional standards in Turkey in the early 1950s, first in USIS and then in the wider community. Officials at the Turkish national library sought her advice on their own collection. Upon her return from the meeting she described her experience to a staff meeting. "I was shocked," she declared. "They catalog their books by *size:* the big books here, the small books there and the middle-sized ones in between." Emily Dean's visit led to the adoption of the Dewey decimal system in Turkish libraries. She also trained local librarians, as did USIS librarians in other parts of the world. Jim Hulbert, mentioned above, gave the first course in library science at the University of Dhaka in Pakistan.

The USIS libraries offered all the services of their stateside counterparts, from bookmobiles to book boxes shipped to schools and cultural centers in outlying areas. Library visitors fingered magazines and other periodicals into shreds. The most pawed-over publications were the Sears Roebuck and Montgomery Ward mail-order catalogues. They were also the most likely publications to be stolen, a formidable undertaking given their bulk. In Berlin, this problem was resolved by chaining the catalogues to a desk. In Helsinki, they were put into hardbound covers and catalogued as reference books.

Another heavily used library service was the reference desk. In the larger libraries, the reference sections served walk-in customers as well as those who sent in queries by phone or by mail. From small beginnings, the reference center at the USIS library in London was upgraded with computer-based facilities to handle the twenty-five thousand queries it received every year, most from media companies and government agencies.[11]

Posts in larger cities sponsored libraries for special audiences. The best known of these was the Centre Culturel Américain, on the Rue Dragon in the university quarter of Paris. Opened in 1958, the center's library, music collection, films, and lectures soon attracted over four hundred students daily. "It is easy to find out why they go, because they know and state the reason," a *New Yorker* correspondent wrote. "They go because it is free, because they are interested in the United States, and because they think what comes from the States is bound to be stimulating, new, valuable, and different from what comes from the rest of the world."[12]

USIS libraries presented a challenge to the agency's congressional mandate to present "a full and fair picture of the United States." This principle suffered grievously during the 1953 McCarthy investigation's attempts to purge the libraries of alleged un-American materials. Some books were actually burned.[13] It took years of bureaucratic dithering before a reasonable policy was worked out. This happened in 1970 with a decision to give USIS public affairs officers at each post wide discretion in ordering books, subject only to the "full and fair picture" rubric.[14] This did not end further attempts, particularly by Congress, to dictate book-selection policy, but the subject faded into the background.

Censorship by foreign governments presented a problem from time to time. Thailand once censored a travel book because it described Bangkok as being known for its Buddhist temples and prostitutes.[15] For years, the Republic of China in Taiwan insisted that any photos of Chinese Communist leaders in imported magazines be stamped with the word "bandit." USIS posts resisted these restrictions in most cases. An exception occurred in Syria in 1967 when the USIS post agreed to black out references to Israel in its library's books. (One of my books in the library, *Television—A World View*, had references to Israel covered over with brown paper.) The practice was halted soon thereafter, but the precedent was unfortunate.[16]

Another USIA-sponsored outlet for cultural activities was the global network of binational centers. A board of directors that included local leaders, resident Americans, and the USIS cultural attaché ran these joint ventures. The first such center was set up in Rio de Janeiro in 1937. Nelson Rockefeller picked up the idea as part of his efforts to strengthen inter-American cultural ties in the early 1940s.[17] The centers flourished throughout Latin America; by the 1960s there were 113 in nineteen countries. USIA usually subsidized the binational centers to the extent of providing an American director and an English-teaching specialist. Most of the centers were otherwise self-supporting. The São Paulo, Brazil, center had its own seventeen-story building, with classroom space for over six thousand students, a theater, lecture halls, a restaurant, and an extensive library.

The Latin American centers were replicated, with variations, in other regions. Manila's Thomas Jefferson Center was founded in 1945, a month after the end of World War II. Athens has its Hellenic-American Union. A number of the Amerika Haus cultural centers set up by the U.S. Army in Germany during the postwar occupation remained in place as locally controlled organizations. In Thailand, the center was founded by an American University Alumni Association with USIA help.

Most of the binational centers relied on revenues from teaching English to sustain their cultural activities. Over the years, USIA officials were ambivalent about whether they should be in the English-teaching business at all. It was a big and growing commercial business overseas in the postwar decades, in response to the intense demands to learn the language. Should USIS posts compete with them? The decision favored a role for the agency. English had become, in both real and symbolic terms, the mother tongue of modern democracy and freedom. There were, in short, good reasons to include language as part of the ideological projection of U.S. strategic interests.

USIA went about this task in two ways. The first involved promoting the language at the mass level. In the 1950s, the Voice of America began broadcasting news in what it called "special English," using a vocabulary limited to about twelve hundred words and speaking them v-e-r-y s-l-o-w-l-y. It was boring stuff, but it caught on with listeners overseas who responded to the VOA's offer of a free "Special English" dictionary. Scripts and tapes of the programs were made available to schools.

The agency's major emphasis, however, was on improving the skills of teachers of English, many of whom had only a limited grasp of the language and no training in how to teach it. A USIA English-teaching division was created in the 1950s to prepare teaching guides and packets of short textbook lessons based on American themes. By the 1960s, the unit was also sponsoring over one hundred seminars abroad each year to help English teachers in dozens of countries improve their skills. At its height, the seminar program involved eight thousand teachers a year worldwide.[18] In 1963, the agency also began publishing *English Teaching Forum,* a quarterly publication sent to over eighty thousand teachers overseas. *Forum* soon became the leading professional magazine in its field. It is still published and can be subscribed to at a State Department web site (www.exchanges.state.gov/forum).

English-teaching programs and USIS libraries served as important channels for spreading American ideas through books. Equally important was the agency's role in producing and distributing books on a mass scale, under its own auspices or in cooperative programs with U.S. publishing companies. Its activities proved critical during the postwar decades in making American books a familiar commodity overseas for the first time, particularly in Asia, Africa, and Latin America.

In the years before 1950, U.S. book exports were a negligible factor in global markets. European publishers dominated the trade, particularly the British and the French. It was not until the 1960s that overseas sales by U.S. publishers exceeded those of a much smaller number of British firms.[19] The U.S. share of the market continued to expand to the point where U.S. book exports now dominate in most overseas markets, either through direct sales or cooperative agreements with foreign publishers.

In large part, this resulted from the publishers' own efforts to promote their wares abroad. But their success owed a lot to the parallel effort of USIA to produce and distribute American books. The agency was the biggest single buyer and distributor of books internationally in the early postwar decades. (Its challenger for this claim was the Soviet government's overseas propaganda program's book-promotion efforts, whose size was a classified secret.) In one year, 1965, USIA distributed over 15 million books for its own libraries, for presentations to individuals and organizations, and for its own publications programs, in which books, in English and in translations, were sold commercially. In this latter category, the agency pioneered the marketing of low-priced paperbacks abroad.

USIA supplemented its own book publication and distribution programs by subsidizing the overseas expansion of U.S. commercial publishers. This strategy had the effect of jump-starting the entry of these publishers into new markets, particularly in developing countries. By the start of the twenty-first century, the volume of foreign sales of U.S. books was over $1.8. billion a year.[20] This commercial expansion also benefited from the parallel activities of USIA book production and distribution programs. The agency's program focused on works that presented a broad picture of American life. American literature was high on the list—from Henry David Thoreau to J. D. Salinger. There was also a heavy emphasis on history, biography, science, and government. Books documenting the faults and failings of communism were a special category. These and other works were translated into over seventy-five languages. Millions of books in basic English, known as "Ladder Books," described American life and culture.

Another specialized series consisted of books published in French by a small agency unit based in Paris. The group, known as the African Regional Service, published and distributed over eight hundred U.S. paperback titles for sale in African and Middle Eastern countries where French was still an important second language.[21]

Inevitably, disputes arose about the way USIA selected the books it produced and distributed. These included complaints about works that contained a naughty word or two. Other protests focused on the agency's alleged failure to sufficiently emphasize hard-hitting anticommunist themes in its book programs.

The biggest controversy involved an ill-considered USIA decision to commission authors to write books that directly supported specific U.S. foreign policy themes because such works were often not available in commercial publishers' lists. The project became publicly controversial in the 1960s when it was discovered that the books were being sold in U.S. bookstores, in addition to being distributed abroad. This raised protests about a Washington bureaucracy that was covertly propagandizing its own citizens.[22]

The chief congressional critic of the "book development program" was Arkansas senator J. William Fulbright. A caustic critic of U.S.

involvement in Vietnam, the senator denounced the agency's subsidy for two commissioned books supporting the Johnson administration's policies on the conflict. Such projects, Fulbright declared, were "subversive of our system."[23] Fearing a congressional response in the form of cuts in its budget, the agency stopped subsidizing books that might wind up on the shelves of U.S. bookstores.

Meanwhile, the agency sponsored programs that subsidized book sales by U.S. publishers in the new nations of Africa and Asia. The first of these was the previously noted Information Media Guaranty program that allowed publishers to exchange their earnings from sales in so-called soft currency countries for dollars from a special Treasury Department fund. The program, which also subsidized other media, gave some large U.S. publishers their first significant entrée into Asian, African. and Latin American markets.

Soft-currency funds also helped expand USIS book programs in some countries through the use of local currencies owned by the U.S. government as a result of PL-480 sales of surplus agricultural products.[24] (PL-480 referred to the congressional legislation that authorized such sales.) In India, where these funds totaled billions of dollars, a relatively small but significant amount was turned over to the local USIS post to produce, in cooperation with the Indian government, American textbooks in English and translated editions for schools.

Similar PL-480 projects were undertaken in Indonesia and other Asian countries. The program produced tens of millions of books, which in addition to improving educational resources had two other important consequences. It blunted an enormous effort by the Soviet Union to establish its textbooks as the standard for Asian schools. It also gave U.S. textbook publishers an important initial advantage in what have since become profitable overseas markets.[25]

The agency's most successful book-promotion project, Franklin Publications, was a unique collaboration with U.S. book publishers that began in 1952 and continued for over a quarter of a century. The enterprise was a nonprofit firm based in New York with the explicit mission of setting up publishing firms abroad to print and distribute U.S. books commercially. Franklin's efforts resulted in the publication of tens of thousands of books in hundreds of millions of copies. More important, it gave U.S. publishers a strong base in Asia and the Middle East, where they had never previously sold books.[26] In the early 1950s, when he was U.S. ambassador in India, Chester Bowles had walked into a New Delhi bookstore and discovered that the only U.S. publication on its shelves was an Uncle Wiggily children's book.[27]

USIA played a small but critical role in Franklin's success. The project's New York operations were funded primarily by commercial publishers and by the Ford Foundation and other nonprofit groups. The agency's contribution was largely in sharing its own experience in overseas book publishing with Franklin. It had no say in how Franklin should be run, or what books its local publishers should publish. The result was a healthy collaboration in which all sides benefited—Franklin, the local publishers, and USIA.

I was running USIS operations in East Pakistan (now Bangladesh) when Franklin decided to create a publishing affiliate in the main city, Dhaka. The project was supervised by Franklin's president, Datus Smith, a former director of the Princeton University Press and a man undaunted by the problems involved in dealing with the arcane art of Asian book publishing. His first success was picking a competent local entrepreneur, A.F.M. Abdul Mateen, to manage the new business.

The two men then toured the countryside to sign up booksellers to market Franklin books. There turned out to be a lot of them. Smith later recalled that they visited one town that had three automobiles and a dozen bookstores. Soon Franklin's Dhaka enterprise had a regional network of distributors for its books. One of the early best sellers was Dr. Benjamin Spock's famous book *Baby and Child Care,* adapted in translation by a Pakistani doctor to suit local baby-raising conditions.

The Dhaka project's biggest initial success, one in which USIS played an important role, was negotiating an agreement with local education officials to supply U.S. textbooks, translated in Bengali, to East Pakistani schools. There were some hitches. In discussing a geography book being considered for the project, it turned out that many teachers in the *madrassi* schools attached to local mosques taught that the earth was flat. Franklin declined to modify the textbook to deal with this theory and lost some textbook outlets as a result.

The loss was a minor one. Franklin's Dhaka branch garnered bulk orders from over six thousand grammar and high schools; the titles of the original ninety books in the project ranged from *All About Electricity* to *Lives of Girls Who Became Famous.* The Dhaka textbook project was one of Franklin's earliest successes in educational publishing. Over the years, more than half of its output consisted of U.S. textbooks translated and adapted for use in local schools from kindergartens to universities.

In their first fifteen years of operation, Franklin affiliates in eleven countries published 43 million copies of twenty-five hundred books. This was accomplishment enough, yet at the same time Franklin was laying the foundation for a substantial U.S. book trade in the Middle

East and Asia. A decade after Franklin began operations, American books had captured 70 percent of the translated book market in Arab countries.[28]

Of all USIA cultural operations, none had more profound long-range influence than the agency's role in an extensive exchange-of-persons program during the Cold War decades. In the sixteenth century, the English philosopher Francis Bacon wrote in his magisterial work, *Novo Atlantis,* about the importance of a new kind of traveling scholars he called "merchants of light." No society can be self-sufficient, he declared; it must send out learned men to bring back new ideas from other cultures. In the last half of the twentieth century, Bacon's concept was expanded dramatically in the worldwide exchange of scholars, students, and artists across borders, thanks in part to the new ease of access provided by jet planes.

No country was more heavily affected by this development than the United States. The two-way flow of visitors in and out of the country involved thousands of projects, from the lightweight to the profound. The largest number of these exchanges were sponsored by private groups—universities, foundations, civic associations, labor unions, and professional societies, among others—sending students and others abroad or bringing them here.[29] It was the biggest single movement of people across borders for educational and other cultural purposes.

The federal government provided substantial help to a wide variety of these private exchanges, through direct grants and other subsidies. Dozens of Washington agencies became involved in such programs after World War II. USIA played a special role in the process, particularly in managing a wide range of exchange operations, both public and private, at its posts abroad. The USIS office was often the first stop for foreign students looking into the prospects of studying in the United States. The larger posts had a special section to handle such queries; by the mid-1960s, USIS London's exchange office dealt with over ten thousand visitors a year.

Before 1945, there were few U.S. precedents for funding cultural exchanges with taxpayer dollars. The idea ran against the tradition of American exceptionalism: if foreigners wanted to see the United States, let them pay their own way. For the most part, two-way travel was limited to a relatively few adventurous souls who had the time, money, and inclination to go abroad, or to come here for cultural or educational reasons.

There were some early exceptions to this rule. Best known was the privately financed Rhodes scholarship program that selected thirty-two U.S. students each year to study at Oxford, beginning in 1902. Although many Rhodes scholars later rose to high positions in and out of government, none was more instrumental in establishing a national cultural-exchanges policy than a 1925 University of Arkansas graduate, Senator J. William Fulbright.[30]

Official recognition of exchanges was slow to develop, however. A small but significant breakthrough had taken place in 1905 in the aftermath of the Boxer Rebellion in China. The Boxers, who had sought to end foreign occupation of their country, were forced to pay indemnification for the damage they had done to U.S. and European installations. The U.S. representative in the negotiations was William Woodville Rockhill, whose eclectic career included a tour in the French Foreign Legion, management of a New Mexico beef ranch, and State Department assignments as envoy to Greece, Russia, and China.

As the Boxer negotiations wound down, Rockhill made a unique proposal to President Theodore Roosevelt: set aside half the U.S. share of the Boxer indemnity to provide scholarships for Chinese students in the United States. Roosevelt agreed. The Boxer scholarships brought a small but steady trickle of young Chinese leaders to U.S. universities. Some later played important roles in the creation of the Chinese Republic and in the complex pattern of Sino-American relations for decades after. The Boxer scholarships were a small but auspicious beginning for official U.S. exchange programs.[31]

Thirty years passed, however, before the United States fully acknowledged the role of cultural exchanges in its foreign operations with the 1938 decision to set up a Division of Cultural Relations in the State Department.[32] The division was charged with developing a modest exchange program with Latin American countries but was starved for funds and never operated effectively before Pearl Harbor.

The big change came in 1946. The U.S. military had left mountains of surplus equipment behind overseas after the defeat of Germany and Japan. Senator Fulbright rose from his chair in the Senate chamber to suggest that the equipment be sold to foreign governments and the proceeds used to help fund scholarships for a two-way exchange of foreign and U.S. college students and professors. It was the beginning of the Fulbright program, the best known and most successful U.S. effort to strengthen cultural links with other societies. It also added a new noun, verb, and adjective to dozens of languages abroad: a Fulbrighter is a Fulbright grantee who Fulbrights during his or her study year abroad.

When USIA was created in 1953, it was made the principal administrator of the Fulbright program overseas. A presidentially appointed Foreign Scholarship Board in Washington had the responsibility for selecting U.S. candidates for the program. Binational commissions set local policies and procedures in the more than 135 countries where Fulbright programs have been active.

A master at Oxford's Pembroke College once turned to Senator Fulbright during a symposium and declared: "You are responsible for the largest and most significant movement of scholars across the face of the earth since the fall of Constantinople in 1463."[33] The hyperbole was probably justified. For more than half a century, over a quarter-million academics, artists, and others have benefited from two-way exchanges under the program. Most were anonymous students or scholars who attended classes or taught during their Fulbright year before returning to their home institutions.

Other Fulbrighters became well known in their later careers. Among the prominent foreigners who took part in the program over the years were former UN secretary-general Boutros Boutros-Ghali, British political leader Shirley Williams, writer Umberto Eco, Swedish prime minister Ingvar Carlsson, and Bangladeshi women's activist Salma Shan. U.S. grantees have included composer Aaron Copland, Librarian of Congress James Billington, writers John Updike and Eudora Welty, poet Maya Angelou, actor Stacy Keach, and opera diva Anna Moffo. The daughter of a Pennsylvania shoemaker, Moffo's career blossomed during her study year in Italy. Complimented on her success, she would reply: "Most of all, I thank God for my Fulbright."[34]

The Fulbright program opened new cultural links with many countries, including South Africa. Against the opposition of the white-dominated government, Fulbright grants were made to black scholars. One of them was Makaziwe Mandela, the daughter of Nelson Mandela, who earned a Ph.D. in anthropology from the University of Massachusetts and returned home to a high-profile academic career. In 1996 she was named a Distinguished Fulbright Fellow at ceremonies marking the fiftieth anniversary of the program.

The Fulbright program continues to flourish more than a half century after its modest beginnings in 1946. In its first year, it sponsored a hundred two-way exchanges; currently the number is over four thousand annually. The original funding arrangements, involving the sale of war surplus equipment, have long since been abandoned. About half the program's costs are now underwritten by the U.S. government. The rest is picked up by foreign governments, educational institutions, and the private sector. The cumulative cost of the Fulbright program for U.S. taxpayers over five and a half decades has been about $1.9 billion—quite possibly the best bargain ever in terms of strengthening American ideological outreach abroad.[35]

Senator Fulbright's original 1946 proposal set the pace and tone of all U.S. cultural-exchange programs since. It has been expanded and reshaped to account for changing conditions, but its reputation for contributing to intercultural understanding remains widespread abroad.

A special tribute to the Fulbright legacy took place in the mid-1990s in Ho Chi Minh City, formerly Saigon. As noted earlier, the senator had been a vociferous critic of the Vietnam conflict. In November 1995, a delegation of U.S. government, university, and private-sector representatives visited the city to mark the opening of full-scale cultural relations between the two countries. The ceremonies were held in a new American cultural building aptly named the Fulbright Learning Center.[36]

Beyond the Fulbright scholarships, the most prestigious USIA exchange operation was the International Visitors (IV) program, a bland name for a project targeted at an elite overseas group. From its beginnings a half century ago, the purpose of the IV program was to bring rising young leaders abroad to the United States for a short but intense exposure to American life and ideas. Its success depended on the ability of USIS officers abroad to spot such leaders early on in their careers. The results were mixed: many who were IV grantees returned home and faded into the background. Overall, however, the program's success ratio was high in identifying those who became leaders in their own societies, whether in government, the media, business, or cultural activities.

Among those who rose to high leadership was Hamid Karzai. An obscure young Afghan journalist when he was selected for an IV grant in 1984, he became the first interim president of his country in 2001. During the USIA years, over forty other IV grantees became heads of government or chiefs of state, including Britain's Tony Blair and Margaret Thatcher, Egypt's Anwar Sadat, Tanzania's Julius Nyerere, and Indian prime minister Indira Ghandi.

The pattern of their visits varied. Tours usually lasted about a month. Each IV grantee made up his or her own program, including a personalized itinerary to wherever they wanted to go. Given the shortness of time, most grantees traveled by plane. An exception was Helen Vlachos, who later became publisher of a leading Athens newspaper, *Kathimerini*. She asked for a thirty-day Greyhound bus ticket and visited big and small towns, meeting with mayors, editors, and ordinary citizens, before returning to Greece where, among other accomplishments, she played an important role in the 1970s in bringing down an authoritarian government led by army officers.

Other USIA-managed exchange programs were built around specialized subjects. One of these is the East-West Center at the University of Hawaii, where thousands of U.S. and Asian students and researchers have come together since 1965 for cross-cultural studies. Alumni of the center now make up a major portion of the international-studies faculties at universities in the Pacific region.

A similar gathering place, oriented toward cultural ties between Europe and the United States, is the Salzburg Seminar in Austria. It began as a pie-in-the-sky idea, dreamed up by a group of Harvard students in 1947. Their determination resulted in a cultural center that has provided a meeting place for over twenty thousand scholars and others since then. The seminar's emphasis is on short conferences, some no longer than a week, at its headquarters, the Schloss Leopoldskron, a resplendent palace where the 1960s musical, *The Sound of Music,* was filmed. The seminar played a special role in allowing East European scholars to meet with their Western counterparts during the difficult years of communist rule in their countries. More recently, participation has been widened to include cultural and academic grantees from the Middle East and Asia.[37]

Increasingly during the postwar decades, privately funded exchange programs supplemented those of the federal government. Nevertheless, Washington agencies remained actively engaged. By the 1990s, thirty-eight agencies managed 130 overseas exchange programs with over 120,000 annual participants and a total budget of $1.6 billion. USIA was the largest federal sponsor of these programs, accounting for 27 percent of their participants.[38] In 1999, the agency's responsibilities for managing exchange operations overseas were transferred to the State Department.[39]

Several attempts were made over the years to bring some order to these diverse (and often overlapping) government exchange programs. The most serious effort was an International Education Act sponsored by the Johnson administration in the late 1960s. The legislation proposed consolidating overseas educational programs, scattered through several dozen agencies, into one integrated effort. The idea was viewed suspiciously by most members of Congress, including Senator Fulbright, who saw it as an attempt to take the shine off his own exchange program. The bill was eventually buried in a swirl of accusations that it was a piece of do-gooder foreign aid legislation that had few benefits for the average member's home district.[40]

Foreign students have always made up the largest proportion of U.S. exchanges. By the turn of the century, about a half-million of them were studying at U.S. schools. Most students are funded by their families or through an intricate system of scholarships, many of them arranged through the New York–based Institute of International Education. All together, foreign students spend about $11 billion annually, making higher education America's fifth-highest service export.[41] Fewer U.S. students study abroad, but their number (about 130,000) has doubled in recent years.[42]

Getting admitted to a U.S. university is a long, painstaking process for most overseas students. Many resort to ingenious tactics. The classic example involved a young Pole, Jerzy Kosinski, who came to New York in the 1960s through a ruse that he later described as "my greatest invention." In Warsaw, he had invented four nonexistent U.S. professors, wrote letters for each in which they recommended that he be given a plane ticket and the money needed to accept a fictional foundation grant in the United States. The documents were convincing enough for a consular officer at the U.S. embassy to give him a student visa. Arriving in New York, Kosinski successfully applied to the Ford Foundation for a graduate scholarship at Columbia University. He went on to become a distinguished novelist, winning a National Book Award for one book, *Steps,* and high praise for another, *Being There,* which was made into a brilliant Peter Sellers movie.[43]

Overall, there is an interesting imbalance in the current foreign student pattern at U.S. schools. Not counting Canada, the largest single national representation comes from China. The biggest regional group comes from Russia and Eastern Europe. Africa is seriously underrepresented, accounting for about 5 percent of the total despite public and private efforts to boost scholarship aid for students there.[44]

The postwar exchange programs developed by USIA, other federal agencies, and the private sector laid the groundwork for the United States' current strong presence in global education. This trend has been reinforced in recent decades by the spread of overseas study centers by U.S. colleges and universities, building on a tradition begun over a century ago by the American University of Beirut and Tokyo's International University.

This overseas expansion has led to charges that the U.S. educational model, particularly in higher education, is stifling other cultures. "Uniform education leads to a uniform world," French cultural minister Claude Allegre declared in 2000. "That our students go to the United States . . . is entirely desirable, but that Americans install their universities throughout the world, all on the same model, and with the same courses, is a catastrophe."[45] His comments, though overwrought, underline the influence that U.S. higher education now has abroad.

Academic exchanges in the postwar decades were supplemented by expanded overseas programs for the performing arts—music, dance, theater, graphic arts, and even sports. As with educational programs, little consideration was given to the idea of U.S. government support for these activities abroad before World War II. This indifference changed as Washington officials began to see how effective the performing arts could be in advancing ideological strategy.

A major turning point was the 1951 decision by U.S. occupation authorities in Germany to ask the State Department to provide a performing troupe for Berlin's first postwar cultural festival. Their purpose was to reinforce the U.S. presence in a city divided between Allied and Soviet forces. The department agreed to send a production of the Rodgers and Hammerstein musical *Oklahoma,* which was a rousing success. *Oklahoma* was followed by an equally acclaimed performance of *Medea,* featuring Judith Anderson, a leading actress of the time.

Washington made no immediate move, however, to mount a large-scale overseas arts program, which would have required a strong effort to convince a suspicious Congress to appropriate money for such a project. This obstacle was eventually overcome by what, in retrospect, was a brilliant ploy by the Eisenhower administration, tied to the president's frequent references to the need for what he called people-to-people diplomacy. In 1956 the White House asked Congress to fund what it called "the President's special international program." Most of the money was to be allocated for U.S. exhibits at industrial trade shows abroad—an idea that appealed to Congress. But the bill also called for modest funds to underwrite the foreign tours of American performing arts groups and individuals.

Eisenhower's stamp of approval for the performing-arts proposal was good enough for the Republicans who controlled Congress at the time. Passage of the legislation opened the way for one of the most effective operations managed by USIA in the Cold War years. Hundreds of individuals and groups were sent abroad, including the New York Philharmonic, American Ballet Theater, the Dave Brubeck jazz quartet, Duke Ellington and his orchestra, the Jose Limon dance company, the University of Minnesota student theater, and several repertory companies presenting plays from *The Grapes of Wrath* to *The Glass Menagerie.* Audience reactions were uniformly favorable, although at times with an unexpected twist. What impressed Polish audiences viewing *The Grapes of Wrath,* over and above the play's artistry, was that unemployed Americans looked for jobs in their own automobiles.

The most successful single event in the new program was a 1957 fifteen-nation concert tour by Marian Anderson in Asia and Europe. "Contralto Marian Anderson won another 8,000 friends here last night," a Hong Kong newspaper declared. "The renowned singer took the hearts and emotions of a shirtsleeved throng of students." A Bangkok music critic wrote: "She brings to all peoples of the world the beauty of music through her God-given voice. She stands as a beacon of light to all, a true daughter of America and a most fitting representative of her people."

USIA posts found themselves in a new business, the care and feeding of large groups of often temperamental artists. Glitches did occur. In Athens, for example, I was in charge of preparations for the arrival of the San Francisco Ballet. The opening performance was planned as a major cultural event, with the king and queen of Greece in attendance. On the day before the opening, I discovered that the ballet scenery had been accidentally routed to a warehouse in Brussels, and the company's musical scores mistakenly sent to Ankara. I reported this to the embassy chargé d'affaires, Samuel Berger. He looked me in the eye and said: "When that curtain goes up tomorrow night, I want to see the scenery on the stage and the music in the orchestra pit. You can do it."

I went out and called the local Belgian airlines office and ordered a plane, in violation of all General Accounting Office regulations, to bring the scenery immediately to Athens. I then called the local CIA station chief and asked him to send the station's airplane to Ankara to pick up the music score. The next night, the curtain went up, the scenery was in place, the music was playing. Sam Berger, seated with the king and queen, looked over at me and winked.

Of all the performing arts programs, jazz made a special impact. In part, this reflected the influence of Willis Conover's VOA jazz programs in acquainting the rest of the world with this special American art form. Jazz icons such as Dizzy Gillespie, Sidney Bechet, Muddy Waters, and Gerry Mulligan all took part in overseas tours under USIA auspices.

The star performer was Louis Armstrong. His 1960 tour of a dozen African countries scored both an artistic and a political triumph. He broke color barriers along the route by his refusal to perform before segregated audiences. In the British colony of Southern Rhodesia (now Zimbabwe), the great "Satchmo" attracted an audience of 75,000 whites and blacks, seated next to each other in a large football stadium. Striding across the stage to play his first number, he looked out at the crowd and said: "It's nice to see *this*." The audience knew what he meant and erupted in applause. Five years later, Armstrong made a similar successful tour in Eastern Europe and the Soviet Union.

USIA had a particular problem in scheduling performing artists in many of its out-of-the-way smaller posts. Cochabamba, Chittagong, and Chiang Mai were important to the agency, but not to musicians, singers, and dancers, who wanted to perform in places like London, Rome, or Tokyo. Dhaka, where I spent several years, was very much off the beaten track for them. One year, we were able to entice only one visiting performer—an American Indian named Tom Two Arrows. Decked out in colorful feathers and beads, he alternately delighted and confused Bengali audiences with his war whoops and dances.

We were more successful the next year, when Washington decided to send us the University of Maine Masquers, a group of enthusiastic and talented young actors. To exploit this opportunity, we promoted Dhaka's first formal drama season in collaboration with local theater groups. The season, alternating American and Bengali plays, was a big success. The British Council, our local counterpart in cultural matters, also joined us with an impressive Bengali-language *Hamlet*.

Taking advantage of the interest stimulated by the University of Maine troupe, USIS helped form a local U.S. drama group, which toured the provinces with such classic plays as Thornton Wilder's *Our Town*. Other USIS posts formed similar groups, often mounting elaborate productions. In Lagos, the American community theater put on the Cole Porter musical *Kiss Me Kate,* which found the U.S. ambassador, Donald Easum, and his wife in the orchestra pit, playing respectively trumpet and flute.

The performing-arts program had its controversial side throughout the Cold War years. Among other critics, playwright Arthur Miller accused USIA and the State Department of manipulating the contents of the productions they sent overseas. Congress often weighed in with critiques that usually focused on alleged improprieties among the touring artists. The revelation that unmarried male and female dancers were sharing hotel rooms during a 1974 Martha Graham dance company tour of Asia set off a flurry of State Department instructions to its embassies along the route, primly laying down rules for assigning rooms. Once, when New York theatrical producer Roger Stevens was testifying before a House of Representative committee in support of the program, he was asked by one congressman whether all ballet dancers were gay. Stevens replied that, while their sexual preferences varied, any of the dancers could throw the congressman through a window.

Congressional support for the overseas performing-arts program tended to fluctuate year to year. In part, this involved attempts by the legislators to bend the program toward their version of how American culture should be represented abroad. This was particularly true of touring exhibits of modern art. It was not difficult for a member of Congress to find something objectionable among the paintings and sculptures selected by the State Department and USIA. In the ensuing controversy, the program's budget usually suffered. At one point in the 1960s, Congress voted only $1.6 million for the program, an amount that barely sustained its activities for the year.

By the 1990s, the cultural-presentations program had largely run its course, a victim of its own success. U.S. artistic productions of all kinds had become familiar in most parts of the world. Equally important, many were commercially self-supporting, obviating the need for federal subsidies. In some instances, private groups, including multinational corporations, have underwritten overseas performances for their own purposes. The arts programs managed by USIA laid the groundwork for this development. The original justification for including these programs in the federal budget tended to emphasize Cold War aims: if the Russians are doing it, we'd better do it.

But these programs involved larger aims, then and now. As stated eloquently by one of the most distinguished U.S. diplomats of the last century, George F. Kennan, cultural exchanges are needed

> just as rain is by the desert and needed . . . for our sakes alone, for our development as individuals and as a nation, lest we fall into complacency, sterility and emotional decay and with it much of the wonder of life itself. . . . Let us by all means have the maximum cultural exchange, even if America had before it no problem whatsoever of outside opinion; even if we had no need of any sort for other people, if all that was concerned was our own development here at home.[46]

Notes

1. Smith made this widely quoted remark in commenting on a book, *Seybest's Annals of the United States,* published in London in 1820.

2. Quoted in Wilson P. Dizard, *The Strategy of Truth: The Story of the U.S. Information Service* (Washington, D.C.: Public Affairs Press, 1961), p. 174.

3. "The Firemen of Africa Feel the Heat of Scrutiny," *Financial Times* (London), August 19, 1999, p. 4.

4. Quoted in Dizard, *The Strategy of Truth,* p. 176.

5. Sylvia Wright, "Self-Consciousness: Culture and the Carthaginians," *The Reporter,* November 25, 1952, p. 34.

6. Frank A. Ninkovich, *The Diplomacy of Ideas: U.S. Foreign Policy and Cultural Relations, 1938–1950* (New York: Cambridge University Press, 1981).

7. Several attempts were made during the USIA years to rearrange the responsibilities of the State Department and USIA, particularly in the cultural area. In the mid-1970s, a high-level panel headed by CBS president Frank Stanton proposed a solution for this problem that was seriously considered in and out of government. However, the panel's recommendations were not adopted.

8. John L. Brown, "But What Do You Do?" *Foreign Service Journal,* June 1964, p. 32.
9. "A Renovated USIA Library," *USIA World,* June 1979, p. 9.
10. Peggy Durdin, "A Model for U.S. Propaganda," *New York Times Magazine,* February 6, 1955, p. 13.
11. "What's New at USIA's European Libraries?" *USIA World,* December 1990, p. 14.
12. Janet Flanner, "Letter from Paris," *New Yorker,* February 15, 1958, p. 116.
13. "Some Books Literally Burned After Inquiry, Dulles Reports," *New York Times,* June 15, 1953, p. 1.
14. "Director Gives CPAOs Book Responsibility," *USIA World.* January 1970, p. 1.
15. "Bachelor Party No Fun for Thai MPs," *Financial Times* (London), February 8, 1993, p. 7.
16. "USIS Center Censors Its Own Books to Survive Syrian Anti-Americanism," *Philadelphia Evening Bulletin,* February 28, 1967, p. 40.
17. "Rio's Binational Center Celebrates 50 Years," *USIA World,* May 1987, p. 8.
18. "English Teaching and Democracy Building," *USIA World,* January 1992, p. 3.
19. "Spring Books," *The Economist* (London), April 15, 1967, p. 55.
20. "Volume of Trade," *Foreign Policy,* July 2001, p. 29.
21. "ARS Paris," *USIA World,* September 1983, p. 11.
22. "Government Book Control: How the USIA and the CIA Use Private Publishers to Influence Public Opinion," *Washington Post Book World,* February 5, 1967, p. 2.
23. Thomas C. Sorensen, *The Word War: The Story of American Propaganda* (New York: Harper & Row, 1968), p. 70.
24. "Books and USIA," *New York Times Book Review,* November 20, 1966, pp. 86–87.
25. For a general survey of the U.S. role in the overseas textbook market at the time, see: Gordon Graham, "The U.S. Textbook Abroad," *International Development Review,* Society for International Development, Washington, D.C., June 1961, pp. 15–18.
26. "Literary Emissaries to Foreign Lands," *New York Times Book Review,* January 17, 1960, p. 3 et passim.
27. Dizard, *The Strategy of Truth,* p. 137.
28. "U.S. Books Leading in Translations," *New York Times,* May 28, 1965, p. 34.
29. No one has ever accurately measured the extent of private nonprofit U.S. organizations' operations abroad. An attempt by a congressional committee in the 1960s listed such organizations and a summary of their activities. The list ran 531 pages. "Overseas Programs of Private Nonprofit U.S. Organizations," Report No. 3 on Winning the Cold War: The U.S. Ideological Offensive. House Report No. 368, 89th Congress, 1st session, May 15, 1965. The list would be much longer now, given the overseas expansion of NGOs in recent years.

30. "Many Rhodes to Washington," *New York Times Magazine*, April 16, 1961, p. 54.

31. Rockhill's role in U.S. diplomacy, including the Boxer scholarship program, is described in: Karl E. Meyer and Shareen Blain Brysac, *Tournament of Shadows: The Great Game and the Race for Empire in Central Asia* (Washington, D.C.: Perseus, 1999), pp. 394–424.

32. For a useful survey of early U.S. involvement in overseas cultural exchanges, see: George N. Shuster, "The Nature and Development of U.S. Cultural Relations," in Robert Blum (ed.), *Cultural Relations and Foreign Affairs* (Englewood Cliffs, N.J.: Prentice Hall, 1963), pp. 8–40.

33. "30 Years of Exchanging Fulbright Scholars," *Washington Post*, November 23, 1976, p. C-1.

34. Quoted in *Fulbright at Fifty,* National Humanities Center, Washington D.C., July 1997, p. 3.

35. The estimate of Fulbright program costs is based on projections made in *Fulbright at Fifty,* ibid.

36. "Historic Visit Launches New Era in U.S.-Vietnamese Cultural Relations," *USIA World*, January 1996, p. 6.

37. Oliver Schmidt, "No Innocents Abroad: The Salzburg Impetus and U.S. Studies in Europe," in Reinhold Wagnleitner and Elaine Tyler May (eds.), *Here, There and Everywhere: The Foreign Politics of American Culture* (Hanover, N.H.: University Press of New England, 2000), pp. 64–79.

38. These figures are from a survey of exchange programs issued in 1994 by the Department of State's Bureau of Educational and Cultural Affairs. See "Report Gives Comprehensive Overview of U.S. Government International Exchange and Training Activities," *USIA World,* February 1995, pp. 17–18.

39. "The Bureau of Educational and Cultural Affairs," *State Magazine,* May 1999, pp. 16–21.

40. The genesis of the bill and its eventual demise are described in: Charles Frankel, *High on Foggy Bottom* (New York: Harper & Row, 1968), pp. 115–136. Frankel, a philosophy professor at Columbia, was assistant secretary of state for cultural affairs at the time the bill was being considered.

41. "Chillier on Campus," *The Economist* (London), November 24, 2002, p. 31.

42. "Foreign Exchange Imbalance," *Foreign Policy,* January-February 2001, p. 18.

43. Kosinski's academic caper is described in "The Painted Bird," *New York,* July 12, 1991, p. 29.

44. "Foreign Students Now Get a Break at Some Colleges," *Wall Street Journal,* February 1, 2002, p. B-1.

45. Quoted in "The Liberating Arts," *New York Times Educational Supplement,* April 9, 2000, p. 27.

46. Quoted in Dizard, *The Strategy of Truth,* p. 172.

10

Sunset Years

BY 1980, THE U.S. Information Agency had reached the highest level of its influence within the U.S. foreign policy community. The agency's strength in Washington was its acceptance as a policy adviser on what was increasingly defined as "public diplomacy." Abroad, its local operations were deeply integrated into the work of embassies and other diplomatic operations.

With this new stature, however, came rumblings of change. The agency's original mission had been defined by the hard edge of Cold War realities, in particular the presence of an identifiable ideological adversary. Slowly, these lines were being blurred. The "postwar" was over, and events were steadily changing the confrontation with the communist powers. Both the Soviet Union and China would remain, in different ways, formidable adversaries during this transition. At the same time, third-world countries added to the complexity with their claims for greater political and economic recognition.

Shifts in international communications patterns that began to emerge in full force in the 1980s complicated USIA's role in this transition.

For most of its history, the agency could claim to play a strong role in the export of American information and cultural products, particularly in third-world countries. This role was now being eroded by the new influence of commercial information firms, aided by advanced communications technologies that brought their products and services to vast audiences across the globe.

This trend was hastened by the mass media's corporate mergers and acquisitions, designed to expand operations at home and abroad. The Internet added a new dimension to these efforts. USIA also began to make use of web sites and other advanced services in its programs.

Progress was often slow, however, in part because of congressional reluctance to fund the costs of adapting agency operations to the new electronic technologies.

Early efforts at restructuring USIA operations began during the Jimmy Carter administration in the late 1970s. The agency was led for the first time by one of its own officers, John Reinhardt, who had long experience in the business, particularly in developing countries. He made a series of changes that reflected the need for new approaches. (One decision, renaming the agency as the U.S. International Communications Agency, was less successful and was soon reversed.) By and large, however, he was hobbled by the Carter White House's general disinterest in exploiting the agency's resources. Carter's foreign policy was increasingly dominated by frustrations, culminating in the 1979 takeover of the U.S. embassy in Tehran by a mob. The embassy staff, which was held hostage for 444 days, included four USIA employees—John Graves, Kathryn Koob, Barry Rosen, and William Royer.

Carter's frustrations affected the 1980 presidential race, which was won by a former Hollywood actor who put his stamp on a decade. Ronald Reagan rode to victory on a feel-good wave, proclaiming a new dawn in the United States. Whatever its faults of omission and commission, the Reagan administration offered coherent if somewhat simplistic ideological messages that struck a popular chord in both domestic and foreign affairs. The new president identified the Soviet Union as an "evil empire," to be dealt with through a mixed strategy of confrontation and cooperation.

Ideological warfare was part of the Reagan plan, and USIA became an important player in its execution. The agency's role was personified in its new director, California executive Charles Wick, who transformed the organization and its operations with a vigor not seen since Ed Murrow led USIA two decades earlier. Wick came to his job largely unknown to the public. A former dance-band leader and theatrical agent, he was the successful head of a healthcare company in California. His greatest asset in his new job was his longtime relationship with Reagan in the fraternity of wealthy West Coast conservatives.[1]

It was not just a casual friendship; it was a close bond. As a member of the Reagan inner circle, one USIA staffer declared, "Charlie Wick was fireproof." The ultimate test of this, by Washington standards, was his influence on the agency's budget.[2] By the time Wick resigned in 1989 as USIA's longest-serving director, the agency's annual budget was $882 million, almost double that in 1981, the year he became director. It was a stunning reversal of the government budget officials' practice of regarding USIA as an easy mark for budget cuts, given the agency's lack of a strong domestic constituency. Wick's White House clout was usually sufficient to change their minds.

His managerial style was activist, and on occasion frenetic. He issued "Z-grams" to the staff expressing ideas that ranged from the insightful to the incomprehensible. ("Z" was Wick's middle initial.) He spent more time visiting overseas USIS posts than any previous director, including four trips to the Soviet Union.

Charles Wick melded the new Reagan policies into USIA operations in ways that were arguably the most successful coordination of White House and agency activities in the agency's history. Occasionally this involved ignoring earlier policies on balanced news treatment. This issue came to a head early in the new administration when a Reagan appointee at the Voice of America, Philip Nicolaides, proposed a tough confrontational approach in broadcasts to the Soviet Union. Its thrust went against the intent of a "VOA Charter" ensuring balanced news presentation that had been negotiated several years earlier with congressional support.[3] The Nicolaides statement was criticized in newspaper editorials, forcing the White House to withdraw it.

In another incident, a blacklist of prominent Americans (including newsmen Walter Cronkite and David Brinkley) deemed unsuitable for USIA speaking programs was drafted by Reagan appointees in the agency. Wick quickly disavowed the list when it provoked congressional charges of censorship.[4] Under Wick's direction, media output soon reflected the Reagan administration's mixed messages of "evil empire" and "trust but verify" in dealing with the Soviet Union. It was a strategy intended to exploit Soviet vulnerabilities that had emerged more strongly in the early 1980s as a result of the maladroit political and economic policies pursued by a series of aging Kremlin leaders.

Seizing the opportunities this situation offered, the Reagan White House reorganized its ideological warfare structure.[5] An ambiguously named Special Planning Group was created in 1983, with a membership that included USIA and the State and Defense Departments. One result, *New York Times* columnist William Safire declared, was that USIA's role in ideological warfare had shifted from mouthpiece to policy participant.[6]

The Special Planning Group developed a series of initiatives to promote its international information agenda. The earliest of these was Project Democracy, intended to enlist U.S. civic groups, labor unions, and other private organizations in projects supporting democratic groups overseas. Originally set up in 1983 under USIA auspices, the project was later restructured as the National Endowment for Democracy, which was still functioning as of 2004 as a primary contact with civic groups abroad.⁷

Other Reagan administration plans to promote understanding of U.S. policies overseas were less benign, and at times illegal. The most notorious of these reflected the White House's obsession with aiding anticommunist groups in Latin America to combat what Reagan officials regarded as Soviet attempts to gain a political and ideological foothold in the Western Hemisphere. The project eventually became part of the larger Iran-contra scandal in which White House officials tried to bypass congressional restrictions on aid to Nicaraguan "contra" rebels by selling arms to a dictatorial regime in Iran and using the proceeds to arm the rebels.

A rogue operation from the start, the project soon involved illegal propaganda operations. The White House's enthusiasm for the Nicaraguan rebels' cause led to the creation of an unauthorized "Office of Public Diplomacy for Latin America and the Caribbean" in the State Department. The office had a small staff of about twenty, headed by Otto Reich, a Cuban-American public relations consultant. The operation also drew on resources from USIA, CIA, and the Department of Defense.

Much of the office's activities involved issuing unclassified background materials on the Nicaraguan situation. However, it also expended considerable effort leaking classified information supporting the contras, as well as preparing biased news stories, editorials, and advertisements on their behalf. One advertisement, allegedly sponsored by a Young Republican group, solicited public funds for the contras with the theme that 39-cent-a-day contributions would keep their operations going. As the Reich operation expanded, it attracted congressional charges that it was an illegal attempt to bypass USIA's role in overseas information efforts. The project was finally closed down in the wake of other revelations about White House manipulation of funds and other resources in the Iran-contra operation.⁸

USIA played a relatively minor role in Otto Reich's State Department operation. Instead, the agency focused primarily on expanding its overseas operations, thanks to the larger budgets Director Wick had wheedled out of Congress. Part of this new money was used to upgrade Voice of America broadcasting facilities around the world. Old transmitters, some dating from World War II, were modernized and new ones added. A special effort was made to shift from shortwave to mediumwave facilities that could send a signal to ordinary household radios.

USIA also acquired a new radio service whose primary purpose was not to provide news and information to foreigners, but to bolster the electoral base of the Republican Party. The service, known as Radio

Marti, was directed at audiences in Cuba where the Voice of America already had a strong medium-wave capability for reaching most of the island. The most popular U.S. programming among Cuban audiences, however, came from commercial Spanish-language stations in Miami that could be heard throughout Cuba at night when atmospheric conditions were optimal. Radio Marti was an interloper, a facility whose primary purpose was to burnish Republican Party credentials among Cuban voters in Florida. The Cuban-American Foundation, a powerful political group in Miami, led the way in lobbying for the new facility.

The Radio Marti project was originally opposed by some State Department officials as an unnecessary provocation.[9] U.S. commercial broadcasters also were cool to the idea, fearing a counteroffensive by the Castro regime to interfere with their broadcast signals. Their hesitations were justified: Cuban stations proved capable of jamming local medium-wave transmissions as far north as Chicago and Boston.[10]

Republican politics overrode these objections, and Radio Marti went on the air in 1985. It quickly became a political sacred cow for both the Republican and Democratic parties; neither was willing to challenge the fact that the station had a relatively small listenership in Cuba. They were equally reluctant to point out that the station's programming was dominated by a shrill anti-Castro tone that violated longstanding U.S. foreign broadcasting practices of achieving credibility through balanced news programming.

The parties' reluctance to stand up to the Cuban-American lobby extended to their unwillingness to resist funding for a television version of Radio Marti.[11] Using an airborne transmitter hung beneath an aerostat balloon 10,000 feet above the Florida Keys, TV Marti began transmitting in 1990. There was only one Cuban television channel where its signal could be seen, and this capability was restricted to the hours between three and six A.M. In effect, the station had almost no audience from the start. Moreover, its transmissions violated an international treaty prohibiting foreign use of domestic channels without an agreement between the two countries involved.[12]

A more purposeful agency broadcasting venture was Worldnet, a service designed to provide television programming worldwide via satellite. Billed as the "world's first global satellite network" when it began operations in 1983, Worldnet preceded Cable News Network's overseas satellite news transmissions by several years. Worldnet was designed primarily to deliver signals to U.S. embassies for redistribution live or by tape to local television stations. (At the time, there were no active prospects for telecasting into homes or other locations through rooftop satellite dishes.)

The Worldnet grid soon spread to 190 cities in 128 countries. Its most successful programming involved live teleconferences in which foreign newsmen quizzed a U.S. official on a current issue. An early example involved Secretary of State George Shultz in an interview with journalists in Tokyo and five other East Asian cities. By 1990, over four hundred of these "dialogues" were being telecast annually.[13]

Interviews with U.S. policymakers were only a small part of Worldnet's daily schedule. Most of its programming involved taped reruns of commercial or Public Broadcasting System programs. The network's most useful product for local TV stations abroad was a daily video news feed in English, French, Spanish, and Arabic. Overall, Worldnet proved to be a significant addition to USIA media resources, primarily because of its interactive live interviews.[14]

Worldnet and other new technologies helped revitalize the activities of USIS posts overseas during the 1980s. Although some smaller posts in Western Europe were cut back or closed, USIS activities in Eastern Europe, particularly in Poland, Hungary, and Czechoslovakia, slowly but steadily increased. This shift was sparked by the political activism of local dissident groups eager to end Soviet domination of their countries. Poland led the way, energized by the rise of the Solidarity trade union movement in the late 1970s. USIA had carried on a fairly active program in the country throughout the Cold War decades. This changed in 1981, when the communist government ordered a cutback in USIS activities after imposing martial law, intended to suppress the Solidarity movement. The popular USIS magazine *Ameryka* and other programs were closed down.

Nevertheless, the USIS post in Warsaw quietly stepped up its contacts with dissident leaders. The exchanges program became a critical part of its operations. As a result, when a Solidarity-led coalition regained power by winning parliamentary elections in the mid-1990s, half of the twenty-two cabinet ministers, including the prime minister, were alumni of USIA exchanges, along with forty-four members of the Polish parliament.[15] The post also coordinated its activities with other U.S. groups, including AFL-CIO trade unions that provided invaluable communications assistance to Solidarity in the form of Xerox-type copying machines, videocassette recorders, and data links to the outside world.[16]

Czechoslovakia presented a different set of challenges for the USIS post in Prague. The post had operated limited programs from cramped quarters in the embassy after its library had been closed down in 1950. Following the ouster of the communist government in 1989, President George H. W. Bush informed his Czech counterpart, Vaclav Havel, that the embassy would open a new cultural center in downtown Prague. For the site, the Czech government offered the building that had housed the Lenin Museum during the Cold War years. An honored guest at the opening ceremonies, in addition to President Havel, was Lubomir Elsner, a former USIS employee who had spent eleven years in labor camps after being arrested by the Czech communist secret police in 1950 on allegations of antistate activities connected with his USIS job.[17] Elsner's experience was replicated, with variations, by dozens of other local USIS employees in Eastern Europe during the communist years.

In other parts of the world, the 1980s were marked by a rise in the level of violence against USIA installations. In 1985 alone there were twelve bombings of USIS buildings.[18] Previously, such attacks had been sporadic. The Vietnam conflict provided several examples of violence directed against USIS offices and employees. Charles Willis, a VOA employee, spent five years as a civilian prisoner of war in North Vietnam. Herbert Timrud, a psychological operations adviser in Phong Dinh province, was seriously wounded in an ambush by Viet Cong forces.

In other terrorist incidents, Barbara Hutchinson, the public affairs officer in the Dominican Republic, was seized by a gang that demanded a $1 million ransom. She was released two weeks later, the ransom unpaid. In Bolivia, USIS officers Michael Kristula and Tom Martin were locked up for twelve days in a storeroom filled with dynamite after being taken hostage by miners during a labor dispute. Over twenty other USIA employees lost their lives in the line of duty; a plaque memorializing them is located in the lobby of the State Department's main building in Washington.[19]

Among the overseas USIS operations that adapted to changing political conditions in the 1980s, the program in South Africa stood out. On the one hand, South Africa was a country that magnified many times over the civil rights struggle in the United States. At the same time, it had become a pawn in the larger arena of Cold War strategy. In Washington, both Democratic and Republican administrations played a cautious game, fueled by fears of Soviet influence that included a significant local communist presence in the African National Congress (ANC), the lead organization in opposing apartheid (the strictly enforced separation of the white and black communities). By 1981, the Reagan administration had settled on an ill-defined program of "constructive engagement," which in practice tilted toward support of the minority white government.

USIA was caught in the middle. It had a story to tell about racial progress in the United States, but this was overshadowed by what South

Africa's black leaders regarded as hypocrisy in dealing with their struggle for political, social, and economic equality. Nevertheless, USIS operations played a special role in clarifying long-range U.S. intentions in the apartheid conflict. It began quietly in 1947 when the USIS post in Johannesburg opened the first integrated library in the country.

The practice was later expanded to libraries at branch posts in Cape Town and Durban. In 1962, the post hired its first black local employee. At the same time, it sent a uniquely symbolic message when it took down the "Europeans Only" sign in the elevator of its Johannesburg building. Soon after, the USIS auditorium was made available to the Union of Black Journalists and the black Social Workers Association for their meetings.[20]

These were small steps, but their intent was clear to both white and black South Africans. The message was amplified when USIS opened a branch in Soweto, the large black township on the outskirts of Johannesburg. The operation was initially disguised as a "music appreciation club," run by USIS officer Susan Wagner Crystal at a community center sponsored by the Anglican Church.[21] The program was later expanded to include a library in a separate USIS facility where a Worldnet television dish on the roof allowed direct contact with the outside world, bypassing the South African national network's controls over black participation in its programs.

The main USIS contribution in aiding the apartheid struggle was through its exchange program. Dozens of black leaders went to the United States under Fulbright grants and other programs during the last apartheid decades. This was done in spite of opposition from the South African government, which used a range of tactics from refusing to issue passports to delaying the necessary exit permits. One of the most prominent grantees was Gatsha Buthelezi, chief of 4 million Zulus. Another was Saths Cooper, a leader in the stridently anti-American Azanian People's Organization, a black power group that considered Nelson Mandela's African National Congress too conservative. Cooper astonished the USIS staff in Johannesburg one day when he walked in and asked for a Fulbright scholarship application. He won the grant, studied psychology at Boston University, and returned home to a new career as a teacher and television producer in addition to his political activities.

Percy Qobozo, editor of *The World,* the leading black newspaper, credited his year as a Neiman journalism fellow at Harvard in the 1970s as crucial in understanding the U.S. civil rights experience and its relevance to South Africa's situation. Speaking of his Harvard experience,

Qobozo recalled: "When I arrived there, I found it hard to adjust to the fact that I was living in a free society. When I went down to Harvard Square for a meal, I was tempted to look in the window of a place to see if there were any blacks inside, before going in. The experience forced me to look at myself, and I was surprised to find that I was an Uncle Tom."[22]

The USIS exchange project also included influential white South African participants. One of these was Frederik de Klerk. As the last president of the white-dominated government in the late 1980s, de Klerk was instrumental in modifying hard-line apartheid policies. Among other actions, he released Nelson Mandela from his long prison sentence. De Klerk later acknowledged that his study visit to the United States strongly influenced his views on civil rights in South Africa.

In addition to USIS, other U.S. organizations played a quiet but important role in ending apartheid rule in South Africa. These included the congressionally funded National Endowment for Democracy, which in the 1980s provided direct support, including vehicles and other equipment, to Nelson Mandela's African National Congress and to the ANC's rival, the Zulu Inkatha movement.[23] South African black union leaders also benefited directly from help supplied by the AFL-CIO, preparing them for the time when their organizations would be able to operate without government harassment.

South Africa was an important USIA concern during the 1980s, but the agency remained primarily focused on the continuing erosion of communist rule in Eastern Europe and the ensuing collapse of the Soviet Union in 1991. Ideological operations played a critical role leading up to both events. In Moscow, the aging gerontocracy of Soviet leaders had failed to adjust old doctrines to new political and economic realities. In Washington, the Reagan administration exploited this weakness. It replaced former Nixon-Kissinger détente policies with a more militant strategy that combined ideological confrontation with political and military actions.

USIA was part of this mix of militancy and persuasion. Its East European posts took advantage of the small steps taken by local communist regimes to allow them more leeway in their local operations. This was especially true in Poland, Hungary, and Czechoslovakia, each with a history of failed popular revolts against Soviet domination during the Cold War decades. As noted above, Poland set the pace of resistance, which involved a unique collaboration of workers, intellectuals, and the Catholic Church that eventually eroded the government's ability to maintain its grip on power.

Among other developments, the late 1980s saw the gradual end of jamming operations against the East European language services of the Voice of America, the BBC, and other Western broadcasters.[24] VOA was soon able to sponsor live call-in shows for East European listeners. It also began transmitting some of its programs on local government and private radio stations in the region. Among others, Radio Warsaw broadcast a daily newscast in English and Polish from Washington.[25]

Expanding USIA activities within the Soviet Union was a different matter. The Kremlin subjected the post in Moscow to continual harassment throughout the Cold War years. A typical tactic was to charge that the USIS operation was a spy center. The embassy's cultural section was a favorite target because of its contacts with Soviet intellectuals, including some dissidents. In a typical attack, cultural attaché McKinney Russell was accused of "drawing American participants of the scientific and cultural exchange program into the sphere of subversion against the Soviet Union."[26]

Slowly, then quickly, this harassment eased up. The central event in bringing this about was internal dissension within the Soviet Communist apparatus that resulted in Mikhail Gorbachev's 1985 election as general secretary of the party. He pledged to reform the economy, with particular attention to the introduction of advanced computers and other information-age technologies.[27]

Gorbachev's promises of more information openness had a slow but positive effect on USIA operations within the Soviet Union. The Kremlin reduced its jamming of Russian- and Central Asian–language broadcasts, although not those of Radio Liberty. By 1989, the VOA Russian service was broadcasting *Music Hotline,* a call-in program during which Soviet listeners could request songs, talk about their favorite pop groups, and ask general questions. The phone charges were substantial—18 rubles for three minutes—but the program never lacked for callers.[28] There were also indications that the unjammed programs were attracting a significant audience among the Soviet ruling elite, including Mikhail Gorbachev.[29]

U.S. ideological strategy during the Gorbachev period focused on expanding information and cultural links with the Soviet people. This took two forms: first, to use international pressure to lower long-standing Kremlin barriers to cross-border cultural and information contacts; second, to negotiate a series of bilateral agreements to increase media flows between the United States and the Soviet Union. Together, these actions helped to hasten the political implosion that led to the collapse of the Soviet Union.

International pressure to expand cross-border contacts focused on revisiting the 1975 Helsinki Accords on easing East-West political, economic, and human rights tensions. The original document called for a periodic review of how the agreements were being carried out. In 1988, the United States, Canada, and the West European democracies invoked this clause to examine compliance with the Helsinki human rights provisions. The result was a new accord, signed in Vienna in January 1989, that included a sweeping revision of the original agreement. It called for stronger protections for civil liberties in each country, emphasizing "the right of their citizens to contribute actively, individually or in association with others, to the promotion and protection of human rights and fundamental freedom."

The Vienna agreement listed specific rights to be protected, including uncensored mail, access to religious education, unfettered travel to another country, and the right to make uncensored telephone calls. The agreement also took notice of the role of advanced media technologies, including cable systems and satellites, in expanding information contacts.[30] Although the new provisions, like the original Helsinki document, were not legally binding, they served as a powerful force for human rights reform within the Soviet bloc, particularly in strengthening local dissident organizations. Among these newly energized groups were the Moscow dissidents who since 1968 had sponsored a typewritten *Chronicle of Human Events,* passed from hand-to-hand. The *Chronicle* documented human rights violations, despite police efforts to close it down.[31]

Meanwhile, the United States pressed the Kremlin bilaterally on human rights issues, including information flows. USIA, and especially Charles Wick, took the lead in managing these efforts. An early result was a U.S.-Soviet cultural agreement, the first since the mid-1970s. Signed at the Reagan-Gorbachev 1985 summit meeting in Geneva, the agreement eventually led to a significant increase in academic exchanges between the two countries. The number had been stalled at forty exchanges annually since the first cultural agreement thirty years earlier. In 1988, in negotiations with the New York–based International Research and Exchanges Board (IREX), Washington's representative in exchange operations with Communist-bloc countries, the Soviet education ministry proposed that the number be raised to three hundred exchanges a year.[32]

The exchange negotiations were followed by U.S.-Soviet talks to open media channels between the two countries. For the first time, U.S. commercial companies participated in the discussions. These talks resulted in a series of agreements that gave U.S. film, television, book, and periodical firms a small foothold in Soviet markets that had been closed to them for seventy years.[33] The agreements allowed U.S. film distributors to distribute their products and to share in the box-office receipts of Soviet cinemas. Television companies made similar arrangements with the state television organization. The result was to make popular American entertainment available to Soviet audiences, who responded by flocking to movie theaters and making Hollywood television productions a welcome staple on their TV screens at home. Another provision in the media agreements authorized the opening of a VOA news bureau in Moscow for the first time.[34]

At the same time, a U.S.-Soviet dialogue was started by Ted Turner, the maverick media executive who founded the Cable News Network (CNN). In addition to his many business deals, Turner had created a nonprofit group, the Better World Society, with a broad mandate to use the mass media to address world problems such as overpopulation, erosion of the environment, and the threat of nuclear war. He soon found himself negotiating with Soviet authorities on joint projects. One of them, the Goodwill Games, was a mini-Olympics in which athletes from over fifty countries competed in Moscow in 1988. Turner also struck deals with Moscow television officials to exchange news, entertainment, and sports programming with his expanding CNN world network, using Soviet communications satellites.[35]

To underline the theme of open information channels, USIA sponsored a major exhibit, "Information USA," which toured nine Soviet cities in 1988. The show was so big thirty tractor-trailers were needed to move it around the country. Over a million Soviet citizens viewed such unfamiliar devices as personal computers, supermarket checkout counters, VCRs, and photocopiers. One grammar school student asked an American exhibit guide to design and print for him a card for his teacher with the words: "Greetings from Little America." "What do you mean? Little America?," the guide asked. "This," said the boy, waving his arms over the pavilion, "is Little America."[36]

Mikhail Gorbachev's attempt to reform Soviet society under Communist Party guidance came to an abrupt end in August 1991. Hard-line Stalinists, calling themselves the Committee for the State of Emergency, mounted a coup aimed at reversing the Gorbachev reforms. They failed, but not before a dramatic confrontation that led to the collapse of the Soviet state, the resignation of Gorbachev, and his replacement by Boris Yeltsin as president in a highly charged new political order.

Although the coup leaders had seized local and national radio and television stations, they had overlooked international telephone circuits, including those transmitted on Soviet satellites that they controlled.

Using a cellular phone, Mark Hopkins, VOA's Moscow correspondent, reported on the crisis from inside the Russian parliament building, where the coup leaders were holed up.[37]

On the night of the coup Allen Weinstein, president of the Center for Democracy in Washington, received a dramatic fax message from the foreign minister of the Russian Federation, whom he had visited only a few weeks earlier. Referring to Boris Yeltsin as "BY," the message said: "The Russian government has no NO way to address the people. All radio stations are under control. The following is BY's address to the Army. Submit it to USIA. Broadcast it all over the country. Maybe the Voice of America. Do it! Urgent!"[38] By the time Weinstein had received the fax, the VOA's Soviet division was operating on a round-the-clock basis, broadcasting ten-minute news updates on the hour in a dozen Soviet languages.

The effectiveness of Voice of America broadcasts was later acknowledged in a statement to VOA officials from the All-Russian State Television and Broadcasting Co.: "Millions of Soviet people, denied the possibility of receiving information from Russian sources, listened to your Voice. It inspired them with faith and determination to fight dictatorship."[39] The failure of the August 1991 coup marked the beginning of a tumultuous era in which the former Soviet Union went through a series of wrenching changes, including tentative steps toward a more open information society. New communications technologies continued to frustrate official attempts to limit dissent.[40]

USIA took advantage of the new openness to expand its operations in the Yeltsin era. Posts were opened for the first time in the newly independent former Soviet republics. New programs were begun, and old ones dropped. USIS/Moscow's venerable magazine, *America Illustrated,* was closed down in 1994 after publishing 454 issues over a thirty-eight-year period. A network of "America House" libraries and cultural centers opened in provincial cities with facilities for direct computer and telecommunications links to academic and other research resources in the United States.[41]

The most dramatic changes took place in the exchanges program. By 1995, Russia and Eastern Europe became the leading geographic region for U.S. government exchange programs, with a total of 31,180 exchanges, a quarter of the worldwide total. This figure did not include many of the private grants arranged by U.S. universities, research groups, and other nongovernmental organizations.

Expanding USIA operations in China was another matter. In the early years of the new Chinese-American relationship, Beijing preferred to deal with private U.S. groups in carrying out its ping-pong diplomacy.

In 1979, the two governments signed a limited cultural agreement covering academic grants, exhibits and what were called "cultural study teams."[42] Beijing authorities treated the new cultural contacts warily. They suspended a small Fulbright program in August 1989 following the Tienanmen Square student uprising but allowed it to resume a year later.[43]

The one program Chinese authorities embraced heartily over the years has been placement of students in U.S. schools. By the turn of the century Chinese students constituted the second-largest single group of foreign students in U.S. universities, after Canadians.[44] Study at U.S. schools remains a major goal for many young Chinese. In 2002, the top-selling book in all of China was *Harvard Girl Yinh Liu,* a how-to-do-it manual by a Chinese mother whose daughter had successfully gained admission to Harvard through what the book called "scientifically proven methods." Copycat books, including *Ivy League Is Not a Dream,* soon appeared in Chinese bookstores.[45]

Meanwhile, other USIA information activities within China remained limited. Government-ordered restrictions on the agency's activities were partially offset by the rapid expansion of the Internet and other technologies capable of bypassing official barriers. Internet web sites became increasingly available to millions of Chinese computer owners and those who frequented the country's twenty thousand cybercafes by the turn of the century. Meanwhile, the VOA began transmitting news on its own Chinese-language web site in 1997. The site was quickly declared off-limits by government censors, as were those of the *New York Times* and other U.S. media. Such prohibitions have had limited effect, given the ability of Chinese computer buffs to work around the restrictions.[46]

The so-called opening to Russia, together with lesser opportunities in China, had the effect of blunting USIA's Cold War focus on its two main ideological adversaries. At another level, a new set of challenges arose in U.S. relations with traditional allies and with third-world countries. U.S. society itself was in full transition from the industrial age to an information-intensive postindustrial order. This new environment was changing U.S. international priorities, particularly as U.S. corporations expanded their information markets abroad. By the turn of the century, information goods and services led U.S. exports for the first time, displacing aviation and agricultural products. Most visible was the new overseas impact of U.S. mass media—from films to computer games.

This shift called for a post–Cold War reordering of policy and operational issues within the U.S. government, including those of the agency created forty years earlier primarily as a response to communist ideological challenges. USIA's place in this new order was debated sporadically throughout the 1990s. A 1998 decision to abolish the agency resulted less as a deliberately arrived-at judgment than as part of a political compromise between the White House and a determined North Carolina senator, Jesse Helms, involving legislation on abortion rights, a chemical warfare treaty, and the payment of back dues to the United Nations.

The task of adapting USIA operations to post–Cold War realities rested with the organization's last three directors—Bruce Gelb, Henry Catto, and Joseph Duffey. To their credit, each supervised important changes in how the agency operated in a new information technology environment. In part, this shift meant revising policies and practices that had served well during the Cold War decades but were increasingly irrelevant in the new global information environment. USIA had been a leader among the foreign policy agencies in adopting computerization and other new technologies; by the early 1970s, it had begun automating many of its operations in Washington and at its larger posts, notably in India and Japan.[47]

At one level, this involved cutting back many of the products and services that had dominated the agency's operations during the Cold War decades. Dozens of small posts were closed down and very few new ones opened. The major exception was in Vietnam, where USIS resumed operations in 1995 after a twenty-year hiatus, with posts in Hanoi and Ho Chi Minh City, formerly Saigon. Programs there emphasized two-way exchange programs, including placing American lecturers in seven universities throughout the country.[48]

Meanwhile, the agency restructured its media operations, closing down magazines and other publications, including such venerable products as the *Free World* illustrated magazine series, published in many translated editions overseas. Documentary film production was cut back sharply, replaced by less expensive television products that could be seen by much larger audiences. Less attention was given to exhibits, including the large shows that had once provided attractive glimpses of American life for enormous audiences abroad.

Their place was taken by a new set of programs that stressed direct electronic contact with overseas audiences, emphasizing greater use of technologies such as the Internet, computers, and communications satellites. As noted earlier, these resources had been gradually built into agency programs over several decades. However, the agency's administrative structure for dealing with these technical innovations had changed very little. Each new technology had, in effect, been stuffed into a bureaucratic framework that was essentially the same as the one created by the Office of War Information a half-century earlier.

This practice ended in the 1990s when the agency's separate media divisions were reorganized to reflect the new realities. An all-encompassing "Information Bureau" was created to oversee the electronic integration of USIA media operations. The "I-Bureau," as it quickly became known, had the initial advantage of being headed by an imaginative, long-serving agency officer, Barry Fulton.

The I-Bureau had its growing pains, not the least of which was dealing with bureaucratic resistance as decades-long practices were modified or eliminated. In the process, the new unit helped redefine the ways in which the business of public diplomacy would henceforth be conducted on electronically driven networks that reached out directly to individuals overseas without passing through intermediary individuals or organizations. Within USIA, the change cut across the old top-down hierarchy, relying instead on a group of multifunctional teams that could summon a wide range of media and cultural resources to specific program tasks.

The I-Bureau's central resource was a large database, with electronic collections of policy documents and background materials on every major foreign policy issue and many other subjects. Overseas users could tap into formatted editions of five policy-oriented electronic journals as well as web pages established at most U.S. embassies and other overseas locations. USIS libraries abroad were transformed into online Information Resource Centers that gave their clients fast access to multiple databases, both governmental and private. The agency's venerable Wireless File, its newsfile to overseas posts, was also accessible to Internet audiences abroad both in its daily editions and as a documentary archive.[49]

The new bureau's capabilities were tested during the events preceding the breakup of Yugoslavia in the late 1990s. When the country's dictator, Slobodan Milosevic, banned rebroadcast of foreign programs from sources such as the BBC and the Voice of America, the I-Bureau developed Serbian- and Albanian-language web sites, which made audio sound bites and printed news materials available to Balkan audiences. The Milosevic regime resorted to Internet "cyber-disinformation" efforts, which led to an I-Bureau project to identify, monitor, and refute the false reports on its web pages. Eventually, USIA set up seven electronically wired information centers within the region to help rebuild its media infrastructure.[50]

These efforts were coordinated with other Washington groups, both governmental and private. The latter included the National Democratic

Institute for International Affairs, which provided technical assistance to breakaway political groups in Yugoslavia, as well as funding public opinion polling and get-out-the-vote campaigns.[51] U.S. labor unions, civic organizations, and other NGOs also played a role in supporting anti-Milosevic groups. The result was a textbook example of how government and private groups could coordinate public diplomacy efforts through separate but compatible programs.

Despite this success, USIA faced a formidable challenge to its operations in the post–Cold War environment. Its budget ($1.3 billion in the mid-1990s) was a fat target for congressional budget cutters. Critics suggested reducing or eliminating Voice of America programming, arguing that the commercial Cable News Network, now telecasting by satellite to all regions of the world, could supplant the Voice. VOA officials pointed out that, at the time, reception of CNN programs overseas was limited primarily to large hotels. "CNN is great," VOA director Geoffrey Cowan pointed out, "but most people don't live in hotels and don't speak English. That's where we come in. We broadcast in 47 languages."

Increasingly these arguments fell on deaf legislative ears. In 1995, the first bill to abolish USIA was introduced into Congress.[52] The agency managed to survive these early congressional moves, but another Washington event proved more threatening. This was the Clinton administration's determination to consolidate all foreign affairs agencies in the State Department.[53] The plan, announced in April 1997, was driven less by bureaucratic efficiency than by the effort to accommodate Senator Helms, chairman of the Foreign Relations Committee and a longtime critic of USIA and other foreign affairs units.[54] USIA, the Agency for International Development, and the Arms Control and Disarmament Agency would each be integrated into the State Department framework. In exchange, Senator Helms would relax his opposition to various Clinton administration foreign policy initiatives, including funding overseas abortion clinics and paying back dues to the United Nations.[55]

Congress passed the reorganization plan in October 1998 in a bill that provided for the wholesale transfer of USIA operations to State except for the Voice of America.[56] The legislation created an independent Broadcasting Board of Governors to manage the VOA, Radio Liberty, Radio Free Europe, Radio Free Asia, and Radio Marti. Within the State Department, the agency's other media units were transferred to a new bureau headed by an undersecretary for public diplomacy and public affairs.[57]

The changeover took place officially on October 1, 1999. It happened under circumstances very different from the period forty-six years earlier, when the overseas information program had, in effect, been drummed out of the State Department. Then, many department officials, from Secretary John Foster Dulles on down, regarded its activities as irrelevant, if not inimical, to the proper conduct of U.S. foreign relations. By 1999, these attitudes had shifted significantly. Among other things, the creation of the public diplomacy undersecretaryship within the department made the function organizationally equal with political, economic, and security concerns at the highest level.

Foreign policy experts will debate the decision to close down the U.S. Information Agency for a long time. USIA was only one of many voices of America that defined the United States to overseas audiences in modern times. Within this context, the agency played a special role in advocating the country's ideas and values. Its legacy took on new meaning in the challenges presented by the events of September 11, 2001, particularly in confirming the continuing relevance of ideology in the transition to a more stable world order.

Notes

1. "Wick Finds High Profile Need Not Be a Target," *New York Times,* June 2, 1988, p. 11.
2. "Talk Not Cheap at Wick's USIA," *Washington Post,* March 31, 1986, p. 1.
3. "Propaganda Role Urged for Voice of America," *Washington Post,* November 13, 1981, p. 1.
4. "Wick Legacy: Making a Difference," *Broadcasting,* November 7, 1988, p. 43.
5. "Fearing Soviet Gains, USIA Counterattacks in the Propaganda War," *Wall Street Journal,* May 17, 1983, p. 1.
6. "Openly Arrived At," *New York Times,* January 1, 1983, p. 17.
7. For the genesis of Project Democracy, see: "Project Democracy," Current Policy No. 456, Office of Public Communications, Bureau of Public Affairs, Department of State, February 23, 1983.
8. "Reagan's Propaganda Ministry," *Propaganda Review,* summer 1988, pp. 25–28; "Iran Contra's Untold Story," *Foreign Policy,* no. 72, fall 1988, pp. 3–30; "Reagan's Pro-Contra Machine," *Washington Post,* April 9, 1988, p. C-1; "Payback Time for Cubans?" *Economist* (London), April 14, 2001, p. 26.
9. "U.S. Diplomats in Cuba Dissent on Radio Plan," *New York Times,* October 29, 1981, p. 7.
10. "Cuban Radio Invades the U.S.," *Business Week,* September 21, 1981, p. 42.
11. "Cuban-American Takes Aim at Castro on TV," *New York Times,* April 1, 1990, p. 13.
12. "TV Marti: Inventorying the Legal Ammunition," *Broadcasting,* August 20, 1990; "Cuba Fights New Telecast from the United States," *New York Times,* March 17, 1990, p. 12.

13. "USIA: A United Voice of America?" *Intermedia* (London), November 1990, p. 6.
14. "The Televised Future of USIA," *Broadcasting*, March 26, 1984, p. 65.
15. "Keeping the Dream Alive," *Foreign Service Journal*, June 1999, p. 36.
16. "TV, VCRs Fan Fire of Revolution," *Los Angeles Times*, January 18, 1990, p. 1.
17. "USIS Prague Moved into Lenin Museum," *USIA World*, June 1993, p. 8.
18. "How to Deal with a Bomb Threat," *USIA World*, July 1986, p. 24.
19. "USIA Unveils Plaque Honoring Employees Killed in the Line of Duty," *USIA World*, August 1990, p. 20.
20. "AP Story Cites USIS 'Activist Program' in South Africa," *USIA World*, January 1977, p. 3.
21. "USIA Johannesburg," *Foreign Service Journal*, October 1997, p. 30.
22. "Editor of Principal Black Newspaper in South Africa Becomes Influential Critic of Apartheid System," *New York Times*, May 17, 1977, p. 9.
23. "Voice Lessons," *New Republic*, July 8, 1991, p. 15.
24. "Growing Clarity on the Shortwave Dial," *Broadcasting*, January 2, 1989, p. 86.
25. "The Changing Role of VOA in Eastern Europe," *USIA World*, March 1990, p. 7.
26. "U.S. Embassy Aide in Moscow Accused of Spying," *New York Times*, May 6, 1971, p. 3.
27. Wilson Dizard and Blake Swensrud, *Gorbachev's Information Revolution: Controlling Glasnost in a New Electronic Era*, Significant Issues Series, vol. 9, no. 8, Center for Strategic and International Studies, Washington, D.C., 1987. See also: "Media Message: Gorbachev Loosens the Reins," *Time*, June 30, 1986, p. 55.
28. "Voice of America Has Some Wondrous Plans," *New York Times*, October 7, 1988, p. 18; "Bridging the Gap: A Soviet Connection," *USIA World*, January 1989, p. 13.
29. Kevin J. McNamara, "Reaching Captive Minds with Radio," *Orbis*, winter 1992, p. 24.
30. "35 Nations Issue East-West Pact to Protect Broad Human Rights," *New York Times*, January 17, 1989, p. 1.
31. "Soviet Heroes," *New York Review of Books*, December 18, 1980, p. 41.
32. "Exchange Quota Increase Agreed," *IREX Update*, International Research and Exchanges Board, summer 1988, p. 6.
33. "USIA and Soviets Sign Historic Agreements at Bilateral Information Talks in Moscow," *USIA World*, January 1989, pp. 4–5.
34. Charles Wick, "Talking to Moscow About Cultural and News Issues," *Washington Post*, October 27, 1988, p. 19.
35. "To Russia with Hope: Ted Turner Tackles Cold War with TV," *Broadcasting*, November 25, 1985, p. 80.
36. "They Are the Exhibit," *USIA World*, March 1988, p. 8.
37. The role of VOA and other media during the coup is described in: "Moscow's Media War Heats Up," *Los Angeles Times*, August 21, 1991, p. 1.
38. "Make It Known," *Washington Post*, August 20, 1991, p. 15.
39. "USIA and the Soviet Crisis," *USIA World*, October 1991, p. 2.

40. "Workers of the World, Fax!" *Washington Post*, December 23, 1990, p. C-13.

41. "America Houses to Open in the Former Soviet Union," *USIA World*, November 1992, p. 3.

42. "U.S.-China Cultural Exchanges," *Gist*, Bureau of Public Affairs, Department of State, November 1981.

43. "Fulbright Program Restored in PRC," *USIA World*, May 1990, p. 5.

44. "Looking Homeward," *Washington Post*, January 28, 2002, p. E-1.

45. "Dr. Spock, Where Are You?" *New York Times Educational Supplement*, April 14, 2002, p. 8.

46. "Click Here for China," *New York Times*, August 4, 2002, p. WK-5.

47. "USIS New Delhi Begins Computerization," *USIA World*, July 1972, p. 5; "USIS Japan Inaugurates Infomat," *USIA Communicator*, September 1972, pp. 24–28.

48. "USIS Vietnam," *State Magazine*, February 1977, p. 32.

49. "I Bureau Is Recasting the Story for a New Era," *Washington Post*, November 10, 1994, p. A-24; "I Bureau: A New Beginning," *USIA World*, December 1994, p. 3; "Inside USIA's Information Bureau," *State Magazine*, February 1988, pp. 12–14.

50. "USIA Sets Its Sites on Yugoslavia," *Washington Post*, April 17, 1999, p. A-15; "Information Bureau Brings High Tech to the Kosovo Crisis," in United States Information Agency, *Commemoration: Public Diplomacy, Looking Back, Looking Forward* (Washington, D.C.: USIA Office of Public Information, 1999), p. 73.

51. "U.S. Funds Help Milosevic's Foes in Election Fight," *Washington Post*, September 19, 2000, p. A-1.

52. "Budget Battles Undercut U.S. Information Effort," *New York Times*, July 7, 1995, p. 2.

53. "The Consolidation Game," *Foreign Service Journal*, May 1995, pp. 36–51.

54. "Clinton Agrees to Shift Foreign Policy Agencies," *Washington Post*, April 18, 1997, p. 1; "A Paradox for Helms on an Abortion Issue," *New York Times*, August 1, 1997, p. 12.

55. The chronology of events leading up to the decision to merge State and USIA is contained in: J. Riley Sever, "Learning from Insiders," *Foreign Service Journal*, December 1997, p. 22.

56. "Senate Kills Two Agencies, Reorganizes Foreign Affairs Roles," *Washington Post*, October 22, 1998, p. A-23.

57. The State Department's official position on the merger is described in: "USIA Merger: Never Was Public Diplomacy Closer to the Policy Center," *State Magazine*, September 1999, pp. 23–25; "USIA-State Integration: A Work in Progress," *State Magazine*, December 2000, pp. 23–26.

11

The Future of Public Diplomacy

WHEN PUBLIC DIPLOMACY operations were returned to the State Department in October 1999, the USIA staff feared that the creativity and energy that marked the program's activities would be stifled within the department's multilayered bureaucracy. Reinforcing their concerns was the popular perception that the agency's chief task, confronting international communism, had been completed. Congressional appropriations after the 1991 collapse of the Soviet state reflected this attitude.

The resulting cutbacks of agency resources worldwide led to missed opportunities, particularly in mounting new programs within the former Soviet Union and its East European client states. Most Cold War restrictions on local USIS operations in the region had been lifted, opening up prospects for responding to pent-up interest about the outside world and the United States in particular.

USIA had already successfully restructured its program activities to exploit the opportunities opened up by advanced information technologies. Its Information Bureau reorganized agency media operations around a new set of computer-based resources, including the Internet. The I-Bureau would continue to be the centerpiece for the information program's operations after the transfer to State.

Other aspects of the shift were less encouraging. As noted, the primary purpose of the move had been to mollify one powerful senator, Chairman Jesse Helms of the Foreign Relations Committee, a longtime critic of USIA operations. Once the transfer was accomplished, the information program received low priority at the White House and State Department and in Congress. Moreover, the transfer to State took place in the lame-duck months of the Clinton administration, when attention was focused on the upcoming presidential election. A transition team was set up to carry out the transfer, with the understanding that the essential decisions on public diplomacy's future would be made by a new president.

Following the 2000 elections, the Bush administration waited nine months before appointing an undersecretary of state for public diplomacy and public affairs. It chose a successful New York advertising executive, Charlotte Beers, who brought new viewpoints to the job that reflected the business orientation of the Bush White House. "I consider the marketing capacity of the United States to be our greatest unlisted asset," she announced.[1] Responding to criticisms of her remarks, Secretary of State Colin Powell declared: "There is nothing wrong with getting someone who knows how to sell something. We are selling a product. We need someone who can rebrand U.S. foreign policy, rebrand diplomacy. . . . Besides," he added, "she got me to buy Uncle Ben's rice."[2]

Branding became the shorthand theme for Charlotte Beers's approach to public diplomacy. "It is almost as though we have to define what America is," she said. "This is the most sophisticated brand assignment I ever had."[3] Carrying out the assignment within the State Department bureaucracy had its hazards, however. One problem was the department's decision to split control over the information program between Undersecretary Beers's office and the regional political bureaus, the traditional centers of most day-to-day decisionmaking within the department. The Beers office would be involved in big-picture planning; the political bureaus would control the details, including decisions on budgetary allocation of resources to overseas posts. It was, at best, an uneasy arrangement.

The greatest challenge to the new public diplomacy effort came in the wake of the September 11, 2001, suicide attacks in New York and Washington by Arab terrorists. Suddenly the mission changed, as the nation faced a different kind of threat: shadowy networks of individuals like Al-Qaeda's Osama bin Laden who operated outside the framework of normal state-to-state relations. Longtime U.S. diplomat Richard Holbrooke asked plaintively: "How can a man in a cave outmaneuver the world's leading communications society?" No longer were the old Cold War rules of containment and deterrence operable. The terrorist threat called for new approaches to winning overseas support for U.S. policies and actions.

Although the effort would be global, its primary focus was on the broad crescent of Muslim nations from Morocco to Indonesia. It was a daunting challenge. A Gallup poll taken in nine Middle Eastern countries after the terrorist attacks in New York and Washington indicated that 61 percent of the respondents did not believe that the attacks were carried out by Arabs. Other polls confirmed a pattern of strong anti-American attitudes throughout the region.[4]

The public diplomacy campaign following the World Trade Center and Pentagon attacks got off to a bad start when President Bush called for a crusade against the terrorists, raising images among Middle Eastern audiences of Christian knights going forth to do battle with the Islamic heathen.[5] The crusade image was summarily dropped, replaced by the theme of respect for Islam and its adherents.

Heavy emphasis was placed on the successful integration of millions of Muslims into U.S. society. It was a credible story, one that had been told in many forms over the years by USIA media. In their new enthusiasm to emphasize U.S. respect for Islam, State Department officials occasionally overstated the theme. One cynical observer suggested a bumper sticker for the effort: "Take a Muslim to Lunch." A series of television programs on Muslim life in the United States was produced for State's public diplomacy unit by McCann-Erickson, the New York advertising firm, at a reported cost of $10 million. The project was only partially successful: many television stations in Islamic countries refused to air the programs.[6]

The activities of other Washington agencies complicated the State Department's efforts to organize a credible public diplomacy response to the terrorist threat. The CIA played a shadowy role, using its own covert resources to influence Middle Eastern public opinion. At the Pentagon, the Defense Department stepped up its extensive psychological operations (psyops). The effort included leaflet drops and radio messages transmitted from specially equipped air force planes during the campaign against Taliban terrorist units in Afghanistan.[7] The Pentagon also dispatched psyops teams to U.S. embassies in the Middle East to back up these operations.

Following the September 2001 terrorist attacks, Defense Department officials made plans for a new "Office of Strategic Influence," whose purpose would be to inform foreign civilian audiences about U.S. military operations. The office would also be authorized to carry out disinformation projects involving dissemination of false information. The project relied heavily on advice from outside consultant firms, notably the Washington-based Rendon Group, already on the Pentagon payroll, to deal with what its founder, John Rendon, called "perception management operations."[8] In the face of opposition from inside and outside the government, the Office of Strategic Influence project was dropped.

The most important change in the new public diplomacy strategy was the Bush administration's decision to take a direct hand in managing it. A special White House task force was formed with the mission of coordinating overseas propaganda efforts to deal with the terrorist threat. It was the first time that any presidential administration had taken such a direct interest in the subject.[9] The *New York Times* described the move as an attempt "to create a 21st century version of the muscular propaganda war that the United States waged in the 1940s."[10]

The first step taken by the new group was to ensure that U.S. government agencies and those of its close allies were "on message" in their policies and operations in dealing with terrorist activities. A Coalition Information Center was set up following the decision to begin military operations against the Taliban regime in Afghanistan. The center resembled a military war room; it was a twenty-four-hour operation, with instant links to similar centers in London and Karachi. A watch committee included officers from the National Security Council, Defense Department, CIA, and Charlotte Beers's State Department bureau.[11]

Meanwhile, plans were under way to expand presidential-level involvement in public diplomacy operations. In July 2002, an Office of Global Communications was created in the White House with a mission "to coordinate the administration's foreign policy messages and supervise America's image abroad." It was a vague charter that had relatively little immediate effect beyond giving an institutional base within the White House bureaucracy to the already existing Coalition Information Center. Nevertheless, the new office represented a significant departure from past presidential practices of assigning low priority to public diplomacy in national-security planning.

At the State Department, the new public diplomacy bureau was strengthened as a result of congressional budget increases tied to the terrorist threat. Although all parts of the operation benefited, the emphasis was on radio programming directed at Islamic audiences in the Middle East. The Voice of America had lost a large segment of its audience in the region as a result of cutbacks in its program schedules during the 1990s. Surveys indicated that fewer than one in fifty Arabs listened to VOA programs.[12] Listenership was even lower among young people under thirty, who made up over 60 percent of the population in Arab countries.

Congress seized upon a proposal advanced by Norman Pattiz, chief executive of Westwood One, the largest chain of U.S. commercial radio stations. Pattiz recommended replacing the VOA's Arabic-language programs with a new service that would rely on Westwood's pop-music format to attract a young Middle Eastern audience. Congress quickly set aside $135 million for the project, Radio Sawa, a name that incorporated the Arabic word for "together." The station began operations in June 2002 with a program schedule featuring Arabic and American pop music interspersed with short news breaks designed to provide information not normally found in Middle Eastern media outlets. Sawa quickly attracted large youthful audiences, drawn to it by the musical format. Less certain has been the station's influence on changing its audience's perceptions about U.S. policies and actions.[13]

Television proved to be a more difficult medium to enlist in the new public diplomacy offensive in the Middle East. The medium's overall influence in the area was widespread, thanks in part to the availability of small reception "dishes" capable of picking up satellite transmissions, including the Atlanta-based Cable News Network (CNN). Although limited to English-language programs, CNN had a small but significant audience throughout the area, primarily because it provided news and other information not available on local government-controlled stations.

The most listened-to TV station in the region, however, was Al-Jazeera, which transmitted Arabic programming by satellite from the Persian Gulf nation of Qatar. From the time it began operations in 1996, Al-Jazeera attracted a wide audience in the region because of its relatively balanced news and a willingness to provide open discussion of controversial issues. It was the only regional station to invite U.S. officials to present their views after the September 2001 terrorist attacks. Meanwhile, the U.S. government made an initial effort in 2001 to reach Middle Eastern television audiences when it provided funds for satellite-based transmissions sponsored by a London-based opposition group, the Iraqi National Congress.[14]

In Washington, Congress showed a new interest in the long-neglected issue of public diplomacy's policy role in U.S. international operations. The terrorist threat had spawned a wide variety of studies on the subject inside and outside the government. The prestigious Council on Foreign Relations proposed a series of reforms, including a public corporation that would encourage government and private-sector efforts to improve the U.S. image abroad.[15] A Defense Department group, the Defense Science Board, recommended better coordination of public diplomacy activities within the Washington bureaucracy.[16]

These studies were grist for congressional efforts to improve public diplomacy policies and practices throughout the government. The House Committee on International Affairs, sparked by the committee's Republican chairman, Henry Hyde of Illinois, and the ranking Democrat, Tom

Lantos of California, took the lead. Their proposed legislation, known as the Freedom Promotion Act, mandated extensive changes within the State Department's public diplomacy structure, including more centralized management of overseas information and cultural operations. Other legislation set a deadline for the department to submit its specific plans for making the changes. In the Senate, Massachusetts Democrat Edward Kennedy proposed a Cultural Bridges Act authorizing a large increase in exchange programs in the Muslim world, including exchanges of high school students.[17]

The Bush administration's new approaches to public diplomacy faced a major test in the months leading up to the invasion of Iraq in March 2003. On the positive side, the White House was better organized to deal with overseas propaganda activities than ever before. Its new Office of International Communications was clearly in charge of coordinating the government agencies involved in public diplomacy strategy, both at the policy and operational levels.[18] For the first time, public diplomacy was given a continuing strong role in carrying out a major U.S. foreign policy initiative.

The effort faced a formidable challenge: the opposition of a large segment of overseas opinion to U.S. plans for war in Iraq. The fiercest protests came from the Middle East, where public attitudes, goaded by government-controlled media, portrayed the U.S. effort to topple the Baghdad regime as an assault on Islam. These opinions overrode the general tendency of Middle Easterners, particularly among educated elites, to admire many aspects of U.S. society.[19]

Despite a strong White House focus on the subject, the effort to influence overseas opinion on the war fell short. The State Department's new public diplomacy office played a useful role in laying out the U.S. case at its overseas posts, although it lacked adequate resources as a result of years of congressional budget cutting. In the circumstances, the lead was taken by the Defense Department, which had the money, the staff, and the will to get involved. Its contribution included vastly expanded psywar operations, from massive leaflet drops to distributing small transistor radios tuned to friendly stations.

The Pentagon's main contribution to public diplomacy during the 2003 Iraq War partially reversed the military's traditional policy of keeping a tight rein on commercial media coverage of its combat operations. Its strategy included setting up an elaborate press-briefing center at its main command post in Qatar, complete with computerized displays of current battlefield operations and other advanced technological aids.[20]

With White House backing, the Pentagon also adopted a policy of allowing media correspondents wide access to combat operations. Hundreds of correspondents and their supporting staffs were (in the Pentagon's phrase) "embedded" with battlefield units and on navy ships. Although the administration touted the project as an example of the military's openness to the media, the overall effect was mixed. Live battlefield reports often provided strong evidence of the effectiveness of individual units. Such reports, however, tended to give a limited and at times false view of the overall military situation. On the whole, Pentagon officials were uncomfortable with the embedment project.[21]

The major public diplomacy breakthrough in the 2003 Iraq War involved television. New video technologies, including small portable cameras, gave media organizations the ability to file live-action reports via satellite.[22] The result was to give new meaning to the phrase "living-room war."

Satellite television, too, played a significant role in the Iraq War in its use by Arab television networks within the Middle East. Although only a small portion of the region's population could receive these programs directly through rooftop video terminals, local television stations rebroadcast the programs widely. This development confirmed satellite television's role as a stunning new factor in international politics in general and in public diplomacy in particular.[23]

As noted, the leading Arab satellite network was Al-Jazeera, a nominally independent operation broadcasting from Qatar. (The government there had a financial stake in what was otherwise a private company.) The station achieved credible prominence throughout the Middle East, primarily because it provided some measure of balanced news, including U.S. viewpoints.[24] The same could not be said of the half-dozen other Arab satellite stations that competed with Al-Jazeera for audiences within the region. By and large, these other stations were propaganda outlets, controlled by local governments.[25]

The U.S. government was slow to recognize the role of satellite television in its public diplomacy strategy for the Iraq War. Although it had funded satellite programs beamed from London before the war by an Iraqi exile organization, it placed greatest reliance on Radio Sawa, its Arab-language radio station that broadcast a mixed schedule of popular music and short news bulletins.

While Sawa was generally successful in attracting a young Arab audience, it soon became clear that television was having a greater impact on regional opinion, particularly after the invasion of Iraq on March 19, 2003. This led to a hurried decision by the Bush administration to fund its own round-the-clock satellite television channel, the Middle Eastern Television Network, featuring American-style morning chat shows, news, sports, and children's programs.[26] The station, managed by the independent Broadcasting Board of Governors in Washington, began full operations early in 2004. "We'll do anything any legitimate organization might do," board member Norman Pattiz declared. "We won't do propaganda."

Beyond satellite television, other advanced communications technologies played a public diplomacy role during the Iraq War and the uneasy standoff that followed. Although the Internet still had a low penetration rate throughout the Middle East, it gave local computer buffs (including those in "cybercafe" coffee houses) a direct connection to world news and opinion, despite efforts by some Arab governments to restrict access to foreign web sites. Cell phones provided similar links, with the Al-Jazeera television network taking the lead in launching a service that sent digests of its news programs to cell phone subscribers in both Arabic and English.[27]

It is too early to measure the effect these changes will have on U.S. public diplomacy. After the September 2001 terrorist events, the initial emphasis was largely on crash-project solutions, reflecting U.S. impatience. Some of this activity may have been useful in drawing attention to public diplomacy. The real need, however, remains a consistent long-term effort to influence attitudes and actions, both public and private, in ways that effectively counter the forces that encourage what political scientist Samuel P. Huntington characterizes as the clash of civilizations.

Another scholar, Akira Iriye at Johns Hopkins University, argues for a new emphasis on what he calls "cultural internationalism," an academic cliché that masks an important reality. As Iriye points out:

> Much has been made of the alleged "chaos" that is said to have ensued in the aftermath of the Cold War. But it is not really a chaos at all if one views international affairs as a cultural phenomenon. It simply means that now military power, strategy, mobilizing for war, and alliance diplomacy have lost their once dominant roles in defining international relations. Other forces, social and cultural, are coming to the fore. They have not been noticed . . . because of the preoccupation with the geopolitical realities of international affairs. But by adopting the cultural perspective, it would be possible to write a different sort of international history.[28]

Professor Iriye's cultural internationalism is an awkward term for describing profound changes in the global political order in general and

U.S. strategic interests in particular. His ideas reflect the evolution of a liberal international order, even in its present early stages, that has strong U.S. roots, beginning with the vision and actions of, among others, Woodrow Wilson and Franklin Roosevelt.

A new way of organizing global order is emerging, and it has profound implications for the future of public diplomacy. The basic structure for this new order has been built by the United States and its democratic allies, strengthened by alliances, formal and informal, that helped turn back totalitarian threats since 1940. At another level of cooperative action, the democracies took the lead in creating a remarkable network of international organizations, inside and outside the United Nations, to deal with problems beyond their national reach.

These actions have also encouraged the fastest-growing challenge to traditional nationalism—the new global role of nongovernmental organizations. NGOs make up a large mixed bag that includes (among others) transnational businesses, academic institutions, professional organizations, and a wide range of narrowly focused advocacy groups. A 1999 United Nations survey of NGOs with global agendas listed almost thirty thousand of them, heavily dominated by U.S.-based organizations.[29]

These groups increasingly tilt the balance of political influence away from traditional government activities in their own countries and in the wider world. The new century has witnessed a particular upsurge in privately sponsored networks monitoring a wide range of cross-border issues, from the eradication of malaria to the depletion of the world's fishing grounds. The World Bank has identified about fifty such major policy-oriented networks, all thriving in a borderless environment beyond the reach of traditional government activities.[30]

Among the many explanations for this new kind of internationalism, the common thread running through all of them is the use that NGOs make of global electronic networks and the digital information that flows through them. This is an essential part of the "soft power" that Harvard's Joseph Nye sees as a defining element of the new internationalism. It is the major factor influencing the role of U.S. public diplomacy in a new era.

Any consideration of this subject begins with the recognition that the United States is setting the pace and direction of efforts to link the world electronically. It is the first society to make the transition to a postindustrial era in which the production, storage, and distribution of information is its primary activity. Currently about 35 percent of global communications traffic originates or terminates in the United States, a country with less than 6 percent of the world's population. A useful measure of information power is the number of databases a nation possesses. At the turn of the century, the United States had five thousand major data banks, double the number installed in all other countries combined.

The rest of the world is catching up, beginning with Europe, Canada, and Japan. The most startling changes are taking place in many so-called third-world nations. A decade ago, mainland China stood near the bottom of the list in terms of per capita telephone penetration—a rough but convenient index. This is no longer true. Thanks to a massive investment in modern telecommunications ordered by the country's Communist leaders, China will have the world's largest national phone network within the next few years. Similar gains are being made throughout the rest of Asia and in Latin America. The exception is Africa, where per capita expansion of information and telecommunications resources is being outpaced by high birth rates and a rapidly rising population.

Despite these overseas developments, the United States will continue to put its unique imprint on global information patterns. Nowhere is this more evident than in its influence on Internet growth. At the turn of the twenty-first century, about half the network's users were Americans. All but 6 percent of the most visited World Wide Web sites are in the United States. Moreover, an American aura pervades the entire network. "The Internet is profoundly disrespectful of tradition, established order, and hierarchy, and that is very American," says foreign policy analyst Fareed Zakaria.[31]

The dominant U.S. role in Internet content has refueled foreign criticism, particularly among elites, about the Americanization of their societies. A French minister of culture, Jack Lang, famously echoed this theme when he described U.S. information exports as part of a "financial and cultural imperialism that no longer grabs territory, or rarely, but grabs consciousness, ways of thinking, ways of living."[32] The accusation suggests that foreign cultures are overwhelmed by a one-way flow of goods and services from Hollywood, New York, and other production centers.

The charge is overwrought. The United States is the world's largest exporter of cultural goods and services, but it is also the world's largest *importer* of such services. In 1998 (the last year for which comprehensive figures are available), the United States had a deficit of over $38 billion in this sector, according to an analysis of global cultural trade by George Mason University economist Tyler Cowen.[33] This massive two-way flow of images and ideas, from the sublime to the silly, suggests a

United States that has established a rough balance in its information and cultural dealings with the rest of the world.

As noted above, the U.S. preeminence in information and cultural exports (broadly defined) will alter over time. However, the United States' influence in this sector will continue to be sustained not only by its own momentum but also by the continuing attractiveness of American images and ideas for overseas audiences. Moreover, the audience for these ideas is expanding in size and in its ability to deal directly with information and cultural services that are no longer controlled (as they have been historically) by governments and/or local mandarin elites.

The Internet is the spectacular example of this new technology-based freedom of individual choice. Attempts by authoritarian governments overseas to control Internet use have been largely futile. Another liberating technology, that of mobile phones, provides pocket-sized global access to voice, data, and visual information beyond the control of the old guardians of information flows. Cell phones are becoming the new instruments of political and social change, particularly among young people overseas, according to information-age guru Howard Rheingold.[34]

These trends are already affecting the shape and direction of public diplomacy. Such diplomacy will operate in an increasingly higher-decibel political environment, here and abroad, where critical information on public policy issues can be lost or ignored in the Babel of competing voices and images. Government-sponsored information and cultural operations play a steadily diminishing role in this pattern.

Do public diplomacy programs still serve U.S. national interests in the new global order? Or are they an anachronism from the Cold War in a new world of information choices? The question is valid, and the answer is clear. The United States still needs to articulate its policies and actions overseas, if only to assure that an official account of them is available. A more difficult question is how to shape public diplomacy operations so that they are effective in reaching an increasingly complex pattern of audiences abroad, particularly in the aftermath of the September 2001 terrorist attacks. Given U.S. impatience, this could prompt an even larger public relations effort, including all the trappings of "branding" and other Madison Avenue techniques. Such a strategy would at best produce minimal results and more probably a backlash from the intended audiences abroad.

The more effective approach is to reshape public diplomacy operations to information-age realities, recognizing that they have a special niche in the complex pattern of U.S. international interests. This means doing a better job of integrating overseas information and cultural factors into strategic decisions affecting the U.S. role in the world. It also means recognizing the validity of Iriye's concept of cultural internationalism, the push-pull role of ideology in moving toward a more stable pattern of global order.

In particular this involves a continuing policy commitment to removing barriers to information and cultural flows throughout the world. Overall, the United States has played a strong role in this area in the past half century, from the 1948 UN Declaration of Human Rights through the Helsinki Accords in the 1970s and, more recently, U.S. advocacy of trade liberalization in information goods and services in the World Trade Organization.

For almost half a century, the U.S. Information Agency played a critical role in establishing and reinforcing policies and programs in this area. Although its day-to-day activities focused largely on short-term political issues, the record suggests that the agency was most effective when it promoted broad U.S. purposes. This legacy includes its cultural operations—libraries, book publishing, and particularly institutional support for exchange programs, from ballet companies to Fulbright scholarships. Although many of these cultural activities now flourish abroad under private auspices, the record of accomplishments argues strongly for a continued official presence in this sector.

The task of presenting the many voices of America, both public and private, remains. The challenge was defined by F. Scott Fitzgerald early in the last century when he wrote: "France was a land, England was a people, but America, having still about it that quality of an idea, was harder to utter."

Notes

1. "From Uncle Ben's to Uncle Sam," *Economist* (London), February 23, 2002, p. 70.
2. "Brand USA," *Los Angeles Times,* March 10, 2002, p. 1.
3. "The USA Account," *Washington Post,* December 31, 2001, p. C-1.
4. "US Message Lost Overseas," *Washington Post,* October 14, 2001, p. 1; "Bush, Congress Need Joint Strategy to Fight Anti-U.S. Propaganda," *Roll Call,* May 9, 2002, p. 1.
5. "A Battle on Many Fronts," *Economist* (London), October 6, 2001, p. 15.
6. "Muslim-as-Apple-Pie Videos Are Greeted with Skepticism," *New York Times,* October 20, 2002, p. 1.
7. "U.S. Beams Its Message to Afghans," *Washington Post,* October 19, 2001, p. A-20.

8. "John Rendon's Shallow PR War on Terrorism: Flack America," *New Republic*, May 20, 2002, p. 12.
9. "Bush to Create Formal Office to Shape U.S. Image Abroad," *Washington Post*, July 30, 2002, p. 1.
10. "In the War on Terrorism, a Battle to Shape Opinion," *New York Times*, November 11, 2001, p. 1.
11. "U.S., Britain Step Up War for Public Opinion," *Washington Post*, November 1, 2001, p. 1.
12. "Towers of Babelaganda," *Economist* (London), August 24, 2002, p. 36.
13. "Radio Sawa: Music as a Tool," *Foreign Service Journal*, November 2002, pp. 53–57.
14. "U.S. Funds Satellite TV to Iraq," *Washington Post*, August 16, 2001, p. A-21.
15. The council's recommendations are described in: Peter G. Peterson, "Public Diplomacy and the War on Terrorism," *Foreign Affairs*, September-October 2002, pp. 74–94.
16. "Managed Information Dissemination," Report of the Defense Science Board task force, Office of the Under Secretary for Acquisitions, Technology, and Logistics, Department of Defense, October 2001.
17. "Building Bridges to Islam," *Washington Post*, June 12, 2002, p. A-23.
18. "Bush Message Machine Is Set to Roll with Its Own War Plan," *Washington Post*, March 19, 2003, p. 1; "White House: Shepherding the Story," *National Journal*, March 22, 2003, pp. 922–924.
19. John Waterbury, "Hate Your Policies; Love Your Institutions," *Foreign Affairs*, January-February 2003, pp. 58–68; "America Inspires Both Longing and Loathing in Muslim World," *New York Times*, September 16, 2001, p. 4.
20. "The Ring of Truth?" *New York Times*, April 8, 2003, p. 12.
21. "Being There: Suddenly the Pentagon Grants Access to the Action but the Devil Is in the Details," *Columbia Journalism Review*, March-April 2003, pp. 18–21.
22. "The High-Tech War," *E-Week*, March 31, 2003, p. 1.
23. "Both Sides Spar with Images and Words," *Chicago Tribune*, March 27, 2003, p. 1; "Across the Arab World: TV Images Stir Anger, Shock and Warnings of Backlash," *Washington Post*, April 10, 2003, p. A-41.
24. "In the Line of Fire," *Washington Post*, April 3, 2003, p. C-1.
25. "Arab TV Stations Gear Up for Home Front Fight in Iraq War," *Financial Times* (London), February 3, 2003, p. 14; "The Arab TV Wars," *New York Times Magazine*, April 27, 2003, pp. 45–47.
26. "Tune In for America's Next Campaign in the Middle East," *Financial Times* (London), April 16, 2003, p. 11.
27. "Cellphone News from Al-Jezeera," *Financial Times* (London), April 3, 2003, p. 5.
28. Akira Iriye, *Cultural Internationalism and World Order* (Baltimore, Md.: Johns Hopkins University Press, 1997), p. 183.
29. "The 'Firemen' of Africa Feel the Heat of Scrutiny," *Financial Times* (London), August 19, 1999, p. 4.
30. Wilson Dizard Jr., *Digital Diplomacy: Foreign Policy in the Information Age* (New York: Praeger, 2001), p. 10.

31. "Welcome to the Internet: The First Global Colony," *New York Times,* January 9, 2000, p. WK-1.

32. "French Minister Cites U.S. Cultural Influence," *New York Times,* November 16, 1984, p. C-26.

33. Tyler Cowen, *Creative Destruction: How Globalization Is Changing the World's Cultures* (Princeton, N.J.: Princeton University Press, 2002).

34. Howard Rheingold, *Smart Mobs: Transforming Cultures and Communities in the Age of Instant Access* (New York: Perseus Publishing, 2002).

Selected Bibliography

Abshire, David, ed. *Triumphs and Tragedies of the Modern Presidency.* Washington, D.C.: Center for the Study of the Presidency, 2000.
Alexandre, Laurien. *The Voice of America: From Détente to the Reagan Doctrine.* Norwood, N.J.: Ablex Publishing, 1988.
Arbatov, Georgei. *The War of Ideas in Contemporary International Relations.* Moscow: Progress Publishers, 1973.
Arndt, Richard T., and David Lee Rubin. *The Fulbright Difference 1948–1992.* New Brunswick, N.J.: Transaction Publishers, 1993.
Barrett, Edward W. *Truth Is Our Weapon.* New York: Funk & Wagnalls, 1953.
Bergahn, Volker R. *America and the Intellectual Cold War in Europe.* Princeton, N.J.: Princeton University Press, 2001.
Bernhard, Nancy E. *U.S. Television News and Cold War Propaganda.* Cambridge Studies in the History of Mass Communications. New York: Cambridge University Press, 2002.
Beshchloss, Michael. *The Crisis Years.* New York: HarperCollins, 1991.
Blum, Robert, ed. *Cultural Relations and Foreign Affairs.* Englewood, N.J.: Prentice Hall, 1963.
Bogart, Leo. *Promises for Propaganda: The United States Information Agency's Operating Assumptions in the Cold War.* Boston: Free Press, 1976.
Borstelman, Thomas. *The Cold War and the Color Line: Race Relations and American Foreign Policy.* Cambridge, Mass.: Harvard University Press, 2002.
Braisted, Paul J., ed. *Cultural Affairs and Foreign Relations.* Englewood Cliffs, N.J.: Prentice Hall, 1968.
Browne, Donald R. *International Radio Broadcasting: The Limits of a Limitless Medium.* New York: Praeger, 1982.
Brzezinski, Zbigniew. *Between Two Worlds: America's Role in the Technotronic Era.* New York: Viking Press, 1970.
Carroll, Wallace. *Persuade or Perish.* Boston: Houghton Mifflin Co., 1948.
Casey, Steven. *Franklin D. Roosevelt, American Public Opinion, and the War Against Nazi Germany.* New York: Oxford University Press, 2001.
Caute, David. *The Dancer Defects: The Struggle for Cultural Supremacy During the Cold War.* New York: Oxford University Press, 2003.

Chace, James. *Acheson.* New York: Simon & Schuster, 1998.
Chandler, Alice. *Obligation or Opportunity: Foreign Student Policy in Six Major Receiving Countries.* New York: Institute of International Education, 1989.
Clark, Keith, and Laurence Legere, eds. *The President and the Management of National Security.* New York: Praeger, 1969.
Coleman, Peter. *The Liberal Conspiracy: The Congress for Cultural Freedom and the Struggle for the Mind of Postwar Europe.* New York: Free Press, 1989.
Council on Foreign Relations. *Finding America's Voice: A Strategy for Reinvigorating Public Diplomacy.* Report of the Independent Task Force on Public Diplomacy. New York: Council on Foreign Relations, 2003.
Cowen, Tyler. *Creative Destruction: How Globalization Is Changing the World's Cultures.* Princeton, N.J.: Princeton University Press, 2002.
Cruickshank, Charles. *The Fourth Arm: Psychological Warfare 1938–1945.* London: Davis-Poynter, 1977.
Cull, Nicholas John. *Selling War: The British Propaganda Campaign Against American "Neutrality" in World War II.* New York: Oxford University Press, 1996.
Daugherty, William, ed. *The Art and Science of Psychological Operations: Case Studies in Military Applications.* Report No. 525-7-1. Department of the Army, U.S. Defense Department, April 1976.
Davison, W. Phillips. *Mass Communcation and Conflict Resolution.* New York: Praeger, 1974.
Davy, Richard. *European Détente: A Reappraisal.* London: Royal Institute of International Affairs, 1992.
Delmer, Sefton. *Black Boomerang.* London: Secker & Warburg, 1962.
Desmond, James. *Nelson Rockefeller: A Political Biography.* New York: Macmillan, 1964.
Dickson, Paul. *Sputnik: The Shock of the Century.* New York: Walter & Co., 2001.
Dizard, Wilson P. *Digital Diplomacy.* Westport, Conn.: Praeger Publishers, 2001.
———. *Old Media, New Media,* 3rd ed. New York: Longman, 2000.
———. *Meganet: How the Global Communications Network Will Connect Everyone on Earth.* New York: HarperCollins/Westview Press, 1997.
———. *The Coming Information Age: An Overview of Technology, Economics, and Politics,* 3rd ed. New York: Longman, 1989.
———. *Television: A World View.* Syracuse, N.Y.: Syracuse University Press, 1965.
———. *The Strategy of Truth: The Story of the U.S. Information Service.* Washington, D.C.: Public Affairs Press, 1961.
Dizard, Wilson, and Blake Swensrud. *Gorbachev's Information Revolution: Controlling Glasnost in a New Electronic Era.* Significant Issues Series, vol. 9, no. 8. Washington, D.C.: Center for Strategic and International Studies, 1987.
Dudziak, Mary L. *Cold War Civil Rights: Race and the Image of American Democracy.* Princeton, N.J.: Princeton University Press, 2002.
Elder, Robert Ellsworth. *The Information Machine: The United States Information Agency and American Foreign Policy.* Syracuse, N.Y.: Syracuse University Press, 1968.

Ellul, Jacques. *Propaganda: The Formation of Men's Attitudes.* New York: Vintage Books, 1973.
Ferrell, Robert H. *American Diplomacy: A History.* New York: Norton, 1969.
Fisher, Glen H. *Public Diplomacy and the Behavioral Sciences.* Bloomington: Indiana University Press, 1972.
Fousek, John. *To Lead the Free World: American Nationalism and the Cultural Roots of the Cold War.* Chapel Hill: University of North Carolina Press, 2000.
Frankel, Charles. *High on Foggy Bottom: An Outsider's Inside View of the Government.* New York: Harper & Row, 1968.
———. *The Neglected Aspect of Foreign Affairs.* Washington, D.C.: Brookings Institution, 1966.
Glendon, Mary Ann. *A World Made New: Eleanor Roosevelt and the Universal Declaration of Human Rights.* New York: Random House, 2001.
Green, Fitzhugh. *American Propaganda Abroad.* New York: Hippocrene Books, 1988.
Grose, Peter. *Operation Rollback: America's Secret War Behind the Iron Curtain.* Boston: Houghton Mifflin, 2000.
Hansen, Allen. *U.S. Information Agency: Public Diplomacy in the Information Age.* 2nd ed. New York: Praeger, 1989.
Heil, Alan. *The Voice of America.* New York: Oxford University Press, 2003.
Henderson, John William. *The United States Information Agency.* New York: Praeger, 1969.
Hitchcock, David I., Jr. *U.S. Public Diplomacy.* Significant Issues Series, vol. 10, no. 17. Washington, D.C.: Center for Strategic and International Studies, 1988.
Hixson, Walter L. *Parting the Curtain: Propaganda, Culture, and the Cold War.* New York: St. Martin's Press, 1997.
Hoffman, Arthur S., ed. *International Communication and the New Diplomacy.* Bloomington: Indiana University Press, 1968.
Holt, Robert T., and Robert W. van der Velde. *Strategic Operations and American Foreign Policy.* Chicago: University of Chicago Press, 1960.
Iriye, Akira. *Cultural Internationalism and World Order.* Baltimore, Md.: Johns Hopkins University Press, 1997.
Jowett, Garth S., and Victoria O'Donnell. *Propaganda and Persuasion.* Newbury Park, Calif.: Sage, 1986.
Keilson, Jerrold, ed. *A Salute to Citizen Diplomacy: A History of the National Council for International Visitors.* Washington, D.C.: National Council for International Visitors, 2000.
Kissinger, Henry M., ed. *Kissinger Transcripts: The Top Secret Talks with Beijing and Moscow.* New York: Free Press, 1999.
Koppes, Gregory, and Gregory D. Black. *Hollywood Goes to War: How Politics, Profits, and Propaganda Shaped World War II Movies.* New York: Free Press/Macmillan, 1987.
Kraus, Max. *They All Came to Geneva and Other Tales of a Public Diplomat.* Washington, D.C.: Seven Locks Press, 1988.
Krugler, David F. *The Voice of America and the Domestic Propaganda Battles, 1945–1953.* Columbia: University of Missouri Press, 2000.
Lasswell, Harold S. *Propaganda Techniques in World War I.* Cambridge, Mass.: MIT Press, 1971.

Latham, Michael E. *Modernization as Ideology: American Social Science and Nation Building in the Kennedy Era.* Chapel Hill: University of North Carolina Press, 2000.
Lerner, Daniel. *Psychological Warfare Against Nazi Germany: The Sykewar Campaign, D-Day to VE Day.* Cambridge, Mass.: MIT Press, 1971.
Lippmann, Walter. *Public Opinion.* New York: Houghton Mifflin, 1922.
Lipset, Seymour Martin. *American Exceptionalism.* New York: W. W. Norton, 1996.
Malone, Gifford D. *Political Advocacy and Cultural Communications: Organizing the Nation's Public Diplomacy.* Lanham, Md.: University Press of America, 1988.
Menges, Constantine, ed. *The Marshall Plan from Those Who Made It Succeed.* Lanham, Md.: University Press of America, 1999.
Miscamble, Wilson D. *George Kennan and the Making of American Policy.* Princeton, N.J.: Princeton University Press, 1992.
Mitchell, J. M. *International Cultural Relations.* London: Allen and Unwin, 1986.
Mitrovich, Gregory P. *Undermining the Kremlin: America's Strategy for Subverting the Soviet Bloc 1947–1950.* Ithaca, N.Y.: Cornell University Press, 2000.
Nelson, Michael. *War of the Black Heavens: The Battles of Western Broadcasting in the Cold War.* Syracuse, N.Y.: Syracuse University Press, 1997.
Newsom, David D. *Diplomacy and the American Democracy.* Bloomington: Indiana University Press, 1988.
Ninkovich, Frank A. *The Diplomacy of Ideas: U.S. Foreign Policy and Cultural Relations, 1938–1950.* New York: Cambridge University Press, 1981.
Page, Caroline. *U.S. Official Propaganda During the Vietnam War.* Leicester, UK: Leicester University Press, 1996.
Persico, Joseph E. *Edward R. Murrow: An American Original.* New York: Da Capo, 1997.
Pike, Douglas. *Viet Cong: The Organization and Techniques of the National Liberation Front of South Vietnam.* Cambridge, Mass.: MIT Press, 1966.
Pool, Ithiel de Sola, and Donald Blackmer, eds. *The Emerging Nations.* Cambridge, Mass.: MIT Press, 1962.
Prevots, Naima. *Dance for Export: Cultural Diplomacy and the Cold War.* Middletown, Conn.: Wesleyan University Press, 2001.
Price, Harry Bayard. *The Marshall Plan and Its Meaning.* Ithaca, N.Y.: Cornell University Press, 1952.
Rawnsley, Gary D. *Radio Diplomacy and Propaganda: The BBC and VOA in International Politics, 1956–1964.* New York: St. Martin's Press, 1996.
Read, William H. *America's Mass Media Merchants.* Baltimore, Md.: Johns Hopkins University Press, 1976.
Remington, Thomas F. *The Truth of Authority: Ideology and Communication in the Soviet Union.* Pittsburgh, Penn.: University of Pittsburgh Press, 1988.
Richmond, Yale. *Cultural Exchange and the Cold War: Raising the Iron Curtain.* State College, Penn.: Penn State University Press, 2003.
———. *From Nyet to Da: Understanding the Russians.* Yarmouth, Me.: Intercultural Press, 1993.

———. *U.S.-Soviet Cultural Exchanges, 1956–1988*. Boulder, Colo.: Westview Press, 1987.
Riegal, O. W. *Mobilizing for Chaos: The Story of the New Propaganda*. New Haven, Conn.: Yale University Press, 1934.
Robin, Ron. *Barbed Wire College: Reeducating German POWs in the United States During World War II*. Princeton, N.J.: Princeton University Press, 1995.
Rosenberg, Emily S. *Spreading the American Dream: American Economic and Cultural Expansion 1890-1939*. New York: Hill and Wang, 1982.
Rowan, Carl. *Breaking Barriers: A Memoir*. New York: HarperCollins, 1992.
Sanders, Francis Stone. *The Cultural Cold War: The CIA and the World of Arts and Letters*. New York: New Press, 2000.
Schiller, Herbert I. *Communication and Cultural Domination*. White Plains, N.Y.: International Arts and Sciences Press, 1976.
Schlesinger, Arthur M., Jr. *A Thousand Days: John F. Kennedy in the White House*. Boston: Houghton Mifflin, 1965.
Schramm, Wilbur. Ed. by Stephen Chaffee and Everett M. Rogers. *The Beginnings of Communications Studies in America*. Thousand Oaks, Calif.: Sage, 1997.
Short, K.R.M. *Film and Radio Propaganda in World War II*. Knoxville: University of Tennessee Press, 1983.
Shulman, Holly Cowan. *The Voice of America: Propaganda and Democracy 1941–1945*. Madison: University of Wisconsin Press, 1990.
Simpson, Howard R. *Bush Hat, Black Tie: Adventures of a Foreign Service Officer*. ADST-DACOR Diplomats and Diplomacy Series. Washington, D.C./London: Brassey's, 1998.
Smith, Anthony. *The Geopolitics of Information: How Western Culture Dominates the World*. London: Faber and Faber, 1980.
Snyder, Alvin. *Warriors of Disinformation: American Propaganda, Soviet Lies and the Winning of the Cold War*. New York: Arcade, 1995.
Soley, Lawrence C. *Radio Warfare: OSS and CIA Subversive Propaganda*. New York: Praeger, 1989.
Sorensen, Thomas C. *The Word War: The Story of American Propaganda*. New York: Harper & Row, 1968.
Spanier, John W., and Joseph L. Nogel. *The Politics of Disarmament*. New York: Praeger Publishers, 1962.
Staar, Richard F., ed. *The Future Information Revolution in the USSR*. New York: Crane Russek, 1988.
Stearns, Monteagle. *Talking to Strangers: Improving American Diplomacy at Home and Abroad*. Princeton, N.J.: Princeton University Press, 1996.
Steele, Richard W. *Propaganda in an Open Society: The Roosevelt Administration and the Media*. Westport, Conn.: Greenwood Press, 1965.
Stephens, Oren. *Facts to a Candid World: America's Overseas Information Program*. Stanford, Calif.: Stanford University Press, 1955.
Taylor, Philip M. *Communications, International Affairs, and the Media Since 1945*. New York: Routledge, 1997.
———. *The Projection of Britain: British Overseas Publicity and Propaganda 1919–1939*. New York: Cambridge University Press, 1981.

Thomas, Daniel C. *The Helsinki Effect: International Norms, Human Rights, and the Demise of Communism.* Princeton, N.J.: Princeton University Press, 2001.
Thomson, Charles A. *Overseas Information Service of the U.S. Government.* Washington, D.C.: Brookings Institution, 1948.
Tuch, Hans N., ed. *USIA: Communicating with the World in the 1990s: A Commemorative Symposium.* Washington, D.C.: USIA Alumni Association and the Public Diplomacy Foundation, 1994.
———. *Communicating with the World: U.S. Public Diplomacy.* New York: St. Martin's Press, 1990.
Tuch, Hans N., and G. Lewis Schmidt, eds. *Ike and USIA: A Commemorative Symposium.* Washington, D.C.: USIA Alumni Association and the Public Diplomacy Foundation, 1991.
Tunstall, Jeremy, ed. *The Media Are American.* London: Constable, 1977.
United States Information Agency. *Commemoration: Public Diplomacy, Looking Back, Looking Forward.* Washington, D.C.: USIA Office of Public Information, 1999.
Wagnleitner, Reinhold, and Elaine Tyler May, eds. *Here, There and Everywhere: The Foreign Politics of American Culture.* Hanover, N.H.: University Press of New England, 2000.
Whitaker, Urban G., ed. *Propaganda and International Relations.* Chandler Studies in International and Intercultural Relations. San Francisco, Calif.: Chandler, 1960.
Wilhelm, Alfred D. *The Chinese at the Negotiating Table.* Washington, D.C.: National Defense University Press, 1991.
Winkler, Allan M. *The Politics of Propaganda: The Office of War Information 1942–1945.* New Haven, Conn.: Yale University Press, 1978.
Winks, Robin. *Cloak and Gown: Scholars in the Secret War 1939–1962.* New York: Quill Publishers, 1987.

Index

ACDA. *See* Arms Control and Disarmament Agency
Acheson, Dean, 52, 163
Afghanistan, 222
Africa: decolonization in, 64; guerrilla warfare in, 92; nonalignment in, 77; resistance to U.S. Information Service in, 92; trade fairs and exhibits in, 133; U.S. Information Agency in, 77, 78, 92, 97, 98, 125, *125;* U.S. Information Service libraries in, 93; U.S. Information Service posts in, 48; wars of national liberation in, 84
African National Congress, 205, 206
African Regional Service, 183
Africa Today (newsreel), 93
AFSA. *See* American Foreign Service Association
Agency for International Development, 215
Aggrey, Rudolph, 90
Agriculture Department, 134
Aldrin, Edmund "Buzz," 112
Al-Jazeera, 203, 215, 223, 225
Allegre, Claude, 191
Allen, George, 47, 66, 76
Alliance for Progress, 84, 130
All-Russian State Television and Broadcasting Co., 211
Al-Qaeda, 220
"America At Home" (exhibit), 71
America Houses, 42, 181, 211

America Illustrated (magazine), 29, 72, 166, 211
American Ballet Theater, 192
American Broadcasting Station, 25
American Civil Liberties Union, 24
American Cowboy (film), 168
American Foreign Service Association, 161
American Information Service, 30
American Institute of Public Opinion, 20
American Legion, 55
American Library Association, 179
"American National Exhibition" (exhibit), 73
American Reporter (newspaper), 64, 156, 165
American Revolution Bicentennial Commission, 114, 115
American Society of Newspaper Editors, 48, 69, 70
Ameryka (magazine), 71, *124,* 204
Anderson, Burnett, 115
Anderson, Judith, 192
Anderson, Marian, 192–193
And Now, Miguel (film), 168
Angelou, Maya, 188
Apollo space program, 109–114
Argentina: U.S. Information Agency in, 130
Armed Forces Network (AFN) radio, 25, 134, 135; addition of television to programs, 135; as alternative to

Voice of America, 135; British Broadcasting System and, 25; credibility of, 136; English-language skills and, 135; as ideological resource, 25; local audiences, 135; medium-wave transmission, 135; mission of, 135; young audience for, 135
Arms Control and Disarmament Agency, 118, 215
Armstrong, Louis, 193
Armstrong, Neil, 112
Aron, Raymond, 57
Asia: decolonization in, 64; nonalignment in, 77; Office of War Information posts in, 29; radio broadcasts to, 25; trade fairs and exhibits in, 133; U.S. Information Agency in, 77, 78, 92, 97, 98; U.S. Information Service posts in, 48; Voice of America in, 25; wars of national liberation in, 84
Asia Foundation, 140
Associated Press, 26, 136, 158, 160
Atlantic Charter, 29, 31
Atoms for Peace plan, 70, 118
Aubin, Henry, 113
Azanian People's Organization, 206

Bacon, Roger, 186
Bay of Pigs invasion, 87
BBC. *See* British Broadcasting Corporation
Bechet, Sidney, 193
Beers, Charlotte, 220, 222
Benton, Thomas Hart, 2
Benton, William, 39, 44, 47, 48; warnings given on Soviet Union expansionist operations by, 40
Berding, Andrew, 146
Berger, Samuel, 193
Better World Society, 210
BIB. *See* Board for International Broadcasting
Bicentennial celebration, 109, 114–117, 121n20
Billington, James, 188
bin Laden, Osama, 220
Bisbee, Roy, 96
Black, Shirley Temple, 156
Black propaganda operations, 11, 31, 32, 141

Blair, Tony, 189
Blondie for Victory (film), 27
Board for International Broadcasting, 144
Bogart, Humphrey, 28
Bogart, Leo, 69
Bogart Study, 80n16
Bolivia: U.S. Information Agency in, 130, *130*
Boutros-Ghali, Boutros, 188
Bowles, Chester, 156, 184
Boxer Rebellion, 187
Boxer scholarships, 187
Brady, Lee, 77
Branding, 220, 229
Brandt, Willy, 42
Brinkley, David, 201
Britain: American bicentennial celebration in, 116; black propaganda operations in, 11, 31, 32; covert assistance to during World War II, 8, 9; Ministry of Information, 32; network development in, 2; Political Warfare Executive in, 31, 32; request for assistance in psychological warfare operations, 9; U.S. support for in World War II, 9
British Broadcasting Corporation (BBC), 23, 35n18, 75; Armed Forces Network radio and, 25; Empire Service, 23; end of jamming operations against, 208; government control and, 23; wartime radio broadcasts by, 24
British Council, 147
Broger, John, 137
Brown, John, 178
Brubeck, Dave, 192
Brumberg, Abraham, 166
Buckley, William, 108
Buenos Aires Convention, 148
Bundy, McGeorge, 86
Burdette, Franklin, 46, 66
Bureaucrats Bowling League, 97
Bush, George W., 220, 224
Bush, George H. W., 204
Buthelezi, Gatsha, 206
Byrnes, James, 39, 40

Cable News Network, 203, 210, 215, 223

Cambodia: communist-led insurgencies in, 77
Campaign of Truth, 48, 56, 64
Carlsson, Ingvar, 188
Carroll, Phil, 156
Carter, Jimmy, 200
Casablanca (film), 27
Casey Jones Special, 169
Castro, Fidel, 87, 89
Catto, Henry, 213
CBS. *See* Columbia Broadcasting System
Censorship, 66, 181; by media, 26; in postwar Germany, 41; in postwar Japan, 44
Center for Democracy, 211
Central Intelligence Agency, 134; Asia Foundation and, 140; Congress of Cultural Freedom and, 140; covert operations, 5, 49, 54, 67, 139, 140, 141, 150$n18;$ creation of, 38; Cuban missile crisis and, 88; current operations, 221; deniability in activities, 139; Directorate of Operations, 11, 139; disinformation programs, 141; Foreign Broadcast Information Service, 141; forerunners of, 11; influence on Italian elections, 51; National Security Council and, 68; National Students Union and, 140; Office of Policy Coordination, 51; Radio Free Europe and, 51, 142, 151$n28;$ Radio Liberation and, 51, 142, 151$n28;$ relations with U.S. Information Agency, 5, 139–145; and Soviet Union, 67, 140; unvouchered funds for, 50, 51
Charter 77 (Prague), 105
Chiang Kai-shek, 30, 107
China: civil war in, 30; closure to world, 106; communist takeover in, 106; diplomatic relations with United States, 107; exchange programs with, 31; ideological conflict with Soviet Union, 103, 104; ideological operations in, 31; information/cultural exchanges with, 108, 191, 211–212; lack of attention to American bicentennial in, 116; modern telecommunications and, 228; Office of War Information posts in, 30, 31; People's Liberation Army in, 107; relations with Nixon, 106, 107; Tienanmen Square uprising in, 212; U.S. Information Agency in, 108, 211, 212; U.S. Information Service posts in, 31; use of Internet in, 211, 212; Voice of America in, 211, 212
Chronicle of Human Events, 209
Churchill, Winston, 10–11, 25, 30, 31
CIAA. *See* Office of the Coordinator of Interamerican Affairs
Civil Rights Act (1964), 120
Civil rights movement, 109, 119–120
Clay, Lucius, 43
Coalition Information Center, 222
Cohn, Roy, 57
COI. *See* Office of the Coordinator of Information
Cold War, 1; expansion of ideological programs and, 3; politics of, 103; science as factor in mobilization of resources in, 110; United States technical edge in, 114
Collins, Michael, 112
Columbia Broadcasting System, 23–24, 47; public opinion polling and, 21
Committee on International Information Activities, 53, 67
Committee on Public Information, 14$n5$
Communications: defining, 19; international, 20; mass, 19; modern telecommunications, 228; pattern changes, 103; social, 20; use of radio for propaganda purposes, 23; worldwide networks, 5
Communication satellites, 89, 90, 91, 103, 135, 203
Communications Satellite Corporation, 98
Communism, 18; China/Soviet Union confrontation over leadership, 103, 104; imperialistic, 48; in Italy, 51
Conference on Security and Cooperation in Europe. *See* Helsinki Accords
Congress of Cultural Freedom, 140
Conover, Willis, 70, 193
Cooper, Saths, 206
Copland, Aaron, 188

242 Index

Counterinsurgency theories, 91
Cowan, Geoffrey, 215
Cowen, Tyler, 228
Cronkite, Walter, 201
Crossley Company, 24
Crystal, Susan Wagner, 205
Cuba: Voice of America in, 89, 203
Cuban-American Foundation, 203
Cuban missile crisis, 69, 87–90
Cultural topics: barriers, 19; exchanges, 148; exports, 8; imperialism, 228; information, 25; internationalism, 226; isolationism, 147; markets, 23; organizations, 6, 7; policy, 22, 23; preservation of, 175; production, 23; programs, 3, 38, 148; rules, 176
Cultural Bridges Act, 224
Culture: American, 22; "American schools," 177; exporting, 175–195
Current Scene: Developments in Mainland China (newsletter), 165
Cutler, Robert, 67
Cutter, Margo, 114
Czechoslovakia: U.S. Information Service in, 203, 204

Dachi, Steve, 155
Davis, Ann, 57
Davis, Elmer, 17–18, 22, 27, 31, 33
Davy, Richard, 106
Dean, Emily, 179, 180
Defense Department, 134, 201; Armed Forces Network radio and, 136, 137; community relations programs, 137; Defense Science Board in, 203, 215, 223; disinformation campaigns, 139; disputes with State Department, 67; "embedded" correspondents in Iraq war, 225; impact on U.S. Information Agency operations, 134; incorporation of War and Navy Departments into, 38; Korean War and, 137; "Militant Liberty: A Program of Evaluation and Reassessment of Freedom," 137; National Security Council and, 68; Office of Strategic Influence, 221; psychological operations, 5, 137, 221; relations with U.S. Information Agency, 5, 134–139; Vietnam War and, 138, 139

De Klerk, Frederik, 207
DeMille, Cecil B., 66
Denmark: American bicentennial celebration in, 116
Department of Commerce, 71, 134
Department of International Public Relations, 55
Der Monat (journal), 140
Desegregation, 119, 120
DeSica, Vittorio, 47
Developing countries: American bicentennial and, 117; claims for share of economic/political power, 103; expansion of services to, 103; ideological operations in, 91, 92; modernization theory and, 84; in nonaligned movement, 103; wars of national liberation in, 91
Die Neue Zeitung (newspaper), 41, 42
Dinsmore, Lee, 158
Diplomacy: branding and, 220, 229; management of, 222; people-to-people, 78; public, future of, 4, 219–230; terrorism and, 220, 221
Disinformation, 139, 141
Disney organization, 12, 164
Donovan, William, 9, 10–11, 12, 13, 18, 30, 38; promotion of black radio operations by, 32
Dos Passos, John, 112
Duffey, Joseph, 213
Dulles, Allan, 32, 33
Dulles, John Foster, 20, 46, 54, 61*n43*, 66, 67, 68, 73, 77, 120, 149, 161

Easum, Donald, 194
Eco, Umberto, 188
Edwards, Herbert, 64
Edwards, India, 64
Egypt: U.S. Information Service in, 61*n47*
Eisenhower, Dwight, 25, 53, 54, 55, 58, 66, 68, 74, 75, 77, 78, 83, 93, 163; Atoms for Peace plan, 70, 118; creation of Armed Forces Network radio and, 25; creation of Psychological Warfare Branch, 32; decision to centralize overseas propaganda activities, 146; foreign policy initiatives, 69; foreign trips by, 78, 94, 161; gradualist policies of, 78;

interest in contacts with Soviet Union, 78; meeting with Khrushchev, 72; people-to-people diplomacy of, 78; proposal for trade fairs, 71; proposal of disarmament talks with Soviet Union, 70; review of psychological operations, 68; special international program of, 192;
Eisenhower, Milton, 144
Ellender, Allen, 90, 161
Elsner, Lubomir, 205
Emerson, Ralph Waldo, 2
Emrich, Duncan, 178
Encounter (journal), 140
English Teaching Forum (journal), 182
Europe, Eastern: information/cultural exchanges with, 211; Radio Free Europe and, 51, 142; trade fairs and exhibits in, 75; unrest in, 83; U.S. Information Agency in, 106; Voice of America in, 70
Exchange programs, 4, 147, 186–195; academic, 190–192; Boxer Rebellion and, 187; with China, 31, 107; cultural, 148; East-West Center, 189–190; Fulbright awards, 7, 148, 177, 187–189; International Visitors, 189–190; military, 134; performing arts, 192–195; Salzburg Seminar, 190; with Soviet Union, 106; student, 190–192
Express Telegraph (press agency), 33

Fairbank, Wilma, 31
Federal Communications Commission, 24
Field, Cyrus, 2
Films, 167–168; *Blondie for Victory*, 28; *Casablanca*, 28; Disney, 12, 164; distribution, 169; documentary, 4, 47, 94, 95, 167, 168, 213; feature-length, 167; Hollywood, 27, 28, 133; newsreels, 4, 169; by Office of War Information, 27; political, 167, 168; *Star-Spangled Rhythm*, 28
FIS. *See* Foreign Information Service
Fisher, McCracken, 30
Fitch, Guy Sims, 159
Five O'Clock Follies, 97
Foreign Broadcast Information Service, 141

Foreign Information Service, 11
Foreign policy: evolution of, 1; ideological and public opinion factors in, 59; Kennedy administration, 83; organizations, 38; public opinion and, 55; Smith-Mundt Bill and, 46; U.S. Information Agency role in, 67, 78
Foreign Press Center, 93
Foreign Scholarship Board, 187–188
Foreign Service Institute, 91
France: American bicentennial celebration in, 115; Centre Culturel Américain in, 180; colonial possessions, 77; cultural traditions in, 175; Marshall Plan projects in, 47; *mission civilisatrice* of, 147; network development in, 2; Office of War Information media in, 28–29; Psychological Warfare Committee sponsorship, 77; radio broadcasting in, 23; U.S. Information Agency libraries in, 57; U.S. Information Service in, 29, 180; withdrawal from colonies, 92
Franklin Publications, 6, 164, 184, 185
Freedom Promotion Act, 224
Free World (magazine), 213
Fulbright, J. William, 108, 143, 144, 149, 183, 187, 189, 190
Fulbright Act (1946), 177
Fulbright awards, 5, 7, 148, 187–189, 206
Fulbright Learning Center, 189
Fulton, Barry, 214

Gagarin, Yuri, 110
Gallup, George, 20
Gaussman, William, 120
Gavin, Leon, 37
Gelb, Bruce, 213
Germany: America Houses in, 42; American bicentennial celebration in, 116; democratization campaign in, 40–44; *Kulturpolitik* in, 147; network development in, 2; occupation by Allied powers, 40, 41; Office of Military Government in, 41, 42; radio broadcasts to, 23, 24, 33; Radio in the American Sector in, 43, 54; reunification, 70; Voice of America in, 43

Germany, East: Soviet military presence in, 53; worker uprising in, 53
Ghandi, Indira, 189
Gillespie, Dizzy, 193
Good Neighbor Policy, 148
Goodwill Games, 210
Gorbachev, Mikhail, 208, 210
Graham, Martha, 194
Graham, Zelma, 179
Graves, John, 200
Greece: aid to, 45; Marshall Plan projects in, 47–48; U.S. Information Service in, 128, 169

Hammett, Dashiell, 57
Hanna, Awad, 171
Harper, Edward, 107
Harriman, W. Averell, 47
Harris, F. Allen "Tex," 161
Havel, Vaclav, 105, 204, 205
Hawaii: Office of War Information in, 33; radio broadcasts from, 25
Hayes, Helen, *127*
Hearst Metronome News, 169
Heath, Don, 5
Helms, Jesse, 213, 215, 219
Helsinki Accords, 105, 106, 209; "baskets" theory in, 105
Helsinki Final Acts, 106
Helsinki Monitoring Group (Moscow), 105
Hemingway, Ernest, 66
Herschensohn, Bruce, 94, 108
Hickenlooper, Bourke, 55
Hickenlooper Report, 58
Hickok, Bob, 29
Hoffman, Paul, 47
Holbrooke, Richard, 220
Hollywood studios, 133; during World War II, 18, 19, 21, 27, 28
Hopkins, Mark, 211
House Committee on International Affairs, 203, 215, 223
Hulbert, Jim, 179, 180
Hummel, Arthur, 155
Hungary: uprising in, 76, 168; U.S. Information Service in, 203, 204
Huntington, Samuel, 1, 226
Hutchinson, Barbara, 205
Hyde, Henry, 203, 215, 223

I-Bureau, 214, 219; website development, 214
Ideological operations, 2, 3; academic community input on, 50; advertising industry input into, 49–50; Cold War, 104; covert, 49, 51; developing countries and, 91, 92; espionage service, 9; expansion of, 3; government ambivalence on, 8; groundwork for, 9; in Japan, 34; against Nazis, 9; overt, 49, 54; post-Pearl Harbor, 12; private input into, 3; Radio Free Europe and Radio Liberation in, 143; in Soviet Union, 40; successes in Germany and Japan, 40–44; U.S. Information Agency and, 4
IIA. *See* International Information Administration
Imperialism, 84; cultural, 228
India: attempts to gain independence, 30; gap between U.S. and British policy in, 30; U.S. Information Agency in, 64; U.S. Information Service in, 154, 156, 165
Information: exports, 6; global networks, 5; operations advancing U.S. interests, 3–4; private networks, 3; programs, 3; revolution, 3; wartime control, 41
Information Media Guaranty, 6, 7, 164, 184
"Information USA" (exhibit), 210
Institute of International Education, 148, 190
Intelligence operations: covert, 13; mandate for, 13; polling techniques in, 20. *See also* Central Intelligence Agency
Interim International Information Service, 38
International Education Act, 190
International Herald Tribune (newspaper), 164
International Information Administration, 44, 48, 49, 54, 55
International News Service, 26
International Research and Exchanges Board, 209
International Telegraph Union (ITU), 2
International Visitors program, 189–190

Internet, 1, 5, 6; in China, 211, 212; growth, 228; Iraq war and, 226; Wireless File site, 158
Internet Society, 5
Iran: U.S. Information Service in, 169
Iran-contra scandal, 202
Iraq, 158, 203, 215, 223; televised war in, 225
Ireland: Office of War Information media in, 29
Isolationism, 2
Italy: Central Intelligence Agency influence on elections in, 51; communism in, 51; Office of War Information programs in, 18; radio broadcasts to, 24
It's All True (film), 168
Ivory, Hugh, 116

Jackson, C. D., 53
Jackson, William, 53, 67
Jackson Committee, 53, 54, 61*n43*, 67
James, William, 2
Japan: American bicentennial celebration in, 116; censorship in, 44; democratization campaign in, 40, 44; ideological operations in, 34; postwar media activities in, 44; radio broadcasts to, 34; U.S. Information Service libraries in, 44; Voice of America in, 25
John F. Kennedy: Years of Lightning, Day of Drums (film), 94, 95, 167
Johnson, Lady Bird, 98
Johnson, Lyndon, 76, 114, 115, 147, 184; overseas trips by, 95; relations with U.S. Information Agency, 96
John XXIII (Pope), 118
Joint U.S. Public Affairs Office (JUSPAO), Saigon, 97, 98, 138

Kaplan, Harold, 163
Karst, Gene, 155
Karzai, Hamid, 189
Keach, Stacy, 188
Kennan, George F., 50, 51, 52, 195
Kennedy, Edward, 224
Kennedy, Jacqueline, 94, *127*
Kennedy, John F., 83, 84, 86, 87, 89, 91, 93, 110, 156, 162, 167; "Ich bin ein Berliner," 94; overseas trips by, 94, 162
Kennedy, Robert, 90, 91
Keogh, James, 109
Khrushchev, Nikita, 72, 74, 75, 76, 77, 84
Kibble, Stepney, 155
King, Martin Luther, 93
Kissinger, Henry, 104, 106, 107
Koob, Kathryn, 200
Korean War, 70; psychological operations in, 137
Kosinski, Jerzy, 191
Kristula, Michael, 205
Krock, Arthur, 19

Ladder Books, 183
L'Amérique en Guerre (newspaper), 28–29
Lang, Jack, 228
Lantos, Tom, 203, 215, 223–224
Laos: communist-led insurgencies in, 77; U.S. Information Agency in, 92, *124*
Larson, Arthur, 76
Lasswell, Harold, 19–20
Latin America: Alliance for Progress in, 84, 130; attempts to undermine U.S. influence in, 9–10; Good Neighbor Policy in, 148; information/cultural exchanges with, 187; radio broadcasting to, 24; trade fairs and exhibits in, 133; traveling exhibitions to, 10; Voice of America in, 10, 24. *See also* Office of the Coordinator of Interamerican Affairs; Rockefeller, Nelson
Lenin, V.I., 23, 115
Lerner, Daniel, 84
Library network, 4, 46, 65, 179–181; in Africa, 93; in Burma, 179; in France, 179; in India, 154; in Japan, 44; McCarthy Committee and, 57; in Mexico, 179; in Morocco, 93; in Nepal, 179; online Information Resource Centers, 214; open-shelf policy, 153; in Pakistan, 179, 180; services offered, 180; staff training in, 154; in Syria, 181; in Thailand, 181; in Turkey, 179, 180
Library of Congress, 134

Limon, Jose, 192
Lippman, Walter, 39
Lipset, Seymour Martin, 2, 147
"Little Annie," 21
Loomis, Henry, 46, 55, 61n43, 67, 68, 140
Luce, Claire Booth, 156, 157

MacArthur, Douglas, 44
Machiavelli, Niccolo, 1
Maddux, John, 155
Malaysia: communist-led insurgencies in, 77
Malraux, André, 167
Mandela, Makaziwe, 188
Mandela, Nelson, 188, 206, 207
Manifest destiny, 2
Mansfield, Mike, 76, 157
Mao Zedong, 30
Markin Parikama (newspaper), 165
Marks, Leonard, 98, 170
Marshall, George C., 40, 46, 65
Marshall Plan, 46, 47
Martin, Tom, 205
Masey, Jack, 75
Mateen, A.F.M. Abdul, 185
May, Karl, 41
Mayer, Gerald, 32, 33
McCarthy, Joseph, 56, 57, 58, 63, 65, 180
McCloskey, Robert, 163
McDermott, Mike, 145
McKnight, John, 155
Mecklin, John, 92
Media: Associated Press, 26, 136, 158, 160; available at U.S. Information Service posts, 165–168; book industry, 6, 7; commercial, 6, 133, 164; commercial cooperation with Office of War Information, 26; companies, 133; corporate mergers/acquisitions, 199; disinformation and, 141; expansion into overseas markets, 37, 182–183; film, 4, 167–168; Franklin Publications, 6, 164, 184, 185; Hollywood studios, 18, 19, 21; International News Service, 26; international sales, 6; lack of strong international markets, 18, 19, 21; markets for, 6, 7, 182–183; Office of War Information staffing and, 18, 19, 21; overseas markets, 163–164, 182–183; print organizations, 26; private vendors, 6; self-censorship in wartime, 26; support for war effort, 26; Time Warner, 164; United Press, 26; United Press International, 160
Mexico: American bicentennial celebration in, 116; U.S. Information Service in, 179
Middle Eastern Television Network, 226
"Militant Liberty: A Program of Evaluation and Reassessment of Freedom" (Defense Department), 137
Miller, Arthur, 194
Milosevic, Slobodan, 214
Modernization theory, 84, 91
Moffo, Anna, 5, 188
Morgenthau, Henry, 40
Morocco: U.S. Information Service libraries in, 93
Moynihan, Daniel Patrick, 5, 115
Muggeridge, Malcolm, 22
Mulligan, Gerry, 193
Mundt, Karl, 45, 55
Murdoch, Rupert, 164
Murrow, Edward R., 5, *123,* 147, 155; and Cuban missile crisis, 87–90; developing country issues and, 91, 92; Foreign Press Center and, 93; interest in communications satellites, 91; nuclear testing campaign, 87; relations with Kennedy administration, 86, 87; as USIA director, 85–93, 96
Murrow Center for Public Diplomacy (Tufts University), 96
Music USA (VOA show), 70

NASA, 110, 111, 112, 113
National Association of Broadcasters, 24
National Broadcasting Corporation, 24, 47
National Committee for a Free Europe, 142
National Democratic Institute for International Affairs, 215
National Endowment for Democracy, 201–202, 207
National Science Foundation, 134

National Security Act (1947), 38
National Security Council, 67, 84; Central Intelligence Agency and, 68; creation of, 38; Defense Department and, 68; Operations Coordinating Board and, 68; psychological warfare operations and, 38, 49, 51, 52; State Department and, 68; U.S. Information Agency and, 147
National Students Union, 140
National War College, 50
NATO. *See* North Atlantic Treaty Organization
Nazis, 9, 10, 23, 24, 33, 40
NBC. *See* National Broadcasting Corporation
Nehru, Jawaharlal, 64
News Review (magazine), *125*
New York Philharmonic Orchestra, 192
New York Times (newspaper), 19, 76, 164, 212
Ngo Dinh Diem, 92
Nicolaides, Philip, 201
Nine from Little Rock (film), 120, 168
Nixon, Richard, 74, 83, 103, 111; Cold War balance and, 104; détente with Soviet Union, 104, 105, 108; exploitation of China/Soviet Union conflict, 104; interest in foreign affairs, 104; "Nixon thaw" and, 104, 105; overseas trips, 162; "playing the China card," 104; relations with China, 106, 107; resignation, 109; SALT I treaty and, 104, 105; Watergate affair, 108, 109
Nonaligned movement, 103
Nongovernmental organizations, 175, 196*n29*, 215, 227
Nordness, Ned, 118
North Atlantic Treaty Organization, 52, 54
Norway: Office of War Information media in, 29
Nuclear issues, 117
Nuestro Barrio (television), 170–171
The Numbers Begin at the River (film), 168
Nye, Joseph, 3
Nyerere, Julius, 189

Office of International Communications, 224
Office of Military Government, 41, 42
Office of Public Diplomacy for Latin America and the Caribbean, 202
Office of Strategic Influence, 139, 221
Office of Strategic Services, 139, 141; creation of, 13; functions transferred to War Department, 38; negotiations between Nationalist and Communist Chinese forces by, 31; in Psychological Warfare Branch, 32; recruitment for, 18
Office of the Coordinator of Information, 11, 30; reconstituted as Office of Strategic Services, 13; wartime expansion of, 12–13
Office of the Coordinator of Interamerican Affairs, 13; creation of, 10; expansion of propaganda efforts by, 11; international editions of print media and, 26; press service, 12; radio broadcasts to Latin America and, 24; wartime expansion of, 12–13. *See also* Rockefeller, Nelson
Office of War Information, 13, 137, 139, 154; American Broadcasting Station and, 25; book publishing markets and, 26; budget, 17, 37; Chinese posts, 30, 31; closure, 37, 38; commercial media views on, 37; competition with commercial news services, 26; cooperation with commercial media organizations, 26; creation of, 3; criticisms of, 18; executive order for, 17; film production by, 27; in Hawaii, 33; Italian programs, 18; London production center, 28; media/advertising staff and, 18, 19, 21; movie-review unit, 27, 28; need for foreign media channels, 22, 23; Overseas Editions and, 26; overseas wartime media output, 31; Pacific operations, 33–34; phase-out of domestic programs, 17; in Philippines, 33; policy differences in, 18; policy guidance from State Department for, 146; production for enemy-occupied areas, 29; production of specialty items, 29; in Psychological Warfare

Branch, 32; psychological warfare operations and, 31; radio broadcasts by, 25, 33, 34; recruitment for, 19, 21; Republican resistance to, 17; setbacks for, 19; smuggled publications of, 33; State Department oversight of, 18; training for propaganda work in, 34n4; U.S./British views on Indian independence and, 30; war activities committee, 27
Operation Backtalk, 43
Operation Kinderlift, 136
Operation Mongoose, 87
Operations Coordinating Board, 68, 84
OSS. *See* Office of Strategic Services
Overseas Editions, 26
Owens, William, 3

"Pacem in Terris," 118
Pakistan, 95, 96; U.S. Information Service in, 89, 165, 180, 185
Panorama Panamericano (newsreel), 130, *130*
Parker, Dorothy, 66
Pattiz, Norman, 222, 226
Patton, George, 32
Peace Corps, 84
Peck, Gregory, 94
Pegler, Westbrook, 18
Philippines: communist-led insurgencies in, 77; guerrilla warfare in, 92; Office of War Information in, 33; radio broadcasts to, 25; U.S. Information Agency in, 92; U.S. Information Service in, 181
Poland: Solidarity Movement in, 143, 204; U.S. Information Service in, 203, 204
Poles Are Stubborn People (film), 168
Policies: counterinsurgency, 91; cultural, 22, 23; ideological, 1; international opposition to, 22; mass media discussion of, 146; public, 7
Policy Coordinating Group, 68, 69
Political: polling, 20; propaganda, 177
Porter, Cole, 194
Posner, Ben, 86
Powell, Colin, 163, 220
Problems of Communism (magazine), 166

Problems of Post-Communism (magazine), 167
Programs. *See* specific agencies
Project Democracy, 201
Propaganda: covert, 11, 49; defining, 20; Disney organization and, 12; early, 2; exploitation of United States race problems by Soviet Union, 76; Foreign Information Service and, 11; by Office of the Coordinator of Interamerican Affairs, 11–12; Office of War Information training for, 34n4; opposition to domestic operations, 17; overt, 49; political, 177; press services, 12; public opinion and, 20; radio as tool for, 22, 23; relevance of, 20; Soviet, 48; techniques, 3; unvouchered funds for, 11; in World War I, 14n5. *See also* Disinformation
Psychological operations, 11, 31, 51, 52, 53; Defense Department and, 5, 137, 221; in Iraq, 224; in Korean War, 137; National Security Council and, 38, 49, 51, 52; Pacific, 33; Eisenhower adminstration review of, 67, 68; of Soviet Union, 46; U.S. Information Agency and, 137
Psychological Strategy Board, 51, 52, 53, 54
Psychological Warfare Branch, 32
Psychological Warfare School, 137
Public Law 402, 46
Public Law 480, 184
Public opinion: Columbia Broadcasting System and, 21; foreign attempts to manipulate, 20; international, 20; "Little Annie" and, 21; political polling and, 20, 21; on propaganda, 20; studies, 19

Qobozo, Percy, 206, 207

Radio: advertising-supported programs, 23; Armed Forces Network, 25; in Asia, 25; black operations and, 11, 31, 32, 141; Columbia Broadcasting System, 21, 23–24; Communist activities and, 23; domestic market, 23; foreign government control of, 23; in Germany, 24; global, 135; in

Hawaii, 25; in Latin America, 24; military, 25; in Nazi Germany, 23; in Philippines, 25; as socializing instrument, 22, 23; in Soviet Union, 23; transmitter shortage, 11, 24, 25; Westwood One, 222–223
Radio, shortwave: atmospheric disturbances and, 135; British Broadcasting Corporation and, 23; broadcasts to Latin America, 10; European, 23; Foreign Information Service on, 11; Soviet jamming, 75, 143; Voice of America, 3
Radio Act (1911), 2
Radio Free Asia: Broadcasting Board of Governors management of, 215
Radio Free Europe, 51, 142; Board for International Broadcasting and, 144; Broadcasting Board of Governors management of, 215; Central Intelligence Agency and, 151n28; credibility of, 143; ideological operations and, 143; jamming by Soviet Union, 143; role in covert operations, 143; staff issues, 142
Radio in the American Sector (RIAS), 43, 54
Radio I Telewizja (magazine), 172n19
Radio Liberation, 51, 142, 208; Board for International Broadcasting and, 144; Broadcasting Board of Governors management of, 215; Central Intelligence Agency and, 151n28; credibility of, 143; ideological operations and, 143; jamming by Soviet Union, 143; renamed Radio Liberty, 143; role in covert operations, 143; staff issues, 142
Radio Liberty. *See* Radio Liberation
Radio Luxembourg, 33
Radio Marti, 202–203; Broadcasting Board of Governors management of, 215
Radio Moscow, 23, 142
Radio 1212, 33
Radio Sawa, 223, 225
Radio Warsaw, 208
Rains, Claude, 28
Reader's Digest (magazine), 140–141, 165

Reagan, Ronald, 200, 201, 202, 207; characterization of Soviet Union as evil empire, 108, 200; "constructive engagement" in South Africa, 205
Reconstruction Finance Corporation, 10
Reich, Otto, 202
Reinhardt, John, 200
Reischauer, Edwin, 157
Rendon, John, 221
Rendon Group, 221
Report from America (television), 170
Reston, James, 85
Rheingold, Howard, 229
Rhodes scholarships, 186–187
RIAS. *See* Radio in the American Sector
Roberts, Ed, 171
Roberts, Walter, 46
Rockefeller, Nelson, 9, 10, 11, 24, 68, 69, 148, 167, 181
Rockhill, William Woodville, 187
Roosevelt, Franklin, 20, 31, 40, 158, 227; establishment of intelligence operations, 11; Good Neighbor Policy, 148; opinion on World War II, 8; psychological warfare activities and, 11; view on Indian independence, 30
Roosevelt, Theodore, 187
Rosen, Barry, 200
Rossellini, Roberto, 47
Rowan, Carl, 96, 97, 98
Royer, William, 200
Rural Electrification Administration, 134
Russell, Bertrand, 75
Russell, McKinney, 208

Sadat, Anwar, 189
SAD (magazine), 166
Safire, William, 201
Salinger, J. D., 183
San Francisco Ballet, 193
Sartre, Jean Paul, 175
Scheer, Julian, 111, 112
Schine, David, 57
Schlesinger, Arthur Jr., 51, 52, 96
Schmitt, Harrison, 5
Schramm, Wilbur, 19
Schwinn, Walter, 49, 50

Senate Foreign Relations Committee, 58, 67, 108, 143, 149, 215, 219
Senate Government Operations Committee, 56
Senior Interdepartmental Group, 147
Shakespeare, Frank, 108, 109
Shan, Salma, 188
Shaw, Glen, 178
Shultz, George, 204
SIG. *See* Senior Interdepartmental Group
Simpson, Howard, 77
Sivard, Robert, 75
Smith, Alexander, 45
Smith, Anthony, 22, 23
Smith, Datus, 185
Smith, Sidney, 175
Smith-Mundt Act (1948), 46, 148, 176
Smithsonian Institution, 134
Snow, C. P., 176
Snowden, Frank Jr., 178
Solidarity Movement, 143, 204
Sorensen, Tom, 86, *123*
South Africa, 120; African National Congress in, 205, 206; "constructive engagement" in, 205; Social Workers Association in, 205; Union of Black Journalists in, 205; U.S. Information Service in, 205, 207
Soviet Union: *America Illustrated* magazine in, 29; American bicentennial and, 116; atmospheric nuclear testing by, 87, 118; collapse of, 1, 210, 211; Committee for the State of Emergency in, 210; Cuban missile crisis and, 87–90; disarmament talks with United States, 70; exchange programs with, 71–75; expansionism of, 50; exploitation of United States race problems, 76; film distribution in, 210; Helsinki Accords and, 105; human rights issues in, 209; ideological conflict with China, 103–104; ideological operations in, 40; information/cultural exchanges with, 105, 108, 208, 209, 210; "Information USA" exhibit in, 210; Kennan analysis of vulnerabilities of, 50; opposition to establishment of U.S. Information Service post in, 29; overseas radio broadcasts from, 142; political relations with occupying powers in Germany, 42, 43; propaganda vulnerabilities, 50; psychological dissolution of power of, 50; psychological warfare operations of, 46; radio broadcasts to, 23, 51; Radio Liberation and, 142; Radio Moscow in, 23; role of propaganda in countering actions of, 45; television in, 210; U.S. Information Agency in, 106, 108, 208; use of friendship societies, 140; Voice of America in, 70, 211; VOKS in, 147
Spain: Office of War Information media in, 29
Span (magazine), 165
Special Planning Group, 201
Spock, Benjamin, 185
Sprague, Mansfield, 79
Sputnik, 76, 83, 110
Stalin, Josef, 53, 167
Standard Oil, 24
Stanton, Frank, 21, 35n9, 195n7
Star-Spangled Rhythm (film), 27
State Department, 134, 201; Bureau of Educational and Cultural Affairs, 177; Bureau of Public Affairs, 39, 145; changes in public diplomacy structure, 224; coordination of information and psychological operations in, 49; "country desks" in, 146; disputes with Defense Department, 67; Division of Cultural Relations, 37, 177, 187; as elite enterprise, 145; Indian independence, 30; information/cultural programs and, 39, 45, 46, 47, 48; National Security Council and, 68; Office of the Coordinator of Interamerican Affairs and, 24; oversight of Office of War Information, 18; policy guidance for Office of War Information, 146; Policy Planning Staff, 50, 51; relations with U.S. Information Agency, 73, 144–149; transfer of cultural functions to U.S. Information Agency, 178
Stearns, Monteagle, 163
Stevens, Roger, 194
Stevenson, Adlai, 88

Stockholm Peace Appeal, 75
Strategic Services Unit, 38
Streibert, Theodore, 64, 65, 66, 68, 72, 73, 76
Switzerland: U.S. Information Service posts in, 32

Taft, Robert, 45
Taliban, 222
TASS (news agency), 88, 93
Taylor, Edmund, 43
Television: Apollo space program coverage, 112, 113; commercial, 133; diplomacy and, 223; global, 135; "Let's Learn English" programs, 129; programming, 91; satellite, 226; in Soviet Union, 210
Telstar, 89
Terrorism, 1, 220, 221, 222; ideologically driven, 3
Thailand: communist-led insurgencies in, 77; guerrilla warfare in, 92; U.S. Information Agency in, 92; U.S. Information Service in, 181
Thatcher, Margaret, 189
Thayer, Charles, 42
Thompson, Dorothy, 9
Thoreau, Henry David, 66, 183
Tienanmen Square uprising, 212
Times Literary Supplement, 27
Time Warner, 164
Timrud, Herbert, 205
Togo: English-instruction program in, 125, *125*
Tom Two Arrows, 194
Towery, Kenneth, 108
Trade fairs and exhibits, 70–75; "America At Home," 71; "American National Exhibition," 73; Apollo space program, 113; in Argentina, 130, *130;* art displays, 74; bicentennial, 115; book displays, 74; commercial, 133; "Education USA," 113; themes, 75; in Turkey, *123;* "The World of Franklin and Jefferson," 115
Truman, Harry, 38, 45, 46, 48, 51, 52; desegregation of armed forces by, 119
Tuch, Hans, 74
Turner, Ted, 210

TV Marti, 203

Uncle Awad's Friends Club (television), 171
United Fruit Co., 24
United Nations, 145–146
United Press, 26, 30
United Press International, 160
United States: American exceptionalism and, 2, 147; civil rights demonstrations in, 76, 93; Cuban missile crisis and, 87–90; cultural exports, 175–195; diplomatic relations with China, 107; disarmament talks with Soviet Union, 70; dominance in information-intensive world, 3; domination in world opinion influence, 3; early disinterest in cross-border communications, 2; effort to showcase American art abroad, 10; exchange programs with Soviet Union, 71–75; global presence in education, 191; global unfamiliarity with, 22; information/cultural exchanges with China, 108; information/cultural exchanges with Soviet Union, 105, 108; international opposition to policies of, 22; involvement in Vietnam, 84; lack of interest in international broadcasting, 23; lag in establishment of global radio presence, 23; modernization theory and, 84; overseas impact of mass media from, 212, 213; overseas study centers by universities, 191; preeminence in information/cultural exports, 227–229; presence in Vietnam, 92; technology as domestic resource in, 2. *See also* specific agencies
University of Maine Masquers, 194
UN Universal Declaration of Human Rights, 119
Updike, John, 188
U.S. Information Agency: academic/cultural organizations and, 7; arms control and, 119; binational centers, 181–182; book publication projects, 182–183; budget, 6, 63, 64, 76, 77, 78, 90, 108, 200, 215; campaign on nuclear testing, 87, 118; censorship

and, 65, 66; challenges in post–Cold War environment, 215; changes in original mission, 199; choice for ideological operations, 4; civil rights coverage, 93, 109, 119–120; closure of, 4; Commerce Department and, 71; communication satellites and, 90, 91, 98; computerization of, 213; congressional criticism of, 8; counterinsurgency projects, 91; coverage of astronauts, 111; creation of, 4, 56; criticisms of, 90, 177; in Cuban missile crisis, 69; cultural officers, 178–179; decision to abolish, 213, 215, 216; downsizing of European posts, 103; early projects, 63–79; electronic integration of media operations, 214; English-instruction program, 4, *125, 129, 182;* establishment of commercial bases for domestic firms overseas, 26; exclusion from role in National Security Council operations, 68; expansion into decolonized countries, 78; expansion of services to developing countries, 103; film operations, 4, 66, 94, 95; as foreign policy resource, 67, 78, 79, 103; information/cultural operations, 39, 70–75, 148, 175–195; input to National Security Council, 58–59; International Visitors program, 189–190; Iran-contra affair and, 202; Kennedy supporters in, 96; in Korean War, 137; Ladder Books, 183; local responsibilities, 155, 156, 158; mandate to present balanced portrait of United States, 177; mobile units, 131, *131;* National Security Council and, 147; in new information technology environment, 213; newsreels, 169; nuclear issues and, 117, 118; origins of, 17–34; overlap with other organizations, 133, 134; overseas markets for media exports and, 6, 7, 182–183; permanent appointments to, 154; permanent career status in, 98, 99; policy guidance from State Department, 58; polling data, 83; post organization, 157; post routines, 158, 162; presidential visits and, 161–162; press officers, 163; pressures upon for artistic conformity, 8; program decisionmaking in, 66; program resources at posts, 165–168; psychological operations and, 137; as public face of United States overseas, 153; reaching younger audiences, 90; Reagan policies in, 201; relations with Armed Forces Network radio, 26, 136; relations with Central Intelligence Agency, 5, 139–145; relations with Congress, 76, 77; relations with Defense Department, 5, 134–139; relations with State Department, 144–149; Republican resistance to, 63; restructuring operations of, 200; role in national security planning, 69; role in reporting Watergate affair, 109; role of radio in missile crisis, 88, 89; Soviet space propaganda and, 110; staff held hostage in Iran, 200; staff resources, 154, 155, 157, 158; surrender leaflets by, 126, *126,* 166; television and, 4, 91, 170–171; tracking overseas opinion by, 20, 21; trade fairs, 70–71; transfer of State Department cultural operations to, 178; use of films, 167–168; use of Internet, 199–200; violence against, 205; visitors to, 160–161; wars of national liberation and, 83, 84; worldwide channel for information on Kennedy death, 94. *See also* specific countries, programs, and regions; U.S. Information Service

U.S. Information Service (USIS), 4; ambassadorial relations with, 156, 157; *American Reporter,* 64; in apartheid struggle, 205, 206; "cocktail circuit" duties, 129, *129;* country team process in, 156; creation of European posts, 29; criticisms of, 161; cultural programs 7, 7; dance programs, 128, *128;* in development of media markets, 163–164, 182–183; effectiveness of, 156; information/cultural operations, 158, 175–195; integration into military-

tactical effort, 32; Worldnet and, 205. *See also* specific countries, programs, and regions; U.S. Information Agency
USIA. *See* U.S. Information Agency
USIS. *See* U.S. Information Service
USSR (magazine), 72

VanDelden, Patricia, 155
Vatican, 51
Venezuela: American bicentennial celebration in, 116
Victory (magazine), 28
Vietnam: communist insurgency in, 77, 92; Fulbright Learning Center in, 189; information/cultural exchanges with, 213; Joint U.S. Public Affairs Office (JUSPAO) in, 97, 98, 138; Popular Self Defense Forces in, 126; surrender leaflets in, 126, *126,* 166; Tet Offensive in, 98; United States presence in, 84, 92; U.S. Information Agency in, 32, 97, 126; U.S. Information Service in, 92, 97, 166, 213
Vietnam, Vietnam (film), 168
Vietnamese Information Service, 98
Vietnam War, 137, 138; psychological operations in, 138, 139
Vlachos, Helen, 189
Voice of America, 4, 34, 54, 135; in Asia, 25; Broadcasting Board of Governors management of, 215; in China, 211, 212; confrontation tones of, 70; content areas, 145; contracts for scripts, 39, 47; creation of, 3, 11, 24; credibility of, 143; criticism of, 142; in Cuba, 89, 203; cutbacks in, 39, 222; in Eastern Europe, 70; end of jamming operations against, 208; expansion of services, 48; facilities upgrades, 202; in Germany, 43; growth of, 47; "Have You a Question?" program, 127; in Japan, 25; in Latin America, 10, 24; loss of audience, 222; master board, *128;* McCarthy Committee and, 56, 57; *Music USA,* 70; as resource in countering Soviet ideological warfare, 45; rise in listenership, 70; Soviet jamming of, 47, 75; in Soviet Union, 70, 211; "Special English" dictionary, 182; State Department guidelines to, 146–147; Watergate coverage, 109

Walesa, Lech, 143
Wars of national liberation, 77, 83, 84, 91
Washburn, Abbott, 46, 55, 61*n43,* 66
Watergate affair, 108, 109
Waters, Muddy, 193
Weinstein, Allen, 211
Weintal, Edward, 108
Welles, Orson, 167
Welty, Eudora, 188
Westwood One, 222–223
Wick, Charles Z., 108, 200, 201, 202, 209
Wilder, Thornton, 178, 194
Williams, Shirley, 188
Willis, Charles, 205
Wilson, Donald, 85, 86, 88, 89, *123*
Wilson, Woodrow, 227
Winks, Robin, 115
Wireless File, 158–160
Wisner, Frank, 51
Wooten, Richard, 121*n20*
World Marxist Review (journal), 166
Worldnet, 203, 204, 205
World Today (periodical), 165
World War I, 14–15
World War II, 1; calls for propaganda campaign in, 9; public opinion favoring neutrality in, 8. *See also* Office of War Information
World Youth Festivals, 90
Wright, Sylvia, 177

Yeltsin, Boris, 210, 211

Zakaria, Fareed, 228
Z-grams, 201
Zorthian, Barry, 97, 138, 163
Zulu Inkatha movement, 20